The Street Politics of Abortion

The Cultural Lives of Law
Edited by Austin Sarat

The Street Politics of Abortion

Speech, Violence, and America's Culture Wars

Joshua C. Wilson

Stanford Law Books

An Imprint of Stanford University Press

Stanford, California

5-16-14

Stanford University Press
Stanford, California

Printed in the United States of America on acid-free, archival-quality paper

Library of Congress Cataloging-in-Publication Data

Wilson, Joshua C., author.
    The street politics of abortion : speech, violence, and America's culture wars / Joshua C. Wilson.
        pages cm. — (The cultural lives of law)
    Includes bibliographical references and index.
    ISBN 978-0-8047-8533-4 (cloth : alk. paper)
    ISBN 978-0-8047-8534-1 (pbk. : alk. paper)
    1. Abortion—Political aspects—United States. 2. Abortion services—Law and legislation—United States. 3. Freedom of speech—United States.
4. Demonstrations—Law and legislation—United States. 5. Pro-life movement—United States. I. Title. II. Series: Cultural lives of law.
HQ767.5.U5W56 2013
363.460973—dc23

                                                           2013011194

ISBN 978-0-8047-8870-0 (electronic)

To my parents, Kathy and Jerry Wilson

Contents

Acknowledgments

There are too many points competing to be the one that marks when this book project began. As a result, the number of people I want to thank for contributing to this book grows the more I think about it. I will take Horace's advice in the *Art of Poetry*, though, and start in medias res, or in the middle of things, as opposed to some preferred ab ovo point. This spares the reader like the music at the Oscars spares the audience, but it upsets me. My first act of thanking the book's contributors, then, is to thank the many friends, family members, and colleagues who are not mentioned here by name.

When people ask me why I chose to work on this topic, I tell them I wanted to find a compelling story about law and society and that I found one in these abortion politics cases. This point leads to the next mention of those that I would like to thank for helping with this project. William Fletcher drew my attention to this interesting set of cases; William Muir inspired me to write the stories that others do not have the time to write; and Kristin Luker showed me the complexity and value of studying abortion politics.

I would also like to thank all of those who helped nurture and transform my early shapeless ideas about these cases into something with form and structure. The usual caveats apply to them and to all other people who have provided valuable advice and commentary on this project. These people contributed their time and thoughts, but I fully own any faults with the book.

That said, I would like to thank those who helped make my time as a graduate student at the University of California, Berkeley's Jurisprudence and Social Policy Program so valuable, specifically, Hadar Aviram, Jack Citrin, Susan Dennehy, Malcolm Feeley, Jackie Gehring, Alejandra Huneeus, Dorit Rubinstein, Shalini Satkunanandan, and Rachel Van-Sickle-Ward. I would also like to thank my colleagues in the John Jay College Political Science Department who have encouraged dedication to research, particularly my chief collaborator, daily "editor," and friend, Erin Ackerman—I'll miss having the office across the wall from you.

It would be remiss of me to not thank the various conference discussants, lecture audiences, and journal peer-reviewers and editors who have read, listened to, commented on, and encouraged parts of this project over the years. Special thanks in these regards needs to be directed to those who, for no reason beyond their own generosity, took the time to give particularly thorough and helpful comments to someone they barely knew. George Lovell, Kwai Ng, and especially Julie Novkov all greatly exceeded their roles as conference discussants and panelists by expressing genuine interest in my work and providing various forms of support for years after our respective conference panels ended. I would also like to express my deep appreciation to Jeffrey Dudas and Laura Beth Nielsen, who both chose to cross the divide from anonymous peer-reviewers to peers and lent their continued help to this book and other scholarly endeavors. Jeffrey and Laura Beth were both profoundly important in helping me reconceive my approach to my interview data. Finally, I would like to thank Lynn Chancer, who helped shepherd my manuscript to a press through our work in the CUNY Faculty Fellowship Publication Program and who gave continuing support after the program had run its course.

I am deeply grateful for and indebted to three additional people who have given more to me and to this project than anyone could reasonably hope for. First, I need to thank Robert Kagan for listening to the unstructured and rambling ideas that preceded this project; for helping me move it to be something beyond storytelling; for caring enough to give incredibly thorough comments on so many early drafts; for opening the door to academia; and, finally, for simply being a friend. No one could ask for a more thoughtful or kinder mentor than Bob.

Second, I must thank both of my parents, to whom I have dedicated this book. While this mention strays, quite literally, into the ab ovo territory that I said I would not enter, I would not have ever written a book, let alone gone to college, without my mother's efforts to address my ever-mounting frustration with grade school and junior high. Returning to the safety of the in medias res position, I cannot say "thank you" enough to my father, who has not only read and reread every draft or product related to this book but also read almost every academic piece that I have written since I left high school. Securing that this book was a true family affair, I also need to thank my sister, Leah, for her help in transcribing some of the early interviews and for providing general encouragement.

Sincere thanks is also given to all of the interviewees who took the time to talk to me on the phone and who invited me into their homes, workplaces, and favorite cafes. Without their kindness the research would not have been as enjoyable as it was, and without their trust and patience this project truly could not exist. I have done my best to honor their trust through honest, accurate, and detailed work.

I am grateful to the University of California, Research Foundation of the City University of New York, Professional Staff Congress–City University of New York Research Award Program, City University of New York Faculty Fellowship Publication Program, John Jay College Research Assistance Program, The Field Psych Trust, and Berkeley's Center for the Study of Law and Society for their financial support at different stages of this project. Their assistance allowed for much-needed time to do field work and write. Speaking of field work, this book would not have been possible without the help provided by court administrators and the opportunity to do research in the University Archives at the University at Buffalo, The State University of New York (SUNY Buffalo). As Kristin Luker and Erin Ackerman have both rightfully noted, we should always take the time to honor librarians.

One should also always thank good editors—especially when one tends to be wordy or is known to frequently digress. I have had the fortune to complete this book under Kate Wahl's guidance. Kate's initial read of the manuscript produced detailed, critical comments that convinced me that I wanted to work with her. The continued care that she and Frances Malcolm have provided through the editing and production process reaffirm that I made the right choice. I hope that we can work together again on the next book. I would also like to thank Austin Sarat for both publishing an earlier article related to this greater project and including this book in his edited series, *The Cultural Lives of Law*. It is an honor to have my work included in a series that I so respect.

Finally, a great thanks is owed to Elisha and Lila—my ever-present and lovely reminders that it is good to step away from projects that can become all-consuming and that I should always find places to stop, or at least break.

1

Abortion Politics, Legal Power, and Storytelling

When the United States Supreme Court decided the case of *Roe v. Wade* in January 1973, it simultaneously struck down state abortion laws and helped fuel the creation of the modern social conservative movement. Up through the early 1970s the legality of abortion was largely seen as a "Catholic issue." That changed in the aftermath of *Roe v. Wade*.[1] While it did not happen immediately, legalized abortion became a central issue for social conservatives who came to see *Roe* as a particularly morally intolerable example of the political Left once again marshaling the unelected federal judiciary to undo the popular will of the states.[2]

In this line of conservative thinking, the Supreme Court, headed by Chief Justice Earl Warren, was seen as forcing racial integration, banning prayer and religion from public life, creating soft-on-crime policies, and liberating sexual taboos.[3] This growing catalog of offenses helped bring Nixon's "Forgotten Americans" to the polls in 1968, but even that was apparently not enough to stop the Court's socially disruptive progressive trend. Nixon was almost immediately able to reform the Supreme Court in his first term with four judicial appointments, including Chief Justice, but the Court persisted in producing progressive rulings. Over two decades of controversial court cases and social turmoil had helped to move the Forgotten Americans and the "Silent Majority" to vote, but *Roe v. Wade* was the ruling that would mobilize a more sustained and not-so-silent movement.

The anti-abortion movement has taken many forms in the four decades since.[4] In the 1980s and 90s one of its identifying hallmarks was

1

clinic-front activism. These protests took various forms, but collectively they served to publicize the cause, gain more members, give participants the feeling of empowerment via direct action, impede clinic access, and tax clinic resources. A less desirable outcome, from the anti-abortion perspective, was that this activism also spurred abortion-rights advocates to organize to directly counter these street-level tactics. While those fighting for abortion rights may have believed that they had reached their goal with the *Roe* decision, it quickly became clear that the Supreme Court case was just one step in a protracted and ongoing movement-counter-movement struggle.[5]

As clinic-front anti-abortion protests grew in frequency, magnitude, and intensity, abortion providers and their supporters sought ways to respond. Their search yielded its own direct action strategies, but it also returned abortion-rights proponents to the state and, in particular, to the judiciary.[6] At times, abortion-rights advocates attempted to use state-based means to win dramatic gains against their adversaries. The National Organization for Women (NOW) tried to use federal anti-racketeering (or RICO) laws, which were created to fight organized crime, to criminalize specific anti-abortion tactics and organizations.[7] More commonly, abortion-rights activists sought to obtain court orders and legislation that governed how anti-abortion protests could occur—for example, establishing specific distances that needed to be maintained between activists and clinic doorways.

When clinics and abortion-rights groups succeeded in securing injunctions and other legal measures against their opponents, anti-abortion activists did not cower. Instead, they fought back with a legal strategy of their own. Anti-abortion activists around the country began challenging the restrictions by arguing that such measures violated their constitutional right to free speech. The combination of pervasive clinic-front activism, available legal resources, and crosscutting First Amendment questions touched off a wave of cases that disproportionately occupied the United States Supreme Court's docket.

The nation's high court has heard and written opinions for eight anti-abortion activism regulation cases since the late 1980s.[8] The most recent of these cases, decided on February 28, 2006, settled the prolonged dispute over the application of RICO laws to anti-abortion activists.[9] In addition to the cases that the Court has heard, individual Justices have gone out of their way to author two concurrences and three dissents for denials of certiorari ("cert") (i.e., instances where the Court has decided to not hear a case).[10] This is a very uncommon step for a Court that rejects roughly 99 percent of the cases that are appealed to it.[11] With these responses to denials of cert included, members of the Court have written opinions for 13 cases related to the regulation of anti-abortion activism in less than 20 years. As the following chapters will show, three of these cases—*Planned Parenthood Shasta-Diablo Inc. v. Christine Williams* (1995), *Schenck v. Pro-Choice Network of Western New York* (1997), and *Hill v. Colorado* (2000)— represent the range of clinic-front activism, the regulatory responses to it, and the period's importance in the progression of abortion politics and the development of the New Christian Right.[12]

Briefly, the *Williams* case represents largely nonviolent, small-scale but repetitive clinic-front protesting. Over the course of this conflict, groups of anti-abortion activists gathered at a clinic in Northern California and typically held signs and attempted to distribute materials to those who were accessing the clinic. This activism was ultimately responded to with a clinic-specific injunction that pushed the anti-abortion activists away from the clinic. While it was twice appealed to the U.S. Supreme Court, the injunction was repeatedly allowed to remain in place.

Similar events led to *Schenck v. Pro-Choice Network of Western New York*, but they occurred on a much larger and more aggressive scale. Instead of relatively small-scale recurrent activism at one clinic, the *Schenck* case included large-scale repetitive protests known as "rescues" at a number of clinics in Western New York State. The nationwide anti-abortion group Operation Rescue popularized rescues. As a form of protest, rescues involved both peaceful and aggressive activities ultimately intended to close the targeted clinics.[13] A coalition of clinic supporters and abortion providers in Western New York organized in response and countered this activism through a collection of direct-action and state-based means. The resulting Supreme Court case centered on the legality of a regional injunction that established both fixed and floating buffer zones around clinics in Western New York. The Court upheld the fixed buffer elements of the injunction, but struck down the floating buffer provision.

The final case, *Hill v. Colorado*, considered the constitutionality of Colorado's "Bubble Bill"—a law governing activism within 100 feet of health care facility entrances.[14] Unlike the previous two cases, the regulation in *Hill* is not in response to a singular event or a particular ongoing conflict. Rather, according to one of the bill's sponsors, the Colorado "Bubble Bill" was born of a feeling that the state needed new "pro-choice legislation."[15] The case is also unique in that it introduces legislative, as opposed to just judicial, responses to anti-abortion protesting. Noting the adverse effect the Bubble Bill could have on their activities, a group of anti-abortion advocates organized to fight the legislation in public hearings and eventually challenged the law in the U.S. Supreme Court. The Court upheld the Bubble Bill in full, opening the door to the federal Freedom of Access to Clinic Entrances Act, which effectively ended the most aggressive forms of clinic-front anti-abortion activism nationwide.[16]

Taken together, these conflicts illustrate the rise and fall of the most visible, participatory, and overtly contentious period of abortion politics in America. The eventual subsidence of the street politics of abortion in response to clinics' and abortion-rights advocates' legal victories, however, did not mark the end of the anti-abortion movement or abortion politics. Like flowing water that hits an obstruction, efforts in the conflict were merely diverted to a different course. Activists from both sides of the conflict have thus—often literally—moved from the streets to continue the fight in state legislative halls and courtrooms around the country.[17] *Williams, Schenck,* and *Hill* trace and explain this path, unpacking reasons for the resilience of abortion politics while also showing how these events matter for the institutionalization of the New Christian Right more broadly.

Through these cases we see how abortion-rights activists have largely taken a defensive stance that reacts to, rather than initiates action against, their opponents. In the decades since *Roe,* the abortion-rights movement has yet to find a way to take the offensive, control the political discussion, or sustain popular involvement. They have come to be both behind and significantly subject to the anti-abortion movement's actions. As a result, they show no signs of being able to slow, let alone end, the ongoing movement-countermovement conflict over abortion. Rather, they can only perpetuate it.

While one side of these cases is illustrative of a movement that faces difficulty in spite of its successes, the other side provides examples of a movement that is in many ways successful in spite of its failures. These cases demonstrate the resilience of anti-abortion activists and show a movement that is both entrepreneurial and developing in ways that have significant ramifications for the broader Religious Right's place in American politics. The anti-abortion movement's lead in transitioning to new "arenas of conflict" is a prime example of strategic creativity, resource development, and the way in which movement-countermovement struggles continue.[18] The anti-abortion movement has been successful at making these transitions because, as these cases show, they have benefited from a combination of passionate, able activists and available resources. The former creates the will and aptitude to develop new strategies in the face of defeat, while the latter provides the means to persist.

The stories surrounding *Williams*, *Schenck*, and *Hill* largely start with local grassroots organizations with limited resources and elite access. They also, however, introduce then-fledgling organizations and emergent leaders that ultimately rose to prominence through their involvement with these cases and led the way to the new institutional and elite politics of abortion. What's more, some of these organizations and associated leaders have used their experience in these conflicts to become important not only within abortion politics but also within the New Christian Right and the modern Republican Party.

First Amendment Doctrine and Anti-Abortion Protests

Before delving into more detail concerning the specific questions and issues that form this book's core, it is useful first to survey some of the legal matters involved in anti-abortion protest regulation cases. While their specific facts and legal arguments vary, all of the cases examined in this book generally address a similar doctrinal constellation within First Amendment law: the regulation of speech within the "public forum."

Public forum doctrine refers to the collection of cases that began in 1939 and address the regulation of speech in public spaces such as in parks and on sidewalks.[19] Because a broad spectrum of the public mixes and interacts in these spaces, they create a natural space in which to disseminate and debate ideas. As a result, the public forum is at the heart of the First Amendment, and speakers correspondingly experience a higher degree of freedom and protection when they are acting within it than when they are acting on privately owned property.

This being said, the same features that make the public forum an ideal space for speech also make it a volatile and potentially dangerous place. Speech and ideas can excite, offend, and instigate. Unpopular speakers can be attacked, mobs can be mobilized, and violence can be fomented. Considering this, the state must not only protect the rights of speakers within these forums but it must also protect the rights of other people to carry on safely and freely in public. Thus a tension exists in finding the balance between these competing rights. Many of the Court's First Amendment decisions and the resulting doctrinal lines are the result of trying to strike a balance between these interests. What spaces are, and are not, public forums? When is it permissible to regulate speech, or aspects of speech, within the public forum? And when it has been determined that speech in the public forum can be regulated, what are the limits on the resulting regulation?

In the anti-abortion protest regulation cases, there is relatively little debate between the parties about what is defined as the public forum. Neither side generally questions that property rights restrict the protesters' activities on clinic property.[20] Instead, the conflicts hinge on the degree to which clinics and the state can regulate the protesters when they are on the public sidewalks surrounding these clinics. This leads to a set of more specific legal questions concerning both "time, place, and manner" and "captive audience" doctrine, as well as the "content neutrality" of the existing regulations.

The question of content neutrality refers to whether a regulation takes direct aim at the content of regulated speech. If a regulation targets the speech because of the speaker, the subject matter, the viewpoint expressed, or the predicted impact of the speech upon the audience, it operates as a form of censorship—an end deemed unacceptable by the Supreme Court. In the words of Justice Marshall, "[A]bove all else, the First Amendment means that government has no power to restrict expression because of its message, its ideas, its subject matter, or its content. To permit the continued building of our politics and culture, and to assure self-fulfillment for each individual, our people are guaranteed the right to express any thought, free from government censorship."[21]

Expressive behavior may, however, be regulated if it is done without reference to content. For example, it is permissible to regulate the conditions of expression, or, in other words, the "time, place, and manner" of speech. At its creation, time, place, and manner reasoning was used by the Court to synchronize the exercise of free speech (in the originating case, a public parade) with other functions of everyday life in order to "conserve the public convenience."[22] While the local government required a permit in order to hold a parade, it was not deemed an unconstitutional restriction on speech rights because the exercise of speech rights needed to be coordinated with other social functions. The Court determined that the way in which the government coordinated the public's and the marchers' needs did not make reference to the parade's content, its participants, or its predicted impact upon observers. As such, the regulation was considered to be a content-neutral regulation of the time, place, and manner of speech. If, however, obtaining the permit were dependent upon the government approving of the parade's message, the regulation would be declared unconstitutional.

The Court has since attempted to detail what may be considered a content-neutral regulation of the time, place, and manner of speech. The standard applied in the abortion cases directly stems from *Ward v. Rock Against Racism* (1989)—a case that involved a dispute over the regulation of amplified sound in a public venue.[23] In brief, the standard holds that time, place, and manner regulations must meet three requirements. First, "the principal inquiry in determining content neutrality . . . is whether the government has adopted a regulation of speech because of disagreement with the message it conveys."[24] Second, the regulation "must be narrowly tailored to serve the government's legitimate content-neutral interests but that it need not be the least-restrictive or least-intrusive means of doing so."[25] Finally, regulation must "leave open ample alternative channels of communication."[26] While the purpose of these regulations is to "coordinate" speech, critics have pointed out that the content-neutrality requirement and the time, place, and manner test still allow the government to "subordinate" speech—a claim also made by those advocating for anti-abortion protesters.[27]

Along with time, place, and manner regulations, the Court has said that intervening on behalf of "captive audiences" is acceptable. The resulting captive audience doctrine is an attempt by the Court to balance the rights of speakers and unwilling audiences. This is a matter of great concern in these anti-abortion protest conflicts. The rights determination in such cases depends upon the speech's context. If the audience is reasonably able to avoid unwanted speech and is in a traditionally defined public forum, the speaker tends to retain a considerable amount of Constitutional protection.[28] If the audience is unable to escape the speech, or is in a place considered insulated from the public forum, "the First Amendment permits the government to prohibit offensive speech as intrusive."[29] The claims made on behalf of clinics and their clients in the cases studied here are: (1) that the patients who are trying to access clinics are captive audiences; and (2) that the inherent medical risks of the abortion procedure require insulation from the public forum.

This brief selection and survey of legal matters at issue in anti-abortion protest regulation cases demonstrates that they are the latest stages in the evolution of some of the First Amendment's core features. This makes apparent that these cases not only affect the specific disputants and the form of abortion politics, but also that they impact the regulation of political speech and expression generally. Furthermore, this survey hints at another point about law. While existing doctrine provides guidelines for action, the presence of court cases reveals that disputes about the application of doctrine remain. Law is thus simultaneously authoritative and incomplete.

This obvious, but seemingly contradictory—and therefore oft-overlooked—dichotomy raises questions about law's claims to legitimately command obedience. It also creates spaces that can be exploited by social movements and other actors. Law's mix of openness and authority allows space for movements to make novel claims that frame their issues, create public notice, and permit them to get into court. If they win in court—and that is a big *if*—they gain the imprimatur of the state, which presumably translates to various policy and other strategic gains. If, however, they lose, the movement can establish precedent that works against their cause and produces other forms of self-inflicted harm. The ways that movements approach and use litigation is thus worth noting for what it can tell us about social change and political institutions.

Movements, Countermovements, and the Law

In general, those who study social movements and the law are interested in the political opportunities and costs of pursuing various legal strategies. While using law might seem attractive for movements, there is widespread academic debate about the utility of doing so. Much has been made of the "myth of rights";[30] the limited conditional nature of judicial power;[31] the structural advantages in litigation enjoyed by established institutions;[32] the ability of court cases to disproportionately consume resources and alienate grassroots activists;[33] and how litigation and "rights talk" escalate conflicts or otherwise backfire on those who use them.[34] Other scholars have noted that while the courts' power might be limited and conditional, it can still produce sought-after political effects;[35] activists can strategically marshal legal resources;[36] and even if movements lose in court, they can still garner indirect benefits from litigation.[37]

Whatever their conclusions, when scholars talk about law and social movements, they characteristically talk about the place of rights and litigation in deliberately planned, but not necessarily strictly controlled or uncontested, strategies meant to advance a social movement's ultimate policy goals. Furthermore, the goals sought are usually some type of equity reform. These features of law and social movement research tend to lead scholars to focus their attention in specific ways.

First, not surprisingly, studies tend to concentrate on social change activists far more than on the other groups involved in a given struggle. Second, the featured social movements are usually organized in opposition to nonmovement entities that control or administer the policies activists oppose (e.g., the state, employers, or other social institutions). What's more, the examination of the activists' opponents is typically limited to asking if, when, why, and/or how the opponents resisted or changed in relation to the advocates' demands. While such research is undeniably important, limiting the approach to social movements in these ways leads to excluding or overlooking other types of social movement conflicts, resulting in an unduly limited view into how social movements, law, politics, and policy interact.

Law and social movement research is also typically constrained through its focus on rights claiming and litigation as tools used—incrementally or immediately—to directly achieve a movement's central policy goals. The popular conception of the National Association for the Advancement of Colored People's (NAACP) desegregation strategy generally, and *Brown v. Board of Education* (1954) specifically, capture this thinking. The belief is that the NAACP brought *Brown* and its predecessors to both immediately (by desegregating specific institutions) and incrementally (by building precedent to overturn the separate but equal standard) achieve the goal of desegregation. Considering the relative success of this strategy, subsequent progressive and conservative movements have followed its form. Given this, it seems logical that if one wants to study social movements and the law one should study groups that use law and litigation in this direct way.

Admittedly the NAACP's desegregation strategy and the surrounding political and social realities were more complex than this example implies. Correspondingly, those who study social movements and the law have more nuanced questions and approaches than this blunt example might suggest. In spite of this, the example's basic point still stands.

Researchers often look at a group's ability or inability to use rights claims and litigation to conceptualize a wrong, mobilize activism, and/or force significant policy change.[38] As with the privileging of activists over their opponents, looking at a movement's use of law to attempt to directly achieve its goals unduly restrains our understanding of law's place in the interaction between social movements, politics, and policy.[39]

Applying the relatively small but compelling movement-counter-movement literature to the study of law and social movements exposes some of the limits of the typical approaches to the latter.[40] In movement-countermovement research, scholars pay attention to how directly competing movements interact with one another—and possibly with a more traditional entity like the state—in a dynamic process where each movement in part creates the conditions within which the other acts. The fight is no longer about one social movement against the state or an established institution. It is now about the competition between rival movements and their fights to control resources, public opinion, policy, and the arenas of conflict.

Among the relevant issues in this literature for law and social movement scholars is how opposing movements prolong conflicts through their ability to shift to new political venues when they have been defeated in another; how such venue shifts (and the resulting changes in tactics and demands) of one movement can force the opposing movement to respond in areas and ways that they did not intend or desire; and how these strategic changes can cause opposing movements to develop parallel internal organizational structures over time.[41]

Similar themes are found in the law and social movement literature. Robert Kagan's work on adversarial legalism explores how federalism and the separation of powers allow for conflicts to be prolonged through venue shifting.[42] Michael McCann and Paul Frymer discuss how movements are able to use the law to force unwilling opponents to listen, appear in court, spend resources, and otherwise respond to their claims.[43] Charles Epp and Steven Teles provide detailed studies of how progressive and conservative movements develop organizational structures that allow them to enter and thrive in the legal realm.[44] More generally, both areas of study are interested in the interaction of movements, politics, and policy.

In spite of this overlap, little if any work in either area specifically concentrates on the role and manifestations of law and litigation in movement-countermovement struggles.[45] This poses a question about what new issues or findings can be produced by deliberately blending the two approaches to social movements. Furthermore, though David Meyer and Suzanne Staggenborg wrote about it over fifteen years ago, there is also still a need within the movement-countermovement literature for "studies comparing the ways in which different conflicts between opposing movements develop . . . within particular contexts . . . and the factors that lead to . . . shifts in strategies and tactics."[46] As court cases that are simultaneously the *result and cause* of changes in rival movements' strategies, structures, and actions, the conflicts examined in this book are fitting means to respond to both of the above concerns.

To back up for a moment, there is much about these cases that is familiar to both law and social movement and movement-countermovement researchers. The cases reflect the trajectory of abortion-rights activists returning to the courts when they needed to address new clinic-front activism—a step that followed their initial legal victory in *Roe*, and that ran concurrently with the need to challenge early post-*Roe* legislative restrictions on abortion. They show how clinics were able to draw from a mix of local lawyers and established legal resources—both from the abortion-rights movements and other left legal networks—when anti-abortion activists adopted clinic-front tactics. The conflicts also show how specific legal strategies to manage and discourage clinic-front activism developed through local trial and error and then spread through nationwide activist networks. Different provisions (e.g., floating and fixed no-entry zones with varying specific requirements) and different legal vehicles (e.g., local restraining orders and injunctions, regional injunctions, and finally legislation) were used in a continual effort to control the conflicts with the right mix of effective and constitutionally defensible regulation. Finally, through the introduction of legislation, the cases demonstrate how the abortion-rights movement was able to shift some of the costs of defending anti-abortion protest regulation to the state.

The abortion-rights movements' actions were spurred by the need to respond to evolving anti-abortion tactics, and they in turn had an effect on the future development of those tactics. The anti-abortion movement developed significant legal resources that began with local lawyers who were loosely connected to the activists that they represented through churches and fledgling anti-abortion networks. Like some of their rivals who represented the clinics, these lawyers predominantly volunteered their time and still had their regular practices to attend to. In order to fully respond to the abortion-rights activists' growing legal network, resources, and corresponding use of courts, the anti-abortion movement developed organizations that could go beyond the immediate criminal defense of those accused of violating regulations. The movement, in conjunction with the greater New Christian Right, created efficient centralized legal institutions and networks that enabled them to challenge the constitutionality of regulations at the appellate and Supreme Court levels (as seen in the three cases discussed here); identify and attempt to preempt potentially harmful state actions (as they did with the Colorado Bubble Bill); and create the means of going on the offensive in a range of institutional arenas (as organizations like the American Center for Law and Justice [ACLJ] have subsequently done). Given the details that the following chapters provide in terms of the strategic legal moves taken by both sides in response to one another, *Williams*, *Schenck*, and *Hill* provide inviting vehicles for microstudies of movement-countermovement conflicts that add to our understanding of such conflicts as well as of social movement litigation.[47]

The application of a movement-countermovement lens to these conflicts, however, specifically draws out a unique aspect of these cases given the majority of law and social movement research. On one level, these cases are all obvious examples of movement litigation in that they involve activists as litigants. If one looks beyond the cases' surface features to the legal details, however, it is also clear that they are unlike the bulk of movement litigation that has been studied. Instead of examining social movements that bring cases as a means to directly achieve their equity reform goals, the litigation that is of interest here is better classified as what I call "secondary movement litigation." As such, it is a largely heretofore-overlooked form of movement litigation that is produced in the movement-countermovement context.[48]

Using the term "secondary" to describe the type of movement litigation seen in *Williams*, *Schenck*, and *Hill* is not intended to suggest that the activists involved were employing multiple litigation-based strategies with varying degrees of importance. That is, they were not simultaneously pursuing a main and a secondary, or backup, litigation strategy. The difference that is being drawn is in reference to two other interconnected features of these cases. The first stems from the fact that the cases were not part of a broader, premeditated strategy by either movement. Rather, they are unplanned reactions to the current form of the dispute. The second way in which they are secondary relates to the indirect relationship between the litigation and the movements' ultimate goals. Both of these features are rooted in the greater conflict's movement-countermovement dynamic.

The back-and-forth exchange of evolving tactics in this ongoing struggle muddles the cases' origins, making it hard to attribute them to a specific movement. The cases are, in a sense, reactive and secondary for each side and thus good examples of why Meyer and Staggenborg consider movement-countermovement conflicts to be circular or spiraling rather than linear.[49] For example, it is true that anti-abortion activists initiated legal proceedings in cases like *Hill*, and thus these actions can appear to be part of a deliberate strategy. These cases, however, respond to local, state, and federal protest regulation laws won by abortion-rights activists. The anti-abortion activists only entered the court because they were compelled to in order to defend their direct action tactics. Turning to state and federal injunction cases like those seen in *Williams* and *Schenck*, abortion-rights activists had to go to court to secure, modify, and enforce temporary and permanent injunctions. As a result, these cases can appear to be part of the clinics' intended litigation strategy. In spite of this, it is important to note that the anti-abortion activists elevated and effectively drove cases like *Williams* and *Schenck* when they decided to raise and pursue First Amendment claims.[50]

Taken together, neither side of these disputes necessarily planned to enter or stay in the courts, but they were essentially compelled to by their rival's actions. These cases show that effective steps taken by a movement in a given forum forces opponents either to enter into, or to continue developing in, that same forum. Being drawn into the same venue—in this case, the legal arena—causes the opposing movements to develop similar institutional capacities that allow them to effectively perform and further tactically innovate.[51] While neither movement may have foreseen or desired to develop along this legal course, both have done so. As a result, the abortion conflict and the greater "culture war" have been profoundly affected.

The spiraling nature of the conflict and the resulting cases also illustrate that so long as each side can continue to marshal the resources necessary to respond, innovate, and change forums, opposing movement disputes can seemingly continue indefinitely. Certain individuals or whole categories of participants may be eliminated with each tactical turn, but the overall dispute continues. These protest regulation cases may have wrought the effective end of popular, street-level anti-abortion activism and activists, but the wider abortion conflict has continued on in new forums and forms. Those who were best positioned to continue on in the new state-legislative-dominated politics of abortion (e.g., activist leaders) have done so, while those who were not similarly situated (e.g., street-level "foot soldiers") either left the movement or found new means to be involved in other arenas (e.g., opening "crisis pregnancy centers" or giving money to established activist organizations on either side).

The next way in which these cases are secondary relates to the disconnect between the cases and the movements' ultimate missions. Instead of addressing the legality of abortion—the central issue for both movements—the *Williams*, *Schenck*, and *Hill* cases are disputes over the legality of the street-level tactics used in pursuit of their goals. The cases are outliers in movement litigation studies in that they are not meant to, nor do they even have the ability to, incrementally or immediately achieve either movement's ultimate policy goals. That is, neither side directly affects abortion policy by winning or losing these cases. Rather, the litigation is one step removed from these goals and is only understood within the context of the sustained interaction between rival movements.

There is no doubt that anti-abortion protest regulation cases are high-stakes, politically passionate affairs that are intimately entwined with broader abortion politics. In the eyes of the protesters, defeat meant the effective end to both the public face of the anti-abortion movement's activism and, in the movement's language, a means to directly save babies and women. For the clinics and their supporters, defeat would not only signal the persistence of clinic-front conflicts and the perceived standing threat to the individuals at clinics but also foreshadow a general threat to the security of abortion rights within the Unites States. In either scenario, the effects upon the two movements are in terms of tactics, not ultimate policy goals.

Furthermore, jurisprudentially, these cases are not about abortion politics. Rather, the case outcomes determine the means by which *any* activists can employ direct action strategies and the extent to which the targets of their activism can use state power to fight back. As such they are First Amendment cases that are substantively secondary for the competing movements. The abortion protest regulation cases' secondary status is made starker through a comparison with what can be termed "primary" abortion politics cases. For example, *Roe v. Wade* (1973) legalized abortion; *Gonzales v. Carhart* (2007) upheld the ban on "partial-birth" abortions;

and *Webster v. Reproductive Health Services* (1989), *Planned Parenthood of Southeastern Pennsylvania v. Casey* (1992), and *Ayotte v. Planned Parenthood of Northern New England* (2006) each directly imposed restrictions on accessing abortion. All of these are examples of litigation that either incrementally or immediately addressed the competing movements' ultimate policy aims.

The secondary free speech issue was introduced into the conflict by the protesters' desire to respond to the clinics' abilities to effectively regulate anti-abortion direct action strategies. This desire forced the anti-abortion movement to enter the judicial system, which in turn required anti-abortion activists to meet certain institutional criteria. The requirements went beyond hiring lawyers and developing a legal infrastructure. The activists' beliefs about the moral duty to resist abortion were not legally suitable to challenge the regulations—a point that chafed some activists. Given this, the anti-abortion activists were suddenly required to become champions of a new cause. They were now in the position of being advocates for an expansive reading of the First Amendment. This, correspondingly, put the clinics and their supporters in the position of being advocates for a limited reading of speech rights. The introduction of this wholly new and foreign issue into the abortion dispute had multiple effects both within and around the existing conflict. In short, the insertion of First Amendment claims modified both what the disputes were about and to whom they were of interest. This sudden shift is entirely due to the disputes' greater movement-countermovement context.

As might be expected, activists on both sides of these disputes had reason to feel uncomfortable with their new roles.[52] The conflict between clinics and anti-abortion activists represents an inherent tension within speech rights—the tug-of-war between (a) the democratic value of allowing ample room for activism and expression and (b) the moral duty (of states and individuals) to ensure safety and (arguably) civility in the public forum. The weight that one assigns to either side of this tension often reflects one's general political ideology. Traditionally, when it comes to potentially volatile political protest, liberals are thought to put more stock in allowing speech to go forward while conservatives emphasize the importance of public safety and security.[53] Like the interpretation of the limits of acceptable free speech, one's stance on abortion policy typically correlates with political ideology.[54] Liberals, championing individual liberty and equality, tend to support access to abortion. On the other side of the political spectrum, conservatives, especially social conservatives, tend to cite moral principles (e.g., the sanctity of human life) as grounds for banning abortion, or at least for closely regulating and discouraging access to it.[55]

In these anti-abortion protest regulation cases, the traditional alignment of ideology and interpretation of the First Amendment can be turned on its head by abortion politics. When clinics try to regulate protests via court orders and legislation, reflective liberal clinic members and supporters are placed in a dissonant situation. They must decide whether to endorse the free speech rights of protesters at the potential cost of clinic and client safety (not to mention the security of abortion rights) *or* to support the litigation at the cost of free speech. Similarly reflective social conservatives confront a related dilemma—that is, whether to defend the movement's direct action strategies at the potential cost of weakening the state's ability to maintain order during protests, or to stand with the state and allow anti-abortion activists to be regulated.

The introduction of a foreign, secondary issue into the existing movement-countermovement conflict not only complicated ideological alignments; it also brought newly interested parties to these cases. The original disputants may not have been particularly committed to, well versed, or interested in speech politics, but others clearly were. Labor unions, the ACLU, and other traditional advocates of speech politics suddenly became invested in these disputes. These new groups played active roles in the cases, and they were split by the ideological tensions brought by the blending of abortion and speech politics. As later chapters will illustrate, anti-abortion activists and the majority of elites on both sides of the conflict largely possessed ways to avoid or minimize these dilemmas, while abortion-rights activists were hamstrung by their inability to do so. These ideological tensions and the difficulties that they can, and did, create for those involved highlight the cases' unplanned nature and the strange fruits born of the movement-countermovement context. They thus feed our understanding of both movement litigation and "the ways in which different conflicts between opposing movements develop."[56]

These secondary-movement litigation cases also possess other features that should be of interest to law and social movement scholars. As mentioned earlier, much of the work in this area is concerned with questions of whether or not litigation is helpful or harmful for movements. One major concern involves movements falling victim to the "myth of rights"—that is, taking victory in the courts as a substantive victory tantamount to policy change.[57] Secondary-movement litigation appears to be immune to the myth of rights and many of its related problems, possibly creating a substantial upside to this type of litigation. Since the rights disputed in these cases are only tangentially related to those that the competing movements are primarily interested in, the litigants are not in a position to mistake these legal victories for substantive policy ones. The same reasoning makes secondary-movement litigation cases insusceptible to the danger of establishing directly harmful precedent for the activists' ultimate policy goals. The greatest risks that the litigants face in secondary-movement cases are those associated with dedicating too many resources to the litigation and surrendering too much power to outside lawyers. Again, however, returning to the indirect goals sought in this type of litigation, movements can presumably withdraw more easily from secondary-movement cases if the associated costs grow too great than they can from cases more directly related to their ultimate policy goals. This leaves movements open to using secondary-movement litigation as a bludgeon, a means to tie up and bleed their opponent's resources, and/or as a means to defend or force changes in movement tactics.

This type of case potentially adds to the list of social movement legal strategies. In doing so, it also expands our understanding of how social movements, law, politics, and policy interact. It remains to be seen, though, if secondary-movement litigation exists in many other movement contexts, or if it is limited to the conditions present in the abortion conflict and possibly others that involve direct action strategies.[58]

Storytelling, Legal Consciousness, and Legal Power

The stories of and from these conflicts also provide the means for another set of lessons—those about the cultural nature of law and legal power. This book builds from the culturalist "Law and Society" premise that law is not simply contested in courts and wholly controlled by the state. Rather, legal power is intimately intertwined with what individuals believe, the stories that they tell, and the ways that they choose to behave.[59] We all know that there is a difference between law as it exists on the books and law as it is lived and discussed. New Yorkers rarely hesitate to cross against the light in front of a police officer, and drivers in Lincoln, Nebraska, have been known to yell at bicyclists who ride in the street as opposed to on the sidewalk where they are largely prohibited from legally riding.[60]

Beyond these more pedestrian examples, social movement conflicts are particularly suited to produce challenges to the state's claim to monopolize law—both in terms of the arguments that movements make and the actions that they take. By narrowing the focus from the larger political story of the Supreme Court abortion cases to the individual and collective stories told *about* them by those involved, these cases present the ability to learn about the decentralized and interactive process of creating law and legal power.[61] The stories told by the various participants from the *Williams*, *Schenck*, and *Hill* cases (i.e., competing street-level activists, their various lawyers, and the legislative members who eventually addressed the issue of direct-action activism) therefore do not just illustrate how they control and respond to the conditions for movement action but also show us how they simultaneously embrace, resist, create, and employ legal power.

These actors are of particular interest because they are not only members of, or otherwise connected to, social movements. They are also all involved as subjects and/or officers in the formal institutional processes of creating and sustaining official state legal power. Legislation and litigation are meant to determine who can legitimately wield and invoke law. Following a fairly traditional understanding of the fundamental roles of the branches of government, legislative bodies create and thus initially define law. On a practical level, judicial rulings clarify existing law and decide who can utilize state law as a tangible coercive instrument and who is subject to it.[62] On a constitutive level, court decisions attempt to limit access to law's symbolic normative powers by announcing the official state understanding of law and discrediting competing conceptions of it.[63] The state, however, often fails to have a complete monopoly on legal meaning.[64]

People regularly assert, and at times continue to live, their own extrastate versions of law before and in defiance of judicial rulings.[65] While this extrastate creation of law can occur in various settings, the social movement context heightens its likelihood. Movement activists who are already seeking to challenge the status quo are surrounded by similarly motivated people who can reinforce decisions to resist the state's interpretation of law. That is, social movements can create communities that support defiance. As a result, social movement actors are primed to dispute the dominant state understandings of law.

When either activists or more common actors create and live in accordance with alternative conceptions of law, it again reveals that law is decentered, reflecting poststructuralist arguments that have dislocated meaning and authority in text more generally.[66] It also suggests that if one wants to more fully understand the law, it is important to examine how various state and nonstate parties construct law in their own ways. As Susan Silbey notes, these personal accounts are important because they are a form of "participation and interpretation through which actors construct, sustain, reproduce, or amend the circulating (contested or hegemonic) structures of meanings concerning law."[67]

The participants' stories from *Williams*, *Schenck*, and *Hill*, coming from a diversity of positions, are well situated to reveal the back-and-forth process of meaning-making that takes place between centralized and decentralized sources. The storytellers thus contribute to our understanding not only of how law is constructed in individual narratives but also of how formal institutions and movement politics relate to the process of creating legal power. The resulting multilayered conception of law, in turn, has implications for understanding both the nature of legal power and social movement behavior.

The interests in the above require that this book employ a modified legal-consciousness approach, focusing attention on individual movement actors' stories rather than on a movement's more publicly aimed work of framing and meaning.[68] The place of law in the participants' stories is revealed by paying close attention to, as Orbuch writes, "the process by which individuals construct these stories and . . . [to] the recognition that stories formulate, control, and represent self, other, and relationships."[69] Stories make sense because they follow certain rules and employ shared assumptions—right or wrong—about how the world works. As a result, if one considers the details of a given story, one can learn about the storyteller's conception of the world.

Given this book's focus, specific attention is paid to how these storytellers construct law in their narratives. Law's construction is identified by looking for patterns of inclusion, absence, amendment, and type of law (state or extrastate) within and between the stories told by activists, lawyers, and legislative members. The speaker describing, invoking, or notably excluding judicial decisions, statutes, "rights talk," constitutional principles, or other legal concepts precisely notes law's presence in the stories. If and when law appears in these narratives, "the complex, often disparate and ambiguous terms of 'how' it matters and what that means for differently situated persons and relationships" is approached by unpacking the role law plays in and across individual narratives.[70] The patterns in how the speakers employ particular language and create coherence and meaning can then explain how law may be both available and off-limits to movement actors; it can be used to identify specific threats that stories pose to state law; and it allows for unpacking how state legal authority is sustained.

Starting with the street-level activists, both sides of these conflicts had significant reasons to challenge the state's official version of law. By overwhelmingly upholding the various regulations, the courts have acknowledged that anti-abortion activists have committed unprotected acts of violence and intimidation, and that elements of the movement present a standing threat to public safety. In short, the courts have labeled these actions and actors as existing outside of state law. These rulings clearly give anti-abortion activists reason to reject and defy the state's understanding of law. The activists' potential for disobedience was increased by the fact that they all possessed a well-developed religious conception of law that was central to their activism and individual identities, and that could replace the state as a legitimating authority.

On the other side of these conflicts, by largely declaring the anti-abortion activists' conception of law void, the courts have supplied abortion-rights advocates and clinic members with the ability to authoritatively invoke state law in their stories. This grant, however, is not limitless. The courts have also proscribed measures that target content or excessively impede activism. By drawing this line, the courts have presumably narrowed abortion-rights advocates' abilities not only to legitimately regulate opponents but also to authoritatively appeal to certain conceptions of law in their personal narratives. Abortion-rights interviewees, like their opponents, are therefore in the position of either affirming state law by constructing narratives that fall within these stated boundaries or of challenging state law by creating, and possibly attempting to act on, competing elaborations of the law.

In spite of their reasons to challenge the state, the street-level activists' stories on both sides of this conflict overwhelmingly affirm state legal authority. The anti-abortion activists' narratives provide the more interesting examples here. "Rescuers," the term to identify anti-abortion activists who employed more aggressive tactics, justify breaking state law by relying on a belief in the legal supremacy of their understanding of God's will. In spite of the importance of God's will for their actions, the rescuers' stories go on to not only accept but also to directly endorse the state's authority to regulate their actions. Alternatively, the anti-abortion picketers who shared the rescuers religious conception of extrastate law, but who did not follow it to the point of intentionally breaking state law, overtly resist the state in their stories by attacking the judiciary's legitimacy. These attacks, however, are carefully limited. The overwhelming bulk of the picketers' stories are constructed to show how state law is fundamentally valid and how the picketers are aligned with it.

The unexpected twists and significant work done in these stories makes them particularly revealing vehicles for learning about the enduring nature of state legal power. The value that the anti-abortion activists derive from preserving and attempting to align with state law apparently outweighs whatever benefits they could obtain from resisting and defying it in their stories. Whether or not this was a conscious choice, the fact that they maintain and align themselves with the state speaks to the hegemonic power of state law.

The stories studied also reveal the converse of a well-established argument concerning law and social movements. Michael McCann's and Douglas NeJaime's work, among others, informs us that losing in the courtroom does not necessarily lead to a movement surrendering the ability to appeal to law.[71] The anti abortion activists illustrate this via their continued ability to effectively harness both extra-state and state law's cultural power in their stories. A surprise comes, however, from noting the dearth of symbolic and rhetorical resources available to the clinics and their supporters.

Although the clinics won these cases, abortion-rights advocates' narratives exhibit that these actors experienced significant difficulty accessing state law as a normative device. Victory in the court provided coercive power on the street, but it did not provide an unambiguous and equally effective "discourse that clarified divisions between right and wrong, and between supporters and opponents of a good cause."[72] Abortion-rights storytellers, for example, bounce between a number of law-like descriptions of problems that they faced and rights that they possessed, but they are not able to settle on one or two powerful and unambiguous claims. The actors' access to law's cultural power was inhibited by the lack of familiar rights talk, but more significantly, by a concern with preserving a liberal conception of the right to free speech. This shows that like the limitations imposed by adverse court decisions, the benefits of legal victories are not total or guaranteed. Just as one can win in spite of losing, it appears that one can lose in spite of winning.

In a break from legal consciousness norms, attention is also paid to how law is constructed in the stories told by the elites (i.e., lawyers and legislators) that the movements appealed to as these conflicts developed.[73] This inclusion is justified because it provides a more complete understanding of how law and authority are created, sustained, or challenged, as well as how these actors, who are often movement outsiders, relate to the activists who seek them out. Legal elites formally participate in the official creation and sustaining of state law through their institutional capacities, but they are still individuals who have the potential to think and act independently, and thus to challenge official state law. This is especially true within the United States' decentralized governmental and adversarial legal systems, and is heightened when competing social movements use these systems and employ these elites.

Legal elites may come late to the movements, but they can play important roles not only in dictating movement strategy—a typical way in which they are examined in the literature—but in forming activists' perceptions and beliefs, and by providing a vocabulary to describe the events that they are experiencing.[74] Furthermore, these elites are potentially susceptible to having their perceptions, beliefs, and language affected by their interactions with the activists.[75] The range of possibilities for legal elites to become part of challenging state legal authority, or alternatively to protect and impose this authority, complicates their position in relation to law and movements. As a result, the stories that elites tell are worth studying to see how they relate to sustaining and possibly challenging legal power—the traditional domain of legal consciousness scholarship.

Thus, a key finding of this book is that the further elite actors are from a movement's core or a conflict's events on the ground, the less likely they are to portray the law in the same way as activists on either side of a dispute. While this may sound unremarkable, its implications are worth noting. The street-level activists all ultimately endorsed state law through their narratives. In contrast, the balance of the elites on both sides of these conflicts painted a portrait of state law that showed it to be powerful, but largely unprincipled and politically saturated. Because of this, the majority of elite narratives seem to attack state law's durability and ideological power. This is significant for several reasons. First, these elites play important formal roles in the same system that they are attacking. Second, elites are well positioned to pass their views of law on to the activists who can use them as a justification for overtly defying the state. Third, the formal legal system does not have a convenient way of discrediting or eliminating these threatening conceptions of law.

Given these points, it is interesting to see that these negative conceptions of state law did not take significant hold in either street-level activist population in the cases discussed here. Instead, activists on both sides have their own reasons to foster a purer version of state law that preserves state legal authority. This final point demonstrates the opposite of what many critical legal scholars claim about the relationships among activists, elites, and law. Traditionally, critical legal scholars argue that elites temper activists' more radical views and tactical preferences.[76] Here we see the activists defending the state and failing to adopt the more radical views of the elites they are associated with. Furthermore, depending on the audience, the elites' legal-realist stories can be read as contributing to *or* as attacking state law's authority. Even though they portray a system that lacks a traditional principled core, their stories include alternative legitimating forces. For all of their talk of the political game of law, elites also appeal to their duty to clients and constituents, and duty springs from principle.

In their seminal book *The Common Place of Law: Stories from Everyday Life*, Patricia Ewick and Susan Silbey persuasively argue that we all possess and employ multiple conflicting schemas to understand and construct law. Law can be seen as something pure and above the tainted political and personal realms (i.e., a "before the law" consciousness); it can be a game played in the naked pursuit of self-interest (i.e., a "with the law" consciousness); and it can be a force to be resisted and undermined in various ways (i.e., an "against the law" consciousness). Our ability to fluidly switch between these understandings of law is one reason that legal power endures. If law was always kept on a pedestal, its evident failures to continually live up to an exalted standard would soon topple it and we would lose our faith in law. If law was solely seen as a tool and product of self-interest we would have no reason to follow its dictates beyond the brute coercive force that lies behind it. However, when we hold more complex conceptions of law it becomes flexible. Law's failures, or instances when it is seen as a product and tool of self-interested power, can be construed as deviations or as being accompanied by higher principles, and thus law's legitimacy and power persist. This fluidity is seen individually and collectively in the activists' and the elites' stories discussed here.

Anti-abortion activists do not simply see law as a coercive force exercised against them by politically powerful opponents. Rather, they recognize and gravitate to law's purer qualities as a legitimating embodiment of American political and cultural tradition. Abortion-rights activists are similarly able to look beyond what they see as law's initial failings in order to use and praise it as an effective tool. The activists' lawyers, the amicus brief authors, and the legislative members involved in these cases tell stories that initially appear to be distillations of particular legal typologies—either entirely pure or wholly power-politics portrayals of law. A closer look, however, unearths the presence of conflicting views of law in their stories.

The conflict participants' capacities to view the law in assorted ways not only contributes to the persistence of legal power in the face of various reasons for it to fail but also returns us to the political implications of these cases by deepening our understanding of the conflict's course. That is, we see how the cultural aspects of law in these conflicts make a difference politically and materially. Clinic members and abortion-rights activists construct and utilize state law as an effective coercive tool, but they are unable to use it in their stories as a means to frame their experiences in coherent and resonant ways. From how their stories demonstrate law's effectiveness, we see the reaffirmation of state legal power. And from their inability to use law as a frame for understanding the conflicts, we see the limits of law's malleability as well as a reason that legal victories have not translated into lasting popular political-mobilizing devices. This then returns to the abortion rights movement's persistent reliance upon an elite institutional strategy over one with more popular elements.

On the opposite side of the conflict, we see anti-abortion activists who are able to resolve adverse court rulings with a belief that they acted within the law and American political and cultural traditions. This ability translates into a second, but admittedly unexpected, affirmation of state legal power. It also creates the grounds for allowing their movement to transition into its current elite institution-based form. That is, instead of being defeated by these rulings, finding fault in themselves, and giving up on the legitimacy and efficacy of state legal institutions, the stories told by anti-abortion activists give them reasons to continue to engage with the state and to prove that they were and are solidly embedded in the political mainstream. These stories are thus clear examples of the real-world political significance of law's cultural aspects.

2

A Common Occurrence
Planned Parenthood Shasta-Diablo v. Williams

In many ways, Jeannette Hammer represents the typical pro-life activist—she is a self-described stay-at-home mom and a conservative Evangelical Protestant who was moved to participate in activism in the early 1980s.[1] Serving as the founder and director of the Birthright of Vallejo-Benicia crisis pregnancy center from 1982 to 1986, Jeanette headed a small volunteer organization that represented one of the two poles of the abortion debate in the northern San Francisco Bay city of Vallejo, California. The local Planned Parenthood, located just across Broadway Avenue, embodied the other pole. The two centers coexisted relatively peacefully during the 1980s, but, reflecting the shift in the tactics of activists on both sides, the peace did not last. In Jeanette Hammer's words:

I had small children and I decided that, well, the Lord was leading me in other directions, to home school and to do other things, so I stepped down from being director there. And, after that it was when I got involved in picketing up at Planned Parenthood.

. . . I found out that Planned Parenthood in Vallejo was doing abortions, so I decided we need to let people know. We need to do something about this. So I called up one friend [Bridget DeMers, a Birthright counselor at the time] and she and I went out there once a week and started picketing.

. . . When we first started, Bridget and I were able to be in the parking lot next to the front door and talk to people as they were walking up to Planned Parenthood, and make an impact by having conversation with them and talking to people who [were] waiting for someone inside. We didn't have signs that were graphic or had pictures on them. We mostly just had pamphlets talking about the structure of the unborn child and the development and the after effects of abortion—psychological problems women could have.

. . . I hoped to be able to talk to some of the women [who were going to Planned Parenthood] and [to] give them correct information about . . . the unborn child— what it was like, that their heart was beating, that they had brain waves. It wasn't just a blob, and that it wasn't just a problem because so many times Planned Parenthood will not tell people the truth about the unborn child. They rename it and they dismiss it as a person so we wanted to let women know that not only when they had an abortion, they were murdering a child, but that they would [be] living with the consequences of that for the rest of their lives.

Jeanette and Bridget, without any prior experience protesting, began their weekly efforts at the Planned Parenthood in the months transitioning from 1989 to 1990. What started with just the two of them steadily grew through word of mouth via church groups and Birthright. According to Jeanette, there were "just a couple of us at first, then three or four . . . [then] more people came when we were by the door [of the Planned Parenthood clinic]. It might have gotten up to, let's see, ten max I'd say, when we were at the door."[2]

In January 1990, the fledgling group asked Christine Williams, the founder of another anti-abortion group known as the "Solano Citizens for Life," to advertise their activities in her organization's roughly triannual newsletter, *Solano Lifelines*. In April of that year, under the headline of "Picketing Begins in Vallejo," the time, place, day of the week, and contact information for those interested in participating were mentioned in the newsletter, along with a testament to the numbers of "babies saved" by the group. In the same edition of *Solano Lifelines*, with the same contact information attached, there was a full-page ad extending the invitation to "Come learn how to be a sidewalk counselor at abortuaries."[3] After being sent to the roughly 1,000 people on the *Solano Lifelines* mailing list, the numbers of those joining Bridget and Jeanette in front of Planned Parenthood spiked. The core of the group grew to around 30 picketers, including Christine Williams. With their increased size, the anti-abortion picketers were now in the parking lot jointly used by Planned Parenthood and the neighboring tax office, as well as on the sidewalk in front of the clinic.

Those interviewed who picketed the clinic in the beginning used words such as "loving," "caring," "respectful," "peaceful," "educative," "informational," and "low-key" to describe what they were doing. "We were able to wander back to the parking lot and as people came out, as they were walking towards us, we said, 'We have literature here, would you like to read it?' And some people would take it and want it, and then more and more people, I think, began drawing in and a lot of times when people would, they would just be praying too and just be walking around quietly praying and handing out literature."[4]

In addition, all of those who were interviewed and picketed the clinic noted that the group originally made a conscious decision not to follow the examples set by the higher-profile groups like Operation Rescue, or even Don Blythe, the man who trained many of them how to sidewalk counsel. "Now Don Blythe . . . was much more aggressive. Not illegal, but much more aggressive. He would get right in their face and say, 'Are you sure you want to kill your baby?' We just, that was not our style. . . . [Deciding whether or not to have an abortion] was difficult, and we didn't want to traumatize the women more."[5] While some of those picketing the Vallejo clinic had participated in Operation Rescue events, and others made a point to note that they saw a place for its style and techniques, all those who mentioned Operation Rescue saw their means as conflicting with the demonstrators' aims at this clinic. Since these activists sought to approach women going into the clinic in order to discuss what the group saw as overlooked concerns in relation to abortion, tactics such as blocking the clinic, using graphic signs, or aggressively approaching others were considered self-defeating.

The firm, and still-held, belief that they were not being aggressive or offensive in any way set the stage for the demonstrators' collective shock when the police told them that they could no longer be in the clinic's parking lot. According to a *Solano Lifelines* article, on May 11, 1990, in the presence of reporters doing a story on the clinic's decision to hire escorts for the women visiting Planned Parenthood, "a pro-abort arrived and created quite a scene by swearing and yelling at one of our young moms pushing her child in a stroller. . . . The police arrived quickly to check out the disturbance and were convinced . . . that we had to get out of the parking lot."[6]

Less than a month later, after a written appeal by Christine Williams to the Vallejo Police Department and city attorney, the group was allowed to reenter the parking lot. The final sentences of the letter readmitting them to the lot, however, foreshadowed what was to come: "I should also advise you that should the property owner or persons in lawful possession of the property obtain an injunction from Superior Court to protect their property, your group will have to obey the terms of the injunction. I hope that this clarifies the issue for both of us."[7]

While the picketers may have understood their activities to be nonthreatening, the same could not be said from the other side of the picket line. According to Heather Estes, the CEO of Planned Parenthood Shasta-Diablo, which runs the Vallejo center, those protesting in front of the clinic were doing much more than just peacefully picketing and calmly approaching women in the parking lot and on the sidewalk.

There seems to be two kinds of picketers, or two kinds of folks, or protesters with different agendas. One group is like out on the street with signs that say "Babies killed here. Isn't that awful." And then the other group doesn't really care if the passers by see it. It's not a political statement. They're there to save you—your baby, your life. It's about, it's about that person, that moment, that time, and then whatever, and whatever, that gives them what they think they're doing for God, or for life, or whatever. So, two different thoughts. You can sort of tell, depending upon where they stand and what their signs say and whether or not they're into signs, or whether or not they're into confronting patients, or who they think are patients.[8]

From the vantage point of the clinic, the protesters that were there to "save you" were different from the strictly political protesters not just in their intent but also in their tactics. The clinics saw these new activists as grabbing patients, making them cry, forcing small plastic fetuses into their hands, and generally being aggressive and unpredictable. "It got . . . gruesome, you know, around then, which led us to go for . . . the injunction. I mean it got more disgusting."[9]

Beyond the picketing itself, a string of other events fueled Planned Parenthood's fears. The clinic was broken into. They experienced a bomb scare when an unclaimed briefcase was left in the office lobby. Anti-Semitic and KKK literature attacking clinic doctors was left on benches outside the clinic. The clinic incurred acts of vandalism including having door locks injected with glue, bent nails strewn in the parking lot, and a sign reading "Murder, Inc." nailed to the regular business sign. Outside of work, staff members received repeated harassing home-phone calls in the middle of the night. While a number of actions were meant to secure the clinic, anxiety was certainly raised when the FBI twice visited the clinic, staff members were encouraged to change their home phone numbers, bulletproof glass was installed at the clinic, and when the local police devised special planned responses for both the clinic and staff members' homes "so that they would be prepared in case anything came up."[10] Taken as a whole, clinic members "felt like we were under assault. We felt like we were, sort of, you know, we didn't feel like we were in an armed camp because we were not armed, and we couldn't [be] . . . we didn't feel terribly secure."[11]

Although the interviewed anti-abortion activists who conducted demonstrations at the Vallejo clinic stated that they tried to employ different tactics than Operation Rescue, for Planned Parenthood there was little to differentiate this group of picketers from such groups as Operation Rescue. As a result, the activists found themselves subject to what was becoming an increasingly common response by Planned Parenthood and other clinics to such high-profile and aggressive groups.

On August 8, 1990 the Vallejo branch of Planned Parenthood, with the assistance of their lawyer Karen Ryer, filed a complaint in the Solano County Superior Court for injunctive relief against the demonstrators. The complaint cited Christine Williams, Solano Citizens for Life, Birthright of Vallejo, and those acting in concert with them for "consistently intimidating and harassing workers and clients of Planned Parenthood" as well as obstructing the driveway, forcing leaflets upon cars and people, excessive noise, attempting to disrupt business, and attempting to gain entrance to the clinic facility. In their complaint, Planned Parenthood asked for relief via enjoining the above groups and individuals from general acts such as trespassing, verbal harassment, and threatening physical conduct, to more specific items, such as blocking the driveway, "shouting words likely to disturb the peace of the plaintiffs . . . restricting defendants to two pickets on the public sidewalk, [and] . . . harassing, intimidating, telephoning, vexing, annoying, or otherwise attempting to intimidate and harass plaintiffs."[12]

No one seemed more surprised at the suit than the only individually named defendant—Christine Williams.

I saw myself as a networker, not necessarily an organizer of these things [the picketing at the Vallejo clinic]. And in fact I *was* a networker and *not* an organizer of those things. . . . How they tracked me down, I don't know. But they found my name somehow. Maybe from my newsletter . . . I don't remember going [to picket the clinic] more than 3 or 4 times. . . . I thought, "Oh my goodness, what has happened?

And why would they name us [Solano Citizens for Life]? We aren't even organizing this." I mean I was horrified. And yet, at the same time, I felt like, well, we can't just let them file it. We have to fight it. . . . And since they did not name individuals, but they named me. I mean I really didn't have a choice, did I? I mean I had to fight, so, I was not happy about it at all. I felt like it was unfair. You know, they were targeting us [Solano Citizens for Life] for some reason and, um, they'd [the picketers] been out there so short a time—I don't think we'd been out there very long.[13]

Faced with the lawsuit, Christine set to work raising funds at local churches and finding an attorney who could take the case. She found specific help for the latter in a local, newly created anti-abortion legal practice organization. "I think I had met Mary Maxen, who is now Mary Riley, who [was the] head of Life Legal [Defense] Foundation. And, they have a list of lawyers who will do pro bono work for Pro-Lifers. So she gave me John Street's number, and that's how we got started."[14]

John Street, a lawyer who describes his practice in the Marin County "bedroom community" of Novato as consisting of "trusts, wills . . . personal injury work, and . . . a smattering of other things," set to work quashing the motion against Birthright and preparing for the fast-approaching hearing and trial dates.[15] On September 12, 1990, after hearing evidence from three witnesses, Judge Dennis Bunting issued a temporary restraining order against Christine Williams and Solano Citizens for Life. The temporary injunction prohibited Christine, her group, and all those associated with it from verbally harassing or shouting at the plaintiffs and their clients, bringing children under 12 to the protests, taking photographs and recording license-plate numbers of those entering and leaving the lot, accosting or addressing any client who refused to take a plastic fetus, and it restricted their activities to two groups of two picketers separated by 10 feet on the sidewalk in front of the clinic.[16] One week later, Planned Parenthood filed to make the temporary injunction permanent.

Obviously displeased with the result, Christine recounted in her newsletter, "Now I understand what others have been through, and let me tell you, it is shocking to watch a judge totally disregard what the law says he is to do, not require any evidence of their [Planned Parenthood's] allegations, and decide against us. It is like looking evil right in the face! (And we do that every Thursday at the abortuary already!)"[17] After reporting their observational data on the demographics of Planned Parenthood's clients and the success that the group had been having "saving babies" while in the parking lot, the newsletter's discussion of the case ended with a plea to the readers. "As a public outcry to the injustice of the court's decision with our injunction, we are asking all area prolifers to join us on SUNDAY, OCTOBER 21, 2–3 pm to line up with signs along Broadway street. We will obey the injunction by having only 4 picketers on the sidewalk at 990 Broadway, but will line up on the adjacent sidewalks and across the street. . . . We'll do nothing illegal. No chance of arrest. Please come. We need your help!"[18]

It is at this time that many of those involved with the group from the start noted a change in the tactics and tenor of the picketing.

At that point, by putting us out on the sidewalk and keeping us away from talking to people who were not in a moving vehicle, they basically forced our hand in [that] you don't have any right at all. We can't share anything. So the only choice we had at that point in order to send any kind of a message to someone was to have the billboards and the posters. . . . If it was just me, I wouldn't have the graphic ones out there, I would have pictures of the baby in the womb that, for some people they felt that we really need to be in their face and we really need to show them what this is and what abortion does.[19]

[A]fter a while with certain personalities, I saw the flesh get a little too involved . . . I didn't want to be someone that, I just didn't want my flesh to get involved because we were getting thrown at and spat at and stuff like that and people can get upset and I didn't want to get involved in that scene. . . . They had different ideas about the kinds of signs and I was led more to do the informational sort of thing and calmly talk. Not that they were overboard or anything, but I just wasn't as comfortable.[20]

I think it changed when we went from being allowed to be in the back and to having to be on the sidewalk. It was a lot more tense. Before there was just, I don't know, it was like, after they kicked us out and we were always being watched and we were always worried about "Oh my God, are we too close to their building?"[21]

While the tension rose in front of the clinic, the legal wrangling continued in the courthouse. A trial date to determine the need for a permanent injunction was set for April 1991. In the passing months, the lawyers for both sides filed dueling motions: for evidence to be excluded; for Birthright to be reconsidered as a party to the case; and to throw the whole injunction out on the grounds that common law and Article 1 of the California State Constitution gave the protesters the right to defend life and others, and that Planned Parenthood, as a criminal organization, cannot bring a suit against others in order to reach its ends.

On April 18, 1991 Judge Dennis Bunting heard testimony from three witnesses called by Planned Parenthood. After cross-examining the witnesses, and feeling that Planned Parenthood's "case was so weak that the judge couldn't possibly grant the relief they were seeking," John Street, the lawyer for Solano Citizens for Life, motioned to get the case dismissed for lack of evidence. "I didn't even put on a witness, although I made lengthy legal argument."[22] After taking the case into consideration, and extending the decision date until August 1, Judge Bunting announced his decision to make the injunction permanent.

While the defendants were the only ones surprised by the initial restraining order and temporary injunction, the permanent injunction was a surprise for both parties in the case in relation to the scope of its most significant part. Where the temporary injunction had limited the picketers to two groups of two on the sidewalk in front of the clinic, the permanent injunction pushed the entire group to the other side of Broadway. The new, permanent injunction effectively replaced the previous buffer of a few feet between activist and intended audience with a busy four-lane street. According to Karen Anderson Ryer, the lawyer representing Planned Parenthood, "what would not fly with the judges . . . at least in my experience, was to put them across the street. It was too far away from the clinic. The people [the intended audience] would not be looking at them. . . . Thus they could not be heard or seen."[23] While she and some members of Planned Parenthood may have expressed surprise or even mild concern over the distance the protesters were pushed, Planned Parenthood was not about to oppose the move. On the whole, it was greeted as a welcome extra buffer—"it was kind of nice that they were on their own side. There was . . . something pleasant about having the thing [the protests] not be an issue."[24]

The same could not be said for the newly relocated group of counselors and picketers. The bright side of the permanent injunction, that "the signs are actually more visible from the new location" and that "we are no longer limited to four [picketers] anymore," could not overshadow the fact that "sidewalk counselors are still severely limited in talking with those going in."[25] The disappointment and anger about the decision that day was repeated over the course of the next few years while the case worked its way up to the United States Supreme Court. As the legal disputes continued in the form of appeals cases, John Street remained the primary lawyer for the anti-abortion activists. Planned Parenthood, however, eventually replaced Karen Ryer with a team of attorneys from the Walnut Creek office of McCutchen Doyle, a large law firm that had more appellate experience and resources.

On February 5, 1993, over 16 months since the case was appealed to the First District Court of Appeals in San Francisco, Christine Williams and the Solano Citizens for Life won their only, and partial, victory in court. The anti-abortion activists took a multipronged approach to challenging the injunction. They fought their exclusion from the sidewalk in front of the clinic on the grounds that the area was a public forum. They challenged their exclusion from the parking lot on the dual grounds that it too was a public forum and that the clinic did not have standing to file for the injunction since they did not have a possessory interest in the parking lot. Finally, they challenged the picket line prohibition on referring to "physicians, staff or clients as 'murdering' or 'murderers,' 'killing' or 'killers'; or to children or babies being 'killed' or 'murdered' by anyone in the Planned Parenthood building in the presence of children under the age of 12" on the grounds that it was a content-based restriction on their speech.[26] In a unanimous decision, the court largely used state law to uphold the exclusions from the parking lot and the sidewalk, but granted the demonstrators their lone victory by striking down the specific picket-line-language regulations as impermissible content-based restrictions on speech.[27]

From here the group went on to the California Supreme Court to challenge the sidewalk restriction only as an impermissible regulation of speech in a public forum. Writing for the majority, Justice Armand Arabian agreed that the sidewalk in front of the clinic was a public forum but that the regulation, after being modified by the Appeals Court, was a valid, content-neutral regulation of the time, place, and manner of speech. The injunction protected a significant state interest by protecting the health and safety of medical clinic patients. In spite of not being the least restrictive means of regulation, it was still narrowly tailored to meet the state interest. Finally, while the protesters were limited to the opposite sidewalk, they still had adequate means of communicating their message.[28]

Justice Joyce Kennard filed the lone dissent in the case, arguing that the facts did not support the grounds necessary for the injunction to be made permanent. She also argued that the court undermined the claim to content neutrality by citing the need to protect the psychological state of women entering the clinic. Justice Kennard went on to contend that the activists' banishment to the opposing sidewalk ended any claims that the injunction was narrowly tailored or allowed for meaningful alternative means of communication.[29] With the hope that Justice Kennard's opinion could be adopted to strike down the injunction, the protesters appealed to the U.S. Supreme Court. While John Street was still the attorney of record, he received help in his appeal in the form of an amicus brief from Jay Sekulow, Walter Weber, and Thomas P. Monaghan—lawyers who would soon help create Pat Robertson's conservative law firm, the American Center for Law and Justice.

One month after the California Supreme Court made its decision in the *Williams* case, the U.S. Supreme Court decided a related case, *Madsen v. Women's Health Center, Inc.* As part of its ruling in *Madsen*, the Court upheld a 36-foot buffer zone around the clinic entrance and driveway because it was found to be "a means of protecting unfettered ingress to and egress from the clinic, and ensuring that petitioners do not block traffic on Dixie Way."[30] However, by focusing on the governmental interest in protecting ingress and egress, the Court went on to strike down the buffer zone as it applied to the clinic property away from the driveway and entrance. Considering this development, the U.S. Supreme Court vacated and remanded the *Williams* case back to the California Supreme Court to reconsider the matter in light of *Madsen*.

Facing the case one more time, the California Supreme Court, again under the pen of Justice Arabian, did not find a conflict between their past ruling in *Williams* and the U.S. Supreme Court's ruling in *Madsen*. Building on their original list of significant government interests forwarded by the injunction, the California Supreme Court pulled from the *Madsen* decision and added the need to protect ingress to and egress from the clinic. Again filing the lone dissent, Justice Kennard cited two conflicts with *Madsen*. First, she found that since the preliminary injunction was performing its intended function, the escalation of regulatory means in the permanent injunction was not warranted by a significant government interest. Second, she felt that the buffer zone in *Madsen* worked to create an area where certain activities could *not* take place, but in *Williams*, the court had created a narrow zone where expressive activities may *only* take place. The result was to stand the buffer zone "concept on its head."[31] These arguments, however, did not work to persuade the rest of the court.

While the Solano Citizens for Life submitted another writ of certiorari to the U.S. Supreme Court, they failed to get the requisite number
of votes needed to grant the appeal. Angered by the California Supreme
Court's majority opinion that would remain standing, Justice Antonin
Scalia, joined by Justices Anthony Kennedy and Clarence Thomas, wrote
a fuming dissent to the denial of certiorari that reiterated Justice Kennard's concerns. The rare written dissent to a denial of cert began by citing *Schenck v. Pro-Choice Network of Western New York*—a case that the
Court had decided in the time between the California high court's affirmation of the injunction and the anti-abortion activists' second appeal
to the U.S. Supreme Court.[32] In Scalia and his fellow dissenters' view,
the *Schenck* case reaffirmed the rules from the *Madsen* case that required
striking down this injunction. In spite of this, the Court had allowed
"an injunction severely curtailing the speech rights of clinic protesters in
a public forum" even though the record was "so devoid of threatening
physical confrontation it would make an old-fashioned union organizer
blush."[33] Justice Scalia went on to blast the California Supreme Court for
effectively fabricating a legal justification for the injunction in order to
intentionally evade the Supreme Court's decrees:

In its second opinion in this case—after our remand in light of *Madsen*—the California Supreme Court for the first time discerned a second state interest in support
of the injunction: an interest in "ensuring unfettered access" to the clinic, 10 Cal. 4th
at 1022, 898 P.2d at 410. This, it should be noted with suspicion, is an interest which
the court had expressly disclaimed in its first opinion, saying that "the critical issue
[is] not access, but health and safety." 7 Cal. 4th at 879, n. 10, 873 P.2d 1235, n. 10.[34]

The protesters were similarly angered, not only by the case's end result but
also by the entire series of losses that they had endured. Like Scalia, they
viewed these cases with suspicion, seeing them as miscarriages of justice
springing from a variety of sources—a misunderstanding of the right of
free speech; the general biases of judges and other elites against the anti-
abortion movement (a bias that many anti-abortion activists collectively
refer to as the "abortion distortion"); a growing anti-Christian movement
in the United States; and the possibility of an insider conspiracy when the
case was in the Superior Court. This anger was immediate, and, as was
evident in many of the activists' interviews, it still lingered years after the
case's conclusion.

Literally based on no evidence that any of the allegations against picketers were true, he [the judge] not only decided we still could not be in the parking lot, but that we could <u>only be</u> on the sidewalk <u>across</u> the street. . . . Does this mean that standing in prayer could be construed as "demonstrating" and Christians could be arrested for praying on a public sidewalk? (I hope that pastors and church leaders are watching and aware of this erosion of freedoms.)[35]

I could have lived with it if the judges said, "Well you know, this parking lot is enough of a private property that you guys just need to stay on the public sidewalk." I could have understood that. And I could have said that the law's kind of gray about that parking lot. And I think that there are cases on both sides that would have supported either decision. But he [Judge Bunting] didn't say that. They [Planned Parenthood] weren't even asking for us to be off the public sidewalk. They were asking for us to be out of the parking lot. And he put us over here. That's what surprised me. That he had the audacity to tell us where we could be free speech people. And that's not legal. I still don't think it's legal.[36]

I want to know who paid the judge. I am serious. I really do think that there is something very, very seriously wrong with the judgment that came out of the Solano Courts. It's too weird. It's too weird. And I feel deep down inside that something happened to cause him to do it the way that he did that had nothing to do with the facts. And nothing to do with his intelligence.[37]

Judges are making decisions not based on constitutionality, but on feelings. They are writing the law from the benches with restraining orders. . . . The saddest thing in this particular case, for me is that case law has been written based on falsehood, on activism by a few judges. . . . That the facts could be so misconstrued that we had pushed women, that we had stood on that six by six slab out in front, that we had barred the doors. That that was allowed to be public testimony and recorded in case law that we had in fact done that, when in fact we had not. It was those days when we turned and we simply said Christ said that if they persecuted you, me, they persecute you. If I was wrongly accused, you will be wrongly accused. And we were wrongly accused that day. We never had the opportunity to clear that record.[38]

I had a pretty good idea you know, which way they [the Judges] were leaning before I ever walked through the door. Because, it's always made to seem like these Pro-Life people are a bunch of rabid extremists that are zealously trying to hinder women from getting a necessary abortion. I mean, philosophically, and this is not just my observation, I have talked to other lawyers that have been down the same path I have, this type of case bears what's known as the "abortion distortion." . . . What I mean by that is . . . you're considered to be in the wrong before you ever walk through the courtroom door. It's an uphill fight. I am not going to say every judge has that mindset, but it tends, tends to work out that [way], at least in my experience, and many other lawyers' experience.[39]

It seems like the Christians are the ones that are prevented from doing things, stopped from doing things.[40]

Years after the case was settled, the Vallejo Planned Parenthood clinic still has occasional picketers. The size and regularity of the activity, however, does not resemble the conditions before the injunction was secured. Of the early group of anti-abortion activists interviewed, Norman Reece was the last to leave the clinic. He reported that he stopped picketing in early 2003. Solano Citizens for Life dissolved shortly after the U.S. Supreme Court denied the second appeal to hear the case. No one said that the group died or that they personally became inactive as a result of the case outcomes. Rather, they maintained that they had decided to move on from picketing to pursue less public and more personal means of fighting abortion. These activities ranged from simply writing checks to pro-life groups to doing one-on-one counseling and abstinence advocacy at crisis pregnancy centers.

Christine Williams, however, is the exception. She does draw a link between her experience with the case and her lack of present-day anti-abortion activism. "I was beat up after this was over. I dropped out. I don't do pro-life right now." As for her organization, the Solano Citizens for Life, she, like the other interviewees, does not directly attribute its demise to the case outcomes. Christine has, however, come to see parallels between the state's treatment of the greater anti-abortion movement and groups like the Black Panthers: "They [the Black Panthers] were pretty much silenced by the U.S. government and the courts. And now I know that that was probably not right. You know, anytime something becomes too much of a threat, we just squelch it. And I think that's a violation of people's freedoms."[41]

3

Going Big
Schenck v. Pro-Choice Network of Western New York

Adeline (Addie) Levine's views on legalized abortion were formed nearly 25 years before the decision in *Roe v. Wade* when she trained and worked as a nurse after World War II. "We always had women on the gynecology ward who were suffering the after effects of botched abortions—pelvic disorders, you know, pelvic inflammatory diseases and all kinds of adhesions, and all sorts of stuff. And every, most of the girls I trained with were Catholic girls. And every one of them, pro-choice. You know, because you can't see that without realizing how stupid it is. . . . Because women are going to do it [get abortions in spite of their legality], that's all."[1] Her activism in relation to abortion rights, however, did not start until after an experience with anti-abortion protesters while on the way to the hairdresser.

I used to go to a hairdresser who was in this plaza called the Elmwood Plaza, or the Bell Plaza [where Marilyn Buckham had operated a clinic, Buffalo GYN Womenservices, that offered abortion services]. . . . I used to see protesters out there. And one time I got so angry because they were screaming at me not to murder my baby. At that time I must have been 50 years old. It was just ridiculous. And I went into the clinic and, I didn't even know what they were talking about "Don't murder your baby." And I asked them [the protesters] and they said, "Well, it's an abortion clinic. They are killing people." So I went upstairs and I offered to give them [the clinic] a contribution. And they were kind of surprised. They said "Well we don't take contributions." You know, but I found out, at that point I found out that they had two good films that I could use [in courses at the University at Buffalo, State

University of New York]. There was one on, on images about themselves called "Killing Us Softly." And after that I used to go back occasionally and pick that film up for my class.[2]

Just as Jeannette Hammer represented the typical pro-life activist, Addie Levine possesses a number of characteristics shared by many pro-choice activists of the time—she became active in political protests during the 1960s, is well educated, and has a professional life outside of the home.[3] More narrowly, Addie Levine is representative of many of the most active members of the Pro-Choice Network of Western New York (PCN), an abortion-rights organization that she later discovered and joined via her affiliation with the academic community in Buffalo, New York. Having lived in numerous places across the East Coast, she finally settled in Buffalo after taking a position in the Sociology Department of the University at Buffalo, State University of New York (SUNY Buffalo). As a professor, she is just one of many in the PCN affiliated with either SUNY Buffalo or the local Jesuit institution, Canisius College.[4]

On the final weekend in October 1988, a few years after her attempt to donate money to the clinic in Elmwood Plaza, Addie got a call from a friend concerning the large anti-abortion protests and blockades that had begun in Buffalo. Her friend said that there was going to be a meeting that afternoon concerning the clinics. Interested, Addie agreed to attend and proposed that afterward the two of them should go out to the movies.

Earlier that year, two events foreshadowed what would happen in Buffalo and gave a sense of urgency to the October meeting. First, the Buffalo-area was made aware of a local anti-abortion group, Project Rescue, when they had blockaded Dr. Paul Davis's clinic in Amherst, a suburb of Buffalo, that summer. Second, Operation Rescue—the national group that the local Project Rescue emulated—grabbed America's attention earlier that October by staging a series of large-scale "rescues" in Atlanta during the Democratic National Convention.

A rescue that had occurred on October 28, 1988 in Western New York was the subject of the meeting that Addie was headed to. While not as large as the rescues in Atlanta, it had resulted in 82 protester arrests and was part of a nationally organized "day of rescue." These facts could only have helped to push the local pro-choice community to begin to realize that Buffalo was becoming a front in this new and powerful manifestation of anti-abortion activity.[5]

Little did I know that my life was going to change [at the meeting]. So we went to the meeting, and when we got through hearing everybody's speeches—there were ministers and all sorts of people speaking—and um, so somebody said, "Well what do we do now?" And somebody else said, "Well let's march down and liberate the clinic."

So we marched down to the clinic, it was about, I don't know, maybe a mile, mile and a half away. We marched down and it happened, there was a band, the Outer Circle Band, and they were all very liberal and they were there with their drums and stuff so we went marching with a tune. Everybody got all jazzed up. One of the things that struck me funny was that a lot of the people were the old warhorses from the Vietnam War protests.

Anyway, so we went down, and this place was mobbed. It was just mobbed with all these protesters and the police were there. It had been going on, evidently, for two days. And the police were there starting to arrest people because the mayor at that time, Mayor Griffin, had told them [the police] to be very cautious about what they were doing because if even one life was saved [by the anti-abortion protests] it was worth it to have. You know, the mayor had a big sign over his desk, "ABC Abortion Kills Children." . . . Anyways, so that was his sentiment. So the police, of course were kind of slow about it [enforcement]. . . . And so we all got kind of jazzed up from it.

And in the paper that night, I think it was that night, there was a picture of Marilyn Buckham . . . looking out, peering out of a window. She was trapped inside the clinic [that she headed]. . . . And they took this picture of her [at the window]. I just got so angry. It just, you know, it just made me so mad to see people interfering with things that I feel are none of their business. Because in my prior trips to the clinic, the general feeling was that when you walked into a clinic like that, you could just feel it in the air. There were all these girls there. And some of their boyfriends, or parents, or whatever, husbands, whatever. The feeling was of such sadness. These people had reached this decision after a lot of agonizing. You know, whatever way, it's not a light decision on their part.

. . . I got really furious when I saw, somebody trapped like that. It just made me angry. She [Marilyn Buckham] seemed such a victim . . . Marilyn had afterwards said she, when she saw us come marching down the street, that it was just such a relief to her to know that there was somebody who cared.[6]

As a result of the spontaneous march to "liberate the clinic," Addie and her friend never made it to the movies that day.

Years earlier, Jane Holland, a local Planned Parenthood volunteer, had created a group with the intent of bringing all local reproductive rights organizations in Western New York into communication with one another. This loose-knit collection of organizations that met infrequently called itself the "Pro-Choice Network." While Jane Holland had since moved away from the Buffalo area, the Pro-Choice Network persisted. On November 8, 1988, one week after the march to "liberate the clinic," the PCN hosted a meeting in the Unitarian Church in the Elmwood district of Buffalo. Approximately 125 pro-choice activists met in order to organize against what they saw as a mounting threat posed by Project Rescue and other local anti-abortion activist groups. Since Addie's name was on a Planned Parenthood member/donor list, she was invited to the meeting and attended, thinking, "I don't want to get too involved in this. After all I am teaching." Once there, though, her resolve crumbled. "First, I signed up for mass mailing. . . . Then I felt, 'well, maybe I ought to help escort girls' [into the clinics past the protesters], because I had seen pictures of escorting. So, I signed up for that."[7] A week or two later she was contacted in order to be an escort at what was supposed to be another large-scale protest at Marilyn Buckham's Elmwood clinic.

At six in the morning, after checking the clinic in response to a bomb threat received the night before, Marilyn Buckham gave Addie and the other eight or nine other escorts identifying aprons. As time passed and no protesters materialized, Addie went to get some donuts—"when in doubt, eat."[8] When she came back and it was evident that the protest was taking place at a different Buffalo-area clinic, Addie asked Marilyn if there was anything else that she could do for her. From going to get donuts, Addie was promoted by Marilyn to organizing the escorts for the Network. As her first move, Addie "approached this little group that I was feeding donuts to and I said, 'Hey, is there anybody here who will help me organize the escorts?' And this white-haired woman said 'Yes, I'll help you.' Turned out to be Babs Conant. . . . And she and I both became extremely active. And I would say that she and I and Helen Dalley were the three most active organizers [in the PCN]. There were many people involved, but we were at the core of the organizers."[9]

From here the Pro-Choice Network of Western New York shed its loose-knit beginnings as a communication network between clinics and began its rapid growth spurt and maturation into a highly organized entity. A series of regular meetings and internal debates led to the group making the conscious decision to be as inclusive as possible. In order to not discourage potential members who were in support of reproductive rights, but not in support of other progressive political agenda items, the

Network decided to limit its focus to domestic reproductive rights issues. Eventually it formally stated its purposes as being "1. to bring people together to preserve and support women's reproductive rights, 2. to educate the general public regarding these rights, and 3. to undertake actions to publicize the significance of these rights and to counter the threats to them."[10]

In order to reach these ends, the Pro-Choice Network developed an organized internal structure to handle all foreseeable aspects of mounting a significant, multifront campaign. The Network first established executive and steering committees that were in charge of creating the PCN's by-laws. They also elected a board of directors to oversee the governance, operation, and evolution of the Network as a whole. A range of other committees and groups were created to conduct specific, ongoing tasks. The Pro-Choice escorts committee was in charge of organizing weekly groups of escorts at area clinics to address the immediate street-level problem of blockades and other clinic-front anti-abortion activism. The political projects committee kept the PCN up to date on relevant legislation, created an "adopt-a-legislator" program, and monitored political candidates' positions on abortion and anti-abortion activism. A speakers bureau managed communication with the press, institutions such as schools, and the general public. The newsletter committee produced the monthly newsletter *SPEAK OUT!* and circulated it to the PCN's members as well as local political figures, judges, and the media. A court watchers committee attended and tracked the various cases brought against protesters, regularly publishing their observations in *SPEAK OUT!*. The signature ad committee organized the collection of signatures for petitions to be published in the local newspaper, the *Buffalo News*. And finally, the letter writing committee focused their efforts on select elected officials. By April 1990 the Network had grown to include over 4,200 people on its mailing list; was conducting regular meetings, rallies, fundraisers, and public education campaigns; and had become incorporated as a 501(c) 4 nonprofit organization. Given this, it is not surprising that the Network's First Annual Report stated that "no week has passed without one or more committees meeting to plan and carry out activities."[11]

At the center of the perceived threat that the PCN was organizing against were the Schenck twins. Moving with their parents from New Jersey to Pennsylvania, and then finally to Western New York, the Schenck brothers began first grade in Grand Island, New York, just north of Buffalo. Activists "from a pretty young age, my brother and I were 'involved.' My first protest action was against the Vietnam War. My brother [Robert] and I were 12 years old and we were the only ones that were not arrested, and left on the sidewalk, because we were underage. Everyone else that I remember was carried off. . . . Also, when we were in the sixth grade we formed a group called Grand Islanders Against Pollution. . . . We handed out fliers and we ran a recycling deal in the local, in the local shopping mall."[12]

Having grown up in a Jewish family, the twin brothers converted to Christianity in their midteens. In the early 1980s Paul Schenck became the senior pastor of New Covenant Tabernacle, while his older-by-ten-minutes brother, Robert, was the church's "minister-at-large." In addition to his duties as the pastor of the church, Paul Schenck had two children with one on the way, "a daily religious radio program . . . hosted a weekly cable television program, and um, I was, good grief, I was 25 years old."[13] He and his brother, however, were not yet active in the anti-abortion movement.

While the exact timing is a little unclear, Rev. Paul Schenck recalls that in either 1987 or 1988 two members of his congregation requested to meet with him. As he tells it, the resulting meeting profoundly changed the brothers' lives.

They brought me, uh, some red bags. I now know what they are. I did not know what they were then. Medical waste bags which they had recovered from a trash dumpster across the street from their home. What they explained to me was that they had moved into a small bungalow house, kind of the quintessential starter home. And they, she was rocking the baby in the front room and she noticed someone in a white lab coat, with two other personnel, come out of the building from across the street, and was holding in his hand the, what appeared to be one bag, but what turned out to be several. And he held it up and pushed it, it appeared to have something in it. He then put it into the trash dumpster and got into his silver Peugeot and drove away. And she was so suspicious of that activity that she told her husband, who worked for a government agency, and he and a friend went into the trash dumpster that night, recovered the bags, and those were the bags that they brought to me.

We opened them and in them were the remains of four unborn children. They were little babies. You could hold them in your hands. They had identifiable features—faces, hands, depressions where their fingernails and toenails would sprout . . . and I could tell the sexes of two of them. Two of the four of them. . . . And this was the first time that I had seen the primary victim of an abortion. Until then I believed abortion was wrong, morally wrong, but people did wrong things and would reap the consequences. I never imagined being confronted with the victim myself. . . .

I said "we'll bury these babies. If necessary we'll bury them on the church property. We are certainly not going to put them back in the trash." And uh, but then, in the ensuing next couple of days after this encounter it occurred to me that if we buried these babies in a cemetery or even on the church property then the doctor who did this would never know that these babies were taken out of his trash bin and given a proper burial. So I changed my plans and I called a few people and we decided to take the funeral to the doctor's front lawn. . . .

I had three caskets for four babies. . . . We had Jewish, Catholic, and Protestant clergy and we had a memorial service with the babies out on the public sidewalk and about 200 people came including half the Town Counsel, the Supervisor, the Mayor, half the police force, two Chiefs of Police for the Town and the Village. And we had the longest motorcade that anyone could remember. We buried the babies at Mount Olivet Cemetery. . . . And we recovered two more babies after that until they got wise to us and stopped putting the babies in the trash. . . . So we buried six of those babies. . . . That was the seminal event for my becoming engaged in pro-life activism.[14]

Paul Schenck remembers the same couple later coming to ask him to lead a prayer service at the clinic. "I told my wife that night . . . and I said, 'I can't do this because I, I am going to get the reputation of being, being an insane agitator. And so my wife said 'If you don't, I will.' So we went together." The Schencks collected a group of about 40 or 50 people and went to the clinic and "we had what had amounted to a sit-in. . . . The police arrived. . . . We declined respectfully to move. We didn't move, and we were arrested en masse. . . . And that led to yet another [demonstration], and another. And we had seven abortion clinics in Buffalo. So we had a wide area and a lot of targets to um, uh, you know, to uh, to demonstrate at."[15]

While the early protests were not well organized, a wide group of activists in Western New York eventually became structured through the Western New York Clergy Council (now the National Clergy Council), headed by Paul Schenck, and other organizations such as Operation Rescue, led by Randall Terry, and Project Rescue Western New York.

During that time I was [also] on the executive committee for the Billy Graham Crusade. And we were bringing Billy Graham to Buffalo. . . . After we did that, we got some publicity. And I started receiving phone calls from Atlanta, Georgia. . . . Some pro-life protesters were organizing for the [1988 Democratic National] Convention. They asked me to come down. They said to me, "You are the pastor of the largest church represented among pro-life activists. There is no church now larger than yours, so you need to lend your leadership." And I was reluctant then because I was involved in the detailed planning of the Billy Graham Crusade, but I recognized the importance of it, and I acquiesced. . . . I flew to Atlanta and I saw what was happening there. . . . And I came home determined to lend leadership. And the first thing that I felt that we needed to do was, was mobilize a national movement of pastors. . . . It came on pretty quickly, you know. It was evolutionary, but it was still a pretty abbreviated evolution.[16]

With the myriad of connections that he developed through his various activities, Paul Schenck used the Clergy Council, a group of "eventually close to 80 clergy from about . . . 50 or 60 churches," to form the foundation from which to build a movement.[17] It was through this group and the help of nationally prominent anti-abortion figures, like Operation Rescue's Randall Terry, that Paul Schenck was able to mobilize pastors and thus to mobilize parishioners. The strategy's effectiveness is clearly evident via its prominence in a number of activists' stories.

He [Paul Schenck] talked to area pastors, and after he had talked to our pastor, our pastor talked to us as a congregation. And uh, suggested that we should, that there should be something done about this [abortion]. . . . It was given to us in such a way that you felt absolutely compelled at that moment to make your mind up about something. . . . At one point Randall Terry came to our church, and he spoke.[18]

Our pastor was a really strong leader, almost evangelistic in a way. . . . He was very inspirational. . . . He was really good like that. Knew how to bring people together. And Randall Terry of course was like that too. But he [the pastor], uh, started getting involved with it [anti-abortion demonstrations] himself, and kind of gave us a better handle on exactly what was going on. . . . Brought it home in such a way that we really felt like, you know, well maybe I should do something about this. I think it kind of started with going out and picketing. . . . At one point I actually built, I bought a poster . . . 16 feet by 8 feet, pretty large.[19]

When he [Randall Terry] spoke what he spoke [at our church], he kind of gave some outlines in the Bible. It was kind of in the Old Testament. And it was specifically about blood that was being shed on this particular land and how it affected the land, and how God cursed that land because of that. You know really, it really made you stop and think "Wow!" You know, we want God to bless America but this [chance of being cursed due to abortion] isn't cool.[20]

The core of Randall Terry's message concerning the fate of the country, abortion, and God's wrath was later published in a Project Rescue Western New York pamphlet meant to recruit more members to the cause.

WHAT IS AT STAKE?

Time is running out for America. If we don't end this holocaust very soon, the judgment of God is going to fall on this nation. Judah was destroyed because some Jews killed their own children and others stood passively by and didn't try to stop them. (See Kings 24:1-6. Ezekiel 16:20, 21, 36, 38, and Leviticus 20:1-5.) We are all guilty of letting this holocaust continue, and we will all share in God's punishment upon America, whether it be drought, war, AIDS, financial collapse or some other calamity.

Your standing for America's pre-born children means you are ultimately standing for the future, your children, your freedom, and the very survival of America. There are sacrifices to be made in order to fight this battle, but the cost of not fighting will be much higher in the long run. The survival of America is at stake. . . .

OBEYING GOD'S WORD

Rescue those who are unjustly sentenced to death; don't try to disclaim responsibility by saying you did not know about it. For God, who knows all hearts, knows yours, and he knows you knew! And he will reward everyone according to his deeds. *Prov.* 24: 11–12

No Supreme Court ruling can ever nullify God's commands, or our duty to obey His commands. The Scriptures concisely teach that when man's law and God's law conflict, "We must obey God rather than men" (Acts 5:29. See also Exodus 1:15 – 2:10, Joshua 2:1-16, Daniel 6:5-10, and Acts 4:15-20).

Even the law of man acknowledges that at certain times people may break certain laws to avoid a greater evil. We are simply being good, moral citizens by preventing the evil of aborting children.[21]

It was through a combination of messages like this one, Rev. Schenck telling the story of how he became a pro-life activist, the publicity generated by Operation Rescue, and the preaching and activism of Randall Terry and Western New York pastors that numerous people came to join the ranks of the movement. By early 1989, clashes between the rapidly growing anti-abortion and abortion-rights groups became regular features both in front of Buffalo-area clinics and in the local media and editorial pages. According to one article in the *Buffalo News*, "Since the first major demonstration last July [1988] when 215 protesters were arrested . . . 477 persons have been charged with a total of 738 non-criminal and misdemeanor offenses on both sides of the abortion spectrum, but only two of them, a doctor and a feminist, have been pro-abortion."[22] The description of what was occurring in front of the clinics and leading to these arrests varies somewhat according to who is telling the story and what kind of day they are recalling. Both sides do, however, generally agree that not all of the protests or protesters were the same. In short, some activities and people would be more aggressive than others.

As with countless other locations around the country, Buffalo-area clinics experienced regular, relatively small-scale picketing and counseling by anti-abortion activists. These were days when groups of people would organize among themselves and gather in front of clinics to carry signs, pray, and attempt to "counsel" those going into the clinics. While these groups were smaller than the crowds that would materialize at a rescue, the weekly groups were still sizable—peaking at around 150 protesters in late 1988 and early 1989, and eventually lessening to around 20 to 50 protesters by late 1989.[23]

In spite of the lower numbers of people in attendance for weekly protests, the clinics noted that these protests could also effectively result in blockades.

It [a regular, smaller-scale protest] was very peaceful but they were completely blocking the ability of anyone to get in and out of the driveway or the door. And I say very peaceful in that there would be maybe 20 people sitting or lying there and they were singing . . . or sitting there quietly. . . .

It would vary who was out on a particular day. Some protesters are much more aggressive than others. Some of the days when the more aggressive protesters were out, the car trying to turn into the driveway, there would be several people either very slowly baby stepping across the driveway so that the car couldn't get in or, and then when the car started to pull in, people coming right up to the windows of the car . . . so that the sign [that a protester carried] is almost blocking the driver's vision.[24]

This type of experience, however, is not what Buffalo became known for. The other type of protest that places like Buffalo, Wichita, and Atlanta experienced were called "rescues." These were large-scale, coordinated events that resulted in crowds of people intentionally blockading the clinics. Targeted clinics were also occasionally "invaded" by protesters who would lock themselves together or to objects inside the clinic. Rescues and invasions resulted in the temporary closing of clinics, numerous arrests, increased press coverage, and detailed preparation by both protesters and clinics.

Protesters who were part of the rescues conducted by Operation Rescue were asked by their leaders to abide by certain ground rules. In the case of at least one rescue in New York, participants were asked to sign an agreement that read:

RULES FOR ON-SITE PARTICIPATION

I UNDERSTAND the critical importance of Operation Rescue being unified, peaceful, and free of any actions or words that would appear violent or hateful to those watching the event on TV, or reading about it in the paper.

I REALIZE that some pro-abortion element of the media would love to discredit this event (and the entire prolife movement) and focus on a side issue in order to avoid the central issue at hand—murdered children and exploited women.

HENCE, I UNDERSTAND that for the children's sake, this gathering must be orderly and above reproach. THEREFORE . . .

1   As an invited guest, I will cooperate with the spirit and goals of Operation Rescue, as explained in this pamphlet.
2   I commit to be peaceful, prayerful, and non-violent in both word and deed.
3   Should I be arrested, I will not struggle with police in any way (whether deed or word), but remain polite and passively limp, remembering that mercy triumphs over judgment.[25]

In general, there were three types of activities that a protester could take part in during a rescue. As described in an Operation Rescue pamphlet, those prepared to risk arrest could directly join the blockade and sit in front of the entrances to clinics, "placing themselves, physically, between women wanting to kill their babies and those inside waiting to commit the crime. This prevents the murder of babies during the time of the rescue. When police come to arrest them, they go limp, which makes it necessary for the officers to carry them away. This may take hours, buying time for the unborn."[26] If one did not want to risk arrest, one could join "prayer support" or carry a sign and picket. Both prayer support and picketing groups were intended to be limited to the sidewalk, out of the way of the blockades, but if anyone felt moved to join the blockade, they could cross over the line and sit in.

[In] some of the larger-scale blockades, what was going on was fairly chaotic. There would be large numbers of people lying down on the driveway across the mouth of the driveway so that cars could not get in and out unless they wanted to run over 25 people. Or they would be sitting or lying down in front of the doorways so that nobody could get in and out of the doorway. And they would be linking arms as they sat or laid down. And they would be chanting. If the police tried to remove them they would link with other people or they would even go limp so that it made it hard for the police to remove them. . . .

When the police would drag 20 away from the driveway the people on the other side of the street would send another wave of 20 over to crawl under the legs of the police who were busy dragging the others away so that they would quickly fill in and keep the blockade going.

There, there were, when somebody would try to drive into the driveway, particularly if they knew it was a car of a staff person or a doctor, there would suddenly be five or six large men banging on the car, jumping on the hood. There would be a lot of jostling, grabbing, um. You know, things, things could get fairly chaotic during the large-scale blockade.[27]

Along with the protests at the clinics, anti-abortion activists sometimes picketed the homes and neighborhoods of the doctors and high-level staff members who worked at or operated the clinics.

On the whole, the pro-choice activists and the clinic members describe the protests as "Serious. . . . To give you some perspective . . . at the end of the [first] year [of protests], December 31st, there is the year in review. The local paper publishes that. And we [Dr. Wortman's Rochester, New York clinic] made one of the top 10 [stories of the year]."[28] "They were really pretty horrendous. Very scary. Very Scary. . . . They really were frightening. . . . I'll tell you, people were really scared."[29] "Long. Tired. Exhausting. Drawn out. And you know . . . you were pumped. You know, it was almost like you were going into battle in some ways. It, it, it was, not exciting, but it was, your adrenaline was pumping and flowing. Very nervous sleepless nights. It was exhausting."[30]

The visceral reaction to the protests was shared on the other side of the rescues. While all of the protesters stressed the themes of the rescues being peaceful and passive, their passionate nature was undeniable. "Certainly emotions ran very high in these events, and uh, it took a lot to be able to control, to control yourself, on both sides I am sure."[31] "During the height of things, we were getting pretty bold."[32]

I felt so passionate when I got there [to a clinic during a rescue]. One time, huh, there was a doctor trying to come into the abortion clinic—I couldn't even believe it

myself sometimes. But you've got to understand, it's like, it's hard for me to understand how a soldier lays down his life in a war situation, and I was never a military
kind of guy, you know, but at this particular instance, I was a militant. I was totally
convinced in this area . . . I was really ready to give my life. I couldn't believe it when
I thought back about that thing. But essentially, that's why I couldn't become a sidewalk counselor or take the next level because I was just too passionate.[33]

Sometimes there was a mixing. If there was a big crowd of escorts, and a big crowd
of us, there was invariably, you know, we kind of mixed, and sometimes mixed it up
a little bit, you know? Maybe it was a little physical, but not, not punching or anything. People were out, holding their ground.[34]

The clinics initially relied on the police to arrest the protesters in order
to combat the blockades. However, as many of those involved with the
clinics at the time attest, they immediately felt that the police were not of
much help on their own. This lack of faith in the local police was due to
a belief that Mayor Griffin had instructed the force to move slowly and
also that individual members of the police force supported the protesters.
On November 12, 1988, only four days after their first meeting, members
of the newly revitalized Pro-Choice Network picketed "in front of the
Buffalo Police headquarters to protest the slow removal of blockaders on
October 28–29 [1988]."[35]
    One year later:

After the blockade of the clinic at 1241 Main St. on Oct. 28, 1989, several of the
escorts complained to their Councilmen about the treatment that we and the patients
received from the Buffalo Police. [Council member] Al Coppola agreed to bring our
problem to the attention of the Common Council at the meeting on Nov. 21, 1989.
Since our grievances were not answered adequately at that time, it was agreed that it
would be discussed at a later time. . . . After hearing both sides on April 6, 1990, the
Council decided to ask the FBI to investigate since they believed that there was strong
evidence of selective enforcement of the law by the Buffalo Police Department.[36]

Further examples of the PCN's internal and external attempts to get more
desirable reactions from the police—which included writing letters to and
having meetings with members of the force, recording the names of officers who yelled at escorts, and creating internal guidelines for how to act
in reaction to the police—can be found in the minutes kept by the Network from its various meetings over the years.

Resorting to methods of self-help to supplement the support (or lack thereof) that they were receiving from the police, the clinic escorts "used to have to make a ring around the patients to get them in [to the clinic]."[37] In addition to forming human rings around patients, the PCN considered erecting temporary mobile walls held up by escorts called "defense boards" in order to create pathways for patients to walk through. The idea was eventually rejected when members cited various potential problems with the plan—that patients may not feel comfortable with the use of the boards, that the use of such tactics could be interpreted "as an escalation of the pro-choice part, that more extreme measures are being taken," and that the use of the boards could lead to various legal problems when wielded by "overzealous" members of the Network.[38]

One of the more creative forms of self-help undertaken by the PCN was to infiltrate the ranks of the picketers in order to undermine their efforts. As one PCN member wrote in the newsletter:

We picketed at Dr. Paul Davis' office along with the anti-choice group, but our signs exposed a hidden agenda: that they are opposed to most forms of contraception, against most sex education, against most human sexuality, and are anti-women. Our signs said, "We oppose all birth control," "Ban the pill," and "Make babies, not love." My sign, "Sex is disgusting and unholy" (an actual quote from one of the pro life leaders), elicited an incredible response. . . . Aside from the fun and raising public awareness, there were other effects. The anti-choice people were put off balance and actually stopped picketing. Not wanting to be associated with us, they put down their signs and just stood around. This meant that they were distracted from harassing patients, so our primary goal was accomplished. This was one of the greatest, most empowering pickets I've ever been involved with and I highly recommend it to everyone.[39]

Along with onsite self-help and police efforts, the clinics also relied on the local courts as a means for fighting back against the protesters. By bringing criminal trespass and other misdemeanor cases against individual protesters, the clinics hoped to use the courts to apply pressure that would force the blockades to stop. This tactic, however, was not fruitful. While the clinics could get the police to arrest protesters, however slow the process, they could not get the courts to consistently follow through with convictions on the charges. Additionally, when the courts would pronounce a sentence, the impact on the protests as a whole was minimal.

The charges against all 82 anti-abortion activists arrested during the October 28, 1988 rescue were quashed and had to be filed again. Of the 109 demonstrators arrested in a protest on November 19, 1988, all charges were quashed, filed again, and then quashed again. Ninety demonstrators were arrested for being inside the High Street Clinic on February 17, 1989, and all 90 demonstrators were found not guilty by the end of April. In February 1989 the court fined a demonstrator for trespass but allowed "him to avoid a 15-day jail term on the condition that he avoid [the clinic at] 260 Elmwood." Eight days later the same protester was arrested for trespass at the 260 Elmwood clinic—a violation for which he later served 20 hours of a seven-day jail sentence.[40]

The sum of such results was deeply felt disillusionment with the local courts on the side of the Pro-Choice Network.

Local courts were awful. I don't know why they are there. I just, not for us. It just was awful. These people might as well, for all of the energy and time that it took, it was just a waste. . . . They [the Judges] were on the Right to Life ticket, and we'd pull that judge [to hear our cases]. I mean it was just awful. They would let them [arrested protesters] walk 90% of the time. "You know, they didn't hurt anyone." And, "You know, so they crossed the line, what's the big deal?"[41]

The courts and abortion have been in the news daily these past weeks . . . we need only read the Buffalo News for a shocking litany of justice denied in our city, the most recent being Judge Mazur's finding on April 27th [1989] that 86 persons jammed into EMC [Erie Medical Clinic] halls could not be shown to be trespassing. Our notoriety as a city that does not prosecute blockaders will inevitably attract bolder harassment activities. . . . To comment on Judge Mazur or others, call . . . the information number of the General Court.

Let's change some faces. Judges Broderick, Romuno and Figliola all took Right-to-Life endorsements at their last election. Judge Mazur did not, but he acts like he is paying an anti-choice debt. . . . *Change their faces, change their places.*[42]

For the protesters, the result was that the courts, at least in the early years, seemed impotent.

I was baffled, in some ways, by the court system and how crazy that was. I got a new perspective of that. Just how crazy that whole thing was. . . . It really affected me in a huge way. I thought, "No wonder they can't convict anybody anymore."

Just some of the things that happened. . . . The police would come and they'd say, after a while they'd say, "OK, we are giving you a warning here. Um, you are trespassing, you know, and we want you to leave." And, um, so then of course, you know, we'd get up and leave and come back a little later. . . . And what it came down to was, in court it said, you know, the arresting officer, "Can you tell me for sure that this guy was here when they made the announcement, you know, you need to get up and leave the premises?" And he said, "No." So we would all get off for some simple little thing like that.

. . . I just saw, you know, how, in a lot of ways, how the police, and how the, you know, other people struggle with, you know. It just gave me the realization of how they must really feel frustrated sometimes when, you know, having to try and convict people that are generally guilty of things that are really wreaking havoc in the, in society, you know. It just amazed me.[43]

Unwilling to accept the current state of affairs, the Network continued to try and develop a means of effectively controlling and combating the protesters. In April 1989, the steering committee for the Network decided that it needed to address the subject of long-term strategies. Despite the PCN's theretofore poor judicial track record, the first indications that the courts would be part of the Network's long-term strategy appeared in the November 1989 steering committee meeting minutes. "It is her [Marilyn Buckham's] feeling that, bottom line, pro-choice forces need an injunction and that no other course would be effective [in controlling the protests]. Marilyn stated that she is looking for a 'lead' attorney to work on an injunction which would legally limit the number of feet protesters could block, the number of protesters allowed, etc."[44]

Shortly before this PCN steering committee meeting, Lucinda Finley, a professor from Yale University Law School, relocated to the Buffalo area to start a one-year visiting professor position at SUNY Buffalo Law School. It did not take long for Lucinda to witness the conflict over abortion in what was to become her adopted city. In October 1989—one year after the blockading began in earnest—Marilyn's clinic was again blockaded.

I had never seen anything like this before. In New Haven, Connecticut they didn't have stuff like this. And I remember watching this blockade and watching the police not do anything to stop it and I was just flabbergasted. And I said "This is outrageous. This, you know, I should help try to stop this." . . . My colleague [at SUNY Buffalo Law School] Isabel Marcus . . . she was active in the Pro-Choice Network and she began bringing me to meetings. And um, introduced me to them. And sort of that's how I got connected and expressed my interest in helping.[45]

While harboring an interest in civil rights and civil liberties issues, Lucinda Finley's primary interest was in feminist legal theory. Up to this point,

Lucinda's work in feminist legal theory had manifested in teaching courses and working on cases about employment discrimination. Given the events in Buffalo, abortion access was quickly added to her areas of interest and she was appointed to a position on the PCN's board of directors.

I got to know Marilyn, and Marilyn and I became friendly. And, you know, I was a law professor, she would generally ask for advice and I was tracking some cases. And I guess around the time that the Second Circuit [Federal Court of Appeals] decided *NOW v. Terry* in '89? Um, I think I told her and the Network people about this case and that it, that it gave the basis for a Federal injunction here.

   . . . [U]nder the auspices of the Center for Constitutional Rights in New York and maybe the NOW [National Organization for Women] Legal Defense Fund, there was a meeting in New York for interested lawyers to come and brainstorm and strategize. . . . And we talked about using 42 USC 1985(3) [a federal anticonspiracy civil rights law] and we kicked around the pros and cons using RICO [federal anti-racketeering law], and state law versus federal law. Just generally a lawyers' strategizing brainstorm.

   I found it very helpful and came back and told Marilyn and some people from the Network about it and that, based on what I'd been told and the things going on here, I thought that we had a good basis for getting an injunction. And Marilyn told me "I don't think so. We had already tried." . . . The head of the local NOW chapter had done it [sought an injunction]. And they had gone to state court, they had done it wholly in state court and they didn't get a preliminary injunction and kind of gave up at that point.

   So I told Marilyn I would go talk to Loraine Kelly [the lawyer who had worked with the local NOW chapter] and sort of find out what was going on. . . . Loraine told me that she didn't think that the general conservative judiciary around here would get anywhere with anything. And she said that . . . when they went before the state judge the day they had their preliminary injunction hearing there was actually a blockade going on. And they were pulling in witnesses from the blockade and he said that he didn't think that they were showing any likelihood of repetition or irreparable harm . . . it wasn't worth pursuing the case.

   And, I remember telling Marilyn, "Hey, I am a law professor. I am not a full time lawyer. I don't have time to, you know, [engage in] major litigation. This case will be time consuming. Um, but I think based on the Second Circuit decision and some of these developments in Federal Law, I think that you've got a good legal ground." And I told her that I didn't think that the state case, it hadn't gone anywhere, would preclude us from going to Federal Court under Federal law, and that I would go around with her and talk to various federal litigators in Buffalo and see if I could interest someone. . . .

I remember my own personal reaction [to the Buffalo legal community] was a couple things—very risk averse, very unwilling to push the legal envelope, very unwilling to stick their necks out. . . . [We] got a lot of, "Gee, I'd love to help you, but I have partners who are anti-abortion and I don't think therefore, that I can take [this case]." . . . I began to get a sense of the general conservatism of the Buffalo legal community. . . .

And also the other problem we were running into was, Marilyn's clinic is a profit clinic [thereby excluding the clinics from getting pro bono legal services] . . . which is an entirely legitimate criterion. And Marilyn could not afford that and she also said the other doctors probably wouldn't join if it was going to cost them a lot of money. . . . So there things sort of stood.[46]

On September 10, 1990 the Pro-Choice Network board of directors met with the intent of discussing "strategy for the Network for the next year."[47] The meeting, however, was quickly refocused onto a more immediate and pressing matter. As Lucinda Finley recalls:

Marilyn came in and sat next to me and shoved a pamphlet in my face and said, "Look! Look! Look what they are going to do." And I looked down at the pamphlet and it was a Project Rescue Western New York [newsletter]. It was announcing that on September 28, 1990 there would be a Rescue at, you know, an unidentified abortuary. . . . And a typical lawyer's reaction, I saw this pamphlet and I said, "Oh good! This is the smoking gun evidence we need to show a judge that something is about to happen to get an injunction."[48]

While aimed at an immediate threat, the ensuing discussion met the meeting's original intent by inadvertently laying the foundation for a significant part of the PCN's long-term strategy in battling the anti-abortion protesters.

The discussion at the September 10 meeting addressed a wide range of concerns about seeking a temporary restraining order that would be followed by the move to secure a standing injunction. The arguments against the strategy focused on two main areas—a mistrust of the legal system and a concern with money. The PCN and the clinic run by Marilyn Buckham—Buffalo GYN Womenservices—were both interested in pursuing the injunction strategy, but they were concerned that other clinics would not join and help bear the estimated financial burden of $5,000 to $15,000. The primary fear with cost stemmed from a concern with free riders. Since the injunction would cover a geographic area instead of just one clinic, those who did not finance the effort would still benefit from it.

Additionally, there were worries about the opportunity costs of the injunction and how it would impact their funding needs in other areas. On the other hand, the Network was also anxious that if they let these fears stop them from pursuing the injunction they "will look foolish to Operation Rescue" and help bolster the opposition's confidence.[49]

Individual PCN members were also concerned with various technical and personal pitfalls that the legal system presented. One member who had witnessed another clinic's attempt to obtain an injunction recalled that she was "appalled at the extensive process because even a typing error could cancel everything."[50] Others posed a range of questions, including: "Can we trust the Federal judges to come through for us?"[51] "How do Federal judges have the leeway to be able to make these decisions?"[52] "Do we rely on the Buffalo police who have shown not to want to enforce the law?"[53] And "are we safe as individuals on the Board [from being countersued]?"[54] At the most basic levels, Network members also noted that "an injunction won't necessarily prevent a rescue."[55] "Escorts have thwarted blockades several times in the past and I don't understand why we're getting so hyper now."[56] And, when faced with all of these concerns, they asked, "Is there anything else we can do instead of this?"[57]

These concerns were countered by listing the possible benefits and the perceived limited costs of beginning the strategy. While the injunctions might not always stop the blockades, the members should "just remember that an injunction does tend to seize up anti[-abortion] activity,"[58] that "it's a symbolic statement,"[59] and that those who violate the injunction "will be in contempt of FEDERAL court. There have been fines of $100–400,000 on individuals in NYC . . . [and that] this was owed to the government (like taxes, so they don't screw around collecting)."[60] Additionally, "a TRO [temporary restraining order] is only for 10 days but an injunction lasts longer" so that pursuing an injunction could be part of a long-term strategy of pressuring the protesters.[61]

Finally, while Network members and other clinics that they knew of had not had much success in the past with local and state courts, the PCN thought it should trust and now try the federal courts for a combination of reasons. In the past, the Network had "often known that something was going to happen, but this is the first time we've had something in print we could use against them [in court concerning a blockade]."[62] In addition to the physical evidence, the law seemed to be on their side since "it was determined by the Second Circuit . . . that a blockade is in violation of a woman's constitutional rights" and that similar New York "cases have won,

[so] legally this is about as open and shut as it could get because of the NYC decisions."[63] This final statement would turn out to be very far from true.

Hearing that they should feel confident with their legal standing, that the "TRO cost is minimal," that "the PCN only has a percentage [financial] responsibility and can withdraw at any time later,"[64] and that they had to make their decision now due to the dual pressures created by the threatened blockade and the fact that they "can't add plaintiffs later on,"[65] the PCN board voted 13–1 to start the suit. The board subsequently voted 12–1–1 to cap their initial financial commitment to $1,000 in two installments.[66] "At that point I [Lucinda Finley] said 'OK. I will throw together the papers, go to Federal Court, at least get the temporary restraining order to stop the protest on the 28th of September, and *then* I will find you a full time practicing lawyer to take over the case.'"[67]

After the meeting, the PCN went to work recruiting a number of clinics and doctors in Western New York to join the move to get a temporary restraining order and, ultimately, a permanent injunction. Over the following weekend at Lucinda's house, with the assistance of a "very primitive word processor . . . , sample complaints from the *NOW v. Terry* case and others," and the affidavits given by escorts, the paperwork was completed and ready to be filed in federal court on September 24. "Through the luck of the [judge selection] wheel, poor [Judge] Richard Arcara got stuck with this mess for the rest of his life. Richard Arcara and *me*. . . . At that point I continued to try to find some other lawyer who, you know, would sort of take over the case. But, I must admit, after doing all that work, it shortly became *my* case and then it wasn't like I was going to hand it over to someone else."[68]

Project Rescue made a strategic decision to not state which clinic would be the site of the September 28 rescue in order to hinder the abilities of the PCN to plan a defense. This move, however, allowed for the temporary restraining order and eventual injunction to cover a wider area. Since no one clinic was specifically threatened, all could be perceived as needing the state's protection. On September 27, 1990, three days after having filed their papers and one day before the planned rescue, Judge Arcara granted a TRO that:

> Enjoined and restrained in any manner or by any means:
> (a) trespassing on, sitting in, blocking, impeding or obstructing access to, ingress into or egress from any facility at which abortions are performed in the Western District of New York, including demonstrating within 15 feet of any person

seeking access to or leaving such facilities, except sidewalk counseling by no more than two persons as specified in paragraph (b) shall be allowed;

(b) physically abusing or tortiously harassing persons entering or leaving, working at or using any services at any facility at which abortions are performed; Provided, however, that sidewalk counseling, consisting of a conversation of a non-threatening nature by not more than two people with each person they are seeking to counsel shall not be prohibited. Also provided that no one is required to accept or listen to sidewalk counseling and that if anyone who wants to, or who is sought to be counseled who wants to not have counseling, wants to leave, or walk away, they shall have the absolute right to do that, and in such event the person seeking to counsel that person shall cease and desist from such counseling of that person. In addition, provided that this right to sidewalk counseling as defined herein shall not limit the right of the Police Department to maintain public order or reasonably necessary rules and regulations as they decide are necessary at each particular demonstration site;

(c) making any excessively loud noise which disturbs, injures, or endangers the health and safety of any patient or employee of a health care facility where abortions are performed in the Western District of New York. . . .

(d) attempting, or inducing, encouraging, directing, aiding, or abetting in any manner, others to take any of the actions described in paragraphs (a), (b) and (c) above; and it is further

ORDERED that nothing in this Order shall be construed to limit Project Rescue participants' exercise of their legitimate First Amendment rights.[69]

Failure to comply with sections (a) –(d) of the TRO would result in civil damages of $10,000 per day for the first violation, with successive violations resulting in a doubling of the previous fine. In addition, if a defendant was found in civil contempt, the guilty party would be responsible for all attorney fees. If convictions could be secured, these penalties gave the TRO a substantial bite.

As the PCN expected, the attorneys for the protesters filed a suit in order to throw out the TRO. In an attempt to broker a compromise, Judge Arcara encouraged the parties to reach a consent settlement. The Network, feeling confident in their stance, approved of the idea since it would "avoid a hardening of lines and [would create] no opportunity for appeal."[70] No settlement, however, was reached. Forging ahead, the PCN, along with the various doctors and clinics that had joined the suit, moved to turn the TRO into a preliminary, and then permanent, injunction.

Over the next year, skirmishes both in the courtroom and on the streets continued. While the litigation strategy remained under Lucinda Finley's control, the PCN enlisted the help of a local trial lawyer, Glenn Murray, in order to enforce violations of the restraining order. Much to the pleasure of the Network and its affiliates, the TRO seemed to be having its desired effect. "It turns out that Rochester had an attempted block at Highland Hospital and two weeks ago there was a standard picket at Geneseo. Someone overheard the anti's say that the TRO that we filed may cover their activities in Rochester. So on Sat. when there was an attempt to enter Highland the Rochester police told the anti's about the TRO and the anti's left!!"[71]

By October 1991, however, "Operation Rescue . . . threatened to invade Buffalo by April 17th [1992]."[72] Much to the dismay of the members of the Network, Buffalo's Mayor Griffin seemed to increase this likelihood by stating that he "welcomes Operation Rescue with 'open arms.'"[73] In accordance with the threat to "invade," Randall Terry and other high-level members of Operation Rescue began a series of visits to the Buffalo area as they prepared for a 15-day series of large-scale rescues that would later be known as the "Spring of Life."

The Pro-Choice Network was also occupied with its own preparations. While satisfied with the initial results of the TRO, Lucinda Finley spotted a hole in the document that she wanted plugged before the TRO became a preliminary injunction.

When I realized that it wasn't tight enough was right after the TRO was enacted by the Federal Court. For that weekend I went out to the clinic to sort of monitor what was going on. I remember there was a leader of the protesters then named Dwight Saunders. He was a lawyer. . . .

There were some Federal Marshals who had come out to sort of monitor things. And I was there. And I remember Saunders was leading protesters in a slow parade back and forth across the mouth of the driveway. And some cars were out on the street sort of waiting to get in. . . . And I am watching this and I [said] "Dwight. Get your people out of the driveway. You know you can't do this." And he goes over to the Federal Marshal and says, "She's telling me, what do you think?" And the Marshall's like, "I'm not here to interpret the injunction. You know, ask your lawyer. Ask her, she's the lawyer. Ask the Judge."

And so Dwight Saunders and I are in this argument in the street. And he is saying, "That car's more than 15 feet away. We're not within 15 feet of that car." And I am sitting there saying to myself, "Shit, he's right. What I really want is for them to not be in the driveway."[74]

In order to solve the problem in the preliminary injunction, Lucinda moved to include a 15-foot no-protest buffer around all clinic entrances and driveways. She did not, however, drop the floating buffer from the injunction. "Once I got the so-called 'fixed buffer' around doorways and driveways, it was like we never needed . . . . Let me put it this way. We never had any occasion or need to enforce or worry about what subsequently became known as the 'floating bubble' [section (a) of the TRO]."[75] As a result of adding the fixed buffers, but not dropping the floating buffers, the eventual preliminary injunction came to possess both elements. This oversight helped to ensure that this injunction case would be more than just the "open-and-shut" matter that it was billed as.

In fact, even when Lucinda was working on the TRO there were signs that the matter was not so straightforward. As she noted:

It [the *NOW v. Terry* decision that the TRO was modeled after] said that people had the right, that protesters had the right to sidewalk counsel. That people also had the right not to accept sidewalk counseling. I remember saying to Alison Wethersfield [a lawyer who worked on *Terry*], "That's really nice. Nice hortatory statement that you have the right to refuse sidewalk counseling, but what the hell good is it without some countervailing restriction on the protesters?"

And I said, "Why didn't you ask for, you know, that if someone refused the counseling, that the sidewalk counselor then had to stop or cease and desist?" And she said, "We didn't ask for it because I didn't think that we could get it, constitutionally." And I said, "Oh really? Because I think I can." And she said, "Well, I don't know about that." And so at that point I said, "Well, I am going to put that in my TRO. And I, I think I can defend a cease and desist requirement if someone has actually said no, leave me alone." And so I thought, so all along, she'd said well, that I was definitely pushing the envelope on that.[76]

The PCN also became aware of how they were potentially heading out on a limb, legally speaking, during their February 11, 1991 board meeting. "From talking to NOW lawyers, we know that no one in the country has focused yet on the legality of 'sidewalk counseling,' especially at this state and in regard to the First Amendment. This potentially could go all the way to the Supreme Court."[77] In that meeting it was also noted, "The ACLU may be on the other side of this case . . . [because] of First Amendment issues."[78] Undeterred, the push for the injunction continued.

On Valentine's Day, 1992, the PCN's legal efforts paid off as Judge Arcara granted the preliminary injunction.[79] There were two significant changes to the TRO in the preliminary injunction. Due to Lucinda's revelation from observing the TRO in action, the first change was the inclusion of the fixed 15-foot buffer around "either side or edge of, or in front of, doorways or doorway entrances, parking lot entrances, driveways and driveway entrances of such facilities." This fixed buffer was in addition to the floating 15-foot buffer around "any person or vehicle seeking access to or leaving such facilities." Second, along with the possibility of being found in civil contempt for the "failure to comply with this Order by any defendant or anyone acting in their behalf or in concert with them," violators were now subject to the possibility of criminal contempt charges for first-time and repeat violations of the injunction.[80]

The Network praised the injunction as "a welcome Valentine's Day present to the interest of law and order and to the health and safety of women seeking abortions" and a protection "against the excesses of clinic blockades such as Operation Rescue."[81] In further explaining the preliminary injunction to the PCN membership, the newsletter stressed the injunction's perceived potency, its legal and normative authority, and the care taken in balancing the rights of protesters, patients, and doctors.

The Judge's thorough and scholarly decision carefully balanced the rights of anti-abortion protesters to demonstrate, with the rights of doctors to practice medicine, and of women and staff to enter health care facilities without obstruction, harassment and intimidation. . . .

Judge Arcara's injunction sends a stern message to Operation Rescue and local anti-abortion activists. . . . The decision and order represent a significant additional weapon to deter the threatened disruption or punish the transgressors.

Arcara's injunction is one of the most comprehensive yet issued against anti-abortion protesters. . . .

While the defendants have protested to the media that this injunction curtails their free speech rights, Judge Arcara thoroughly considered that claim and rejected it. The Judge carefully analyzed extensive Supreme Court case law establishing that the right to demonstrate and express one's views must be balanced against other rights—such as public safety and privacy. . . . The February 14th decision and Preliminary Injunction are amongst the most significant developments yet in the Network's ongoing struggle to maintain unfettered and safe access to needed reproductive health care services in western New York. The court's decision also underscores that no one i[n] this country can put themselves above the law without expecting consequences . . . neither strength nor depth of feeling on an issue, nor religious conviction, nor moral certainty gives anyone the right to trample on the rights of others or on the laws designed to maintain mutual rights and peaceful co-existence despite social disagreements.[82]

While adamantly disagreeing with much of the portrayal of the injunction presented in the Network's newsletter, the protesters and their lawyers must have shared some of the sentiment expressed in the article's conclusion—"neither strength nor depth of feeling on an issue, nor religious conviction, nor moral certainty gives anyone the right to trample on the rights of others or on the laws designed to maintain mutual rights and peaceful co-existence despite social disagreements." Using a similar argument to a different end, the protesters soon filed an appeal with the Federal Second Circuit Court of Appeals, the main element of which was the claim that the First Amendment rights of the protesters were being trampled on by the injunction's terms.

As with the year following the TRO's pronouncement, the months after the preliminary injunction were marked by arrests at the clinics for violations of the court order and maneuvers in court concerning the injunction's future. Undeterred by the injunction, the Spring of Life began on April 20, 1992. On the following day Judge Arcara issued bench warrants for the arrest of six Operation Rescue leaders, and the PCN had a two-page ad in the *Buffalo News* with the signatures of over 1,500 people denouncing Operation Rescue tactics.

The following two weeks secured Buffalo's Spring of Life alongside Wichita's 1991 Summer of Mercy and Atlanta's rescues in 1988. In addition to the now-standard blockades, Operation Rescue customized their Buffalo efforts in multiple ways that circumvented the injunction. The group aired advertisements that included radio spots listing the names of local abortion providers and the plea that listeners "beg them to stop." Seemingly following the request of the ads, "a local pro-life activist was accused of asking [Dr.] Slepian's wife why she couldn't persuade her husband to stop murdering children. The activist then apparently pointed to the couple's four children, saying she hoped they wouldn't grow up murdering children as their father does."[83]

Protests sprung up in the neighborhoods where providers and doctors lived. Picketers carried banners with the names of the targeted people followed by the phrase "Kills Children." These same neighborhoods were canvassed by anti-abortion activists leading "to the distribution of at least 2,000 brochures that name one of the doctors, graphically depict the abortion procedure, and list the fees charged." Finally, there were also "demonstrations at places where abortion providers shop, eat meals or do business." According to one protester, "We know where they shop. . . . We follow them everywhere. If it's embarrassing them, we're glad."[84] None of these tactics violated the regional injunction.

In what became one of the more infamous events during the Spring of Life, Rob and Paul Schenck "walked by abortion-rights activists, and held out the [real] fetus that has been on display all week" during the protests.[85] This was not the first time that the twin brothers had used actual fetuses in their activism. According to Paul Schenck, the reason for using fetuses "is to present the reality of abortion—that abortion results in a dead child."[86]

The two-week Spring of Life ended on May 4 after numerous arrests, criminal contempt charges that led to jail time for some of the organizers, and fines for many other participants. Anti-abortion activism, however, continued in the area and thus the sparring over the injunction similarly went on. To the pleasure of the protesters, a significant crack appeared in the foundation of the injunction when the United States Supreme Court decided *Bray v. Alexandria Women's Health Clinic*, an anti-abortion protest regulation case from the Washington, D.C. area.[87]

In its ruling, the Court majority stated that anti-abortion protesters could not have their activities enjoined as illegal conspiracies to deny the civil rights of women seeking abortions under 42 U.S.C. §1985(3), otherwise known as the Klan Act. While the PCN's injunction was based on trespass law and a state civil rights law, both of which are New York state laws, the Network's federal link in the injunction was based on §1985(3). As a result, there was the possibility that the *Bray* decision could undermine the jurisdiction of the federal court and become grounds to vacate the injunction. Noting the potential impact of *Bray*, the protesters filed an "instant motion to dismiss the complaint and vacate the injunction."[88]

While Judge Arcara agreed with the protesters that the §1985(3) claim should be dismissed, the Court granted the

Plaintiffs leave to amend their fourth amended complaint to attempt to bring their §1985(3) claim within the Supreme Court's holding in *Bray*. . . . [And] in conjunction with its ruling on defendants' motion to dismiss, the Court denies defendants' motion to vacate the injunction, and continues, regardless of the ultimate disposition of the §1985(3) claim, to exercise pendent jurisdiction over plaintiffs' state-law claims.[89]

In short, the protesters did not succeed in either vacating the injunction or removing it from federal jurisdiction.

Up to this point, Project Rescue, Operation Rescue, Project Life of Rochester, and the various individually named defendants in the injunction had primarily relied upon the help of two local attorneys—James Duane and Lawrence (Larry) Behr—in order to defend violators and challenge the injunction on free speech grounds. As it became apparent that their local court options were drying up and the decision was made to continue appealing the case up the legal chain, the local anti-abortion activist leaders also decided to bring in outside legal help. The first Second Circuit Court of Appeals opinion lists a total of eight lawyers working to bring down the injunction. The group's second time in front of the same circuit court saw the addition of one more lawyer. Most notable in their legal ranks were the additions of Jay Sekulow and James Henderson of Pat Robertson's Virginia-based conservative public interest law firm the American Center for Law and Justice (ACLJ).

On the opposite side of the case, the PCN, along with the individually listed clinics and doctors, saw their legal team decrease in size. Lucinda Finley had continued to seek a way to hand the appeals case off to full-time litigators so that she could concentrate on her academic commitments. However, she was not able to find what she considered to be a suitable legal team for the Network. Isabelle Marcus, the other lawyer and SUNY Buffalo professor who had contributed to the original complaint, was forced by her academic obligations to drop out of the case. This left the PCN with a two-person legal team that consisted of Lucinda Finley handling the appeals process and Glenn Murray managing the related local trials.

In their first appearance before the Second Circuit in 1994, Project Rescue and the associated named parties to the case won their largest legal victory. By a vote of 2–1, the Second Circuit struck down both the floating and fixed buffer zones as well as the cease and desist provision pertaining to the two sidewalk counselors who were allowed to breach the 15-foot bubble zones. The court majority found that the injunction was content-neutral and aimed at protecting a significant government interest. In spite of this, two of the justices found that the injunction failed to meet the "Supreme Court's newly enunciated test [in *Madsen*] for determining the constitutionality of content neutral injunctions restricting expression in a public forum: 'whether the challenged provisions of the injunction burden no more speech than necessary to serve a significant government interest.' *Madsen*, 512 U.S., 114 S.Ct. at 2525."[90]

The reasons why the court felt that the injunction did not meet the *Madsen* standard were twofold. First, the majority found that "unless and until the record [in *Schenck*] supports a finding that the prohibition against obstructing or impeding access to the facilities is ineffective to protect access," which the majority did not think that the record did, "the bubble zone provision does not pass constitutional muster."[91] Second, the cease and desist provision in the *Schenck* injunction was judged unconstitutional since the court found that it ran counter to the "established principle that 'in public debate our own citizens must tolerate insulting, and even outrageous, speech in order to provide adequate breathing space to the freedoms protected by the First Amendment.' *Boos*, 485 U.S. at 322, 108 S.Ct. at 1164 (quoting *Hustler Magazine v. Falwell*, 485 U.S. 46, 56, 108 S.Ct. 8476, 822, 99 L.Ed.2d41 (1988) (internal quotation marks omitted)."[92] Although the injunction was not vacated, missing these elements, the PCN felt that it was now effectively gutted.

The celebration on the side of the anti-abortion protesters was, however, relatively short-lived. One year later, the Second Circuit Court reheard the case *en banc* and reversed itself. In three opinions, 13 of the total 15 justices sitting on the Second Circuit Court found that the 15-foot buffer zones as well as the cease and desist provision *were* constitutional. Justice Oakes, the lone dissenter in the Second Circuit's first round, wrote an opinion joined by eight other justices that reinstated the voided provision. Justice Winter, joined by nine other Justices, and Justice Jacobs, joined by Justice Mahoney, wrote two concurring opinions. The main split in the majority stemmed from Justices Winter and Jacobs feeling that Justice Oakes was too narrow in his defense of the injunction and, as a result, producing an opinion with two substantial negative side-effects.

The first negative effect, according to Justice Winter, of "Judge Oakes's opinion is an application of a somewhat broader principle than it acknowledges, namely that the First Amendment does not, in any context, protect coercive or obstructionist conduct that intimidates or physically prevents individuals from going about ordinary affairs."[93] By categorically excluding the protection of such conduct, Justice Winter believed that his colleague inadvertently created a conception of the First Amendment that was too narrow and thus unsupportable in light of the need for an open and active marketplace of ideas.

Second, according to Justice Jacobs, "Judge Oakes' opinion invokes a set of governmental interests so narrowly drawn . . . [that] the Appellants are to be forgiven if they suspect that the opinion and rationale can have no realistic application other than the regulation of anti-abortion protest."[94] An injunction built and defended on such grounds would be so blatantly unconstitutional that upholding it would show the court to be controlled by political biases and not law, thereby undermining the institution's authority—a possibility that members of the court could not allow to exist. While these judges could find broader grounds on which to defend the injunction, and therefore preserve a broader view of First Amendment protections, the two justices from the majority in the original Second Circuit Court decision could not be swayed. Still finding that the *Schenck* injunction's record did not meet the *Madsen* standard, both filed dissenting opinions.

On March 18, 1996, almost seven-and-a-half years after the first blockades in Buffalo, the United States Supreme Court granted a writ of certiorari for the case of *Schenck v. Pro-Choice Network of Western New York*. By this point in time the protests in Buffalo continued, but on a smaller scale, and the original protest leaders had left the area in pursuit of other political opportunities. In the summer of 1994, Robert Schenck announced his intent to move to Washington, D.C., to "become organizing pastor of the National Community Church on Capitol Hill" with the intent of attracting "mid-level Capitol Hill workers and develop a national network of pastors engaged in 'Christian lobbying' on Capitol Hill."[95] Paul Schenck also announced his intended move to Virginia Beach where he would initially become the managing editor of an ACLJ publication and then, in 1995, assume the executive vice president and chief operating officer positions of that organization—the same one that was leading the fight against the injunction in the case that now bore his name. Glenn Murray, one of the PCN's two attorneys, summed up his clients' reaction to these announcements in two words: "Good riddance."[96] However, while the Schencks may have left the Buffalo area, they did not leave the abortion fight. Rather, they used their experience and connections to move to organizations that allowed them to both transition into the next phase of abortion politics and become involved in a much broader range of conservative politics.

As with most Supreme Court cases, part of the run-up to the actual arguments included a period of organizations submitting amicus, or friend of the court, briefs in order to inform the Court how they understood the case and felt that it should be decided. While one could easily discern which party some of the briefs would be in support of—as was the case with the briefs submitted by the Life Legal Defense Foundation and Family Research Council—it was not readily apparent who the American Civil Liberties Union (ACLU) would support. As noted years prior in the Network's board minutes, while the ACLU officially supported a woman's right to choose, they "may be on the other side of this case, anyway, [because] of First Amendment issues."[97]

The decision of which side the ACLU would support in the case was not only difficult for outsiders to predict, it was somewhat difficult for ACLU insiders to decide. As Richard Waples, a member of the ACLU of Ohio, stated, "It was a point of contention for a while in the organization as a whole about where we ought to come down on this. There were people on both sides."[98] While it may have been "a point of contention," the debate over how the organization should treat the case was not overly divisive or injurious to the organization.[99] By September 1996, the New York State Civil Liberties Union and the National ACLU filed a brief along with the American Jewish Congress, the American Jewish Committee, and the People for the American Way in support of the PCN's injunction. According to Marjorie Heins, a lawyer who worked on the brief for the National ACLU, "I don't remember in that case really a lot of conflict over which position to take within the National [ACLU] . . . Schenck was really a question of line drawing. I don't think anybody disagreed that on the one hand there were First Amendment rights of the protesters, and on the other hand there were public safety interest, and anti-harassment concerns, and privacy and medical health concerns, and it was just a question of where to draw the lines."[100]

The lines, however, were drawn differently by the American Civil Liberties Unions of Ohio and Florida and the Indiana Civil Liberties Union. According to one of the lawyers from the Indiana Civil Liberties Union who worked on the brief,

I thought in this case, it was a close case, in that there certainly were, there was a need for government intervention to stop violence at clinics. I fully support a woman's right to choose, and for that right to be meaningful, and to not have that unduly interfered with by others. And I thought government had a legitimate interest in making sure that people had access to the clinics, but where I thought that they went too far in this case was to, where it went beyond just access.[101]

Instead of filing for the protesters directly, however, the three state ACLU affiliates submitted a brief in support of *neither* party that recommended the reversal of the Second Circuit's *en banc* decision. According to James Green, a lawyer with the Florida ACLU, this move was taken with the idea "to remind the court that we have a position that may, that is driven more by the First Amendment than by the . . . the plaintiff's support for abortion, or the protesters', defendant's opposition to abortion."[102]

As the PCN had predicted, First Amendment issues were somewhat problematic for the ACLU, but the resulting rift was treated by many as an illustration of the strength of the ACLU as an organization. "They [the National Branch of the ACLU] were pretty good about it. . . . The National does not control the affiliates. . . . It is recognized that there is diversity in opinion on the issues sometimes and the affiliates have the right to do their own issues . . . I can't recall any pressure or anything *not* to do it. There might have been discussions, but I can't recall them specifically at all."[103]

Of those in the PCN who were carefully following the case, and were aware of the amicus briefs, the general feeling was one of happiness in relation to the ACLU outcome. That is not to say that there was not some amount of bitterness in relation to the state affiliates recommending reversal, but the overriding reaction was positive.

That's their choice. You know, it's like, you know, not everyone was. I mean I was thrilled to get the ACLU. I was not sure we would.[104]

When I knew that the ACLU was opposed, I heard that. I thought, "They don't understand what they are talking about! They should come out and see what is going on." Because in the abstract it's one thing, but when the reality, when you see what's happening on the street, it's another thing.[105]

I was actually quite pleased that the National ACLU was able to keep all but a few affiliates from [filing briefs]. Because it started out and we thought there would be quite a few. I was given the impression that they had quite an internal debate. Much more so with their affiliates, but that they had some delicate maneuvering to do within the National with their board members . . . I tried to stay out of that. . . . One of the things that I delegated out to the NOW Legal Defense fund was to manage the amici.[106]

The fact that two different ACLUs come up with different . . . analysis, uh, I think means that reasonable minds can disagree.[107]

On October 16, 1996, Lucinda Finley, splitting time with Walter Dellinger III, the Acting Solicitor General for the United States, faced off against Jay Sekulow of the ACLJ in the Supreme Court of the United States. As with other cases argued in that forum, the lawyers scrambled to make their points between the Court's constant barrage of questions. Although the appeal targeted both the fixed and floating buffer zones, the overwhelming majority of Jay Sekulow's argument focused on the constitutionality of the injunction's floating buffer zone as well as the cease and desist provision. The question that the Court seemed most interested in having him answer, however, was how the injunction's 15-foot buffers stopped speech. As one Justice bluntly put it, "How does it stop? I mean, we're 15-feet apart now. Even without this microphone I think that I could hear you perfectly well. . . . What is the problem? I mean, here we are. We are having a conversation. And we are 15-feet apart and the Judge's decree allows everybody to go 15-feet apart, doesn't it?"[108]

On the other side of the case, the respondents sought to stress how the injunction was a regulation of space and not speech. In spite of this, the majority of their time was occupied with a discussion of the relevance of the documented medical effects of stress on those seeking access to health care facilities. These effects were submitted in their briefs and mentioned in their opening oral argument. In one hour's time the arguments for both sides were completed. The participants would now have to wait until February 19, 1997 to know the results of their efforts. When the opinions were released, both sides found reasons to declare victory and mourn defeat.

With the exception of Justice Stephen Breyer, who wrote a separate opinion on the point, the Court agreed with the protesters and struck down the floating buffer as being unconstitutional. The Court noted that the types of speech affected by the floating buffer were "classic forms of speech that lie at the heart of the First Amendment, and speech in public areas is at its most protected on public sidewalks, a prototypical example of a traditional public forum."[109] The case record, however, also made it evident to the Court that violence and abusive conduct occurred at some of the protests. This made usually protected speech subject to regulation. The question for the Court then became whether the measures taken in the injunction to regulate speech were acceptable. The Court started with the floating buffer zones.

With clinic escorts leaving the clinic to pick up incoming patients and entering the clinic to drop them off, it would be quite difficult for a protester who wishes to engage in peaceful expressive activities to know how to remain in compliance with the [floating buffer zone in the] injunction. This lack of certainty leads to a substantial risk that much more speech will be burdened than the injunction by its terms prohibits. That is, attempts to stand 15-feet from someone entering or leaving a clinic and to communicate a message—certainly protected on the face of the injunction—will be hazardous if one wishes to remain in compliance with the injunction.[110]

Finding this provision of the injunction to be a greater burden on speech than was necessary, the majority struck it down in accordance with the *Madsen* standard.

The remainder of the case went to the PCN. Justice Breyer joined Justices Rehnquist, Stevens, O'Connor, Souter, and Ginsburg in upholding both the fixed buffer zone and the cease and desist provision as it pertained to the fixed buffer. While the protesters had argued that the injunction's prohibitions on "blocking, impeding or obstructing" were independently sufficient to ensure access to the clinics, the Court felt that the record ran counter to such a claim. "Based on [the defendants'] conduct, the District Court was entitled to conclude that protesters who were allowed close to the entrances would continue right up to the entrance, and that the only way to ensure access was to move *all* protesters away from the doorways."[111] In upholding this provision, the Court made the assumption that fixed 15-foot buffers around entrances and driveways can be clearly understood by protesters (in fact, the clinics painted lines on the sidewalk in order to make these borders evident), thus immunizing them from the speech-chilling flaw that caused their floating counterparts to perish.

The question of the cease and desist provision, which was arguably more complicated, was similarly dispensed with. Noting that some people were concerned that the cease and desist provision was a content-based form of regulation—a state-backed personal right to be left alone when one found another's speech to be offensive or unwanted—the Court reminded them that the cease and desist provision was part of an attempt to "enhance *petitioners'* speech rights" by allowing a limited number of anti-abortion protesters into the buffer zone. Given that, the provision should be "assessed in that light."[112] The Court thus concluded:

The District Court found that "[m]any of the 'sidewalk counselors' and other defendants ha[d] been arrested on more than one occasion for harassment, yet persist in harassing and intimidating patients, patient escorts and medical staff." 799 F.Supp., at 1425. These counselors remain free to espouse their message outside the 15-foot buffer zone, *and the condition on their freedom to espouse it within the buffer zone is the result of their own previous harassment and intimidation of patients.*[113]

In short, the protesters' record of harassing and intimidating behavior permitted the District Court to completely clear out an area around clinic entrances. When the Court permitted two counselors into that buffer zone subject to a cease and desist provision, the Court was being particularly accommodating where it did not have to be. The fact that the permitted entry into the zone was conditional, therefore, was a nonissue.

Justice Scalia, joined by Justices Kennedy and Thomas, vigorously dissented from the majority's upholding of the fixed buffer zone and the cease and desist provision. At the core of the minority's argument is the belief that the injunction was founded upon an unconstitutional premise—that there is a right to be free of unwanted speech. Since the injunction's core was rotten, the dissenters believed that the whole of it needed to be thrown out.

[T]he District Court in this case (like the Court of Appeals) believed that there *was* such a right to be free of unwanted speech, and the validity of the District Court's action here under review cannot be assessed without taking that belief into account. That erroneous view of what constituted remediable harm shaped the District Court's injunction, and it is impossible to reverse on this central point yet maintain that the District Court framed its injunction to burden "no more speech than necessary."[114]

Of particular concern for Justice Scalia is what he termed the "magic" of the majority's opinion—the ability of the Supreme Court to uphold the injunction by finding an alternative foundation than what it had been built upon.[115]

The Court candidly concedes that the nonexistent "right to be left alone" underlay the District Court's imposition of the cease-and-desist provision. *Ante,* at 870. . . . Thus, the Court's statements about what "the District Court was entitled to conclude" are not only speculative (which is fatal enough) but positively contrary to the record of what the District Court *did* conclude—which was that permitting a few demonstrators within the buffer zone was perfectly acceptable, except when it would infringe the clinic employees' and patrons' right to be free of unwanted speech on public streets. . . . Thus, if the situation confronting the District Court *permitted* "accommodation" of petitioners' speech rights, it *demanded* it. The Court's effort to recharacterize this responsibility of special care imposed by the First Amendment as some sort of judicial gratuity is perhaps the most alarming concept in an opinion that contains much to be alarmed about.[116]

Scalia, however, was only able to convince two other Justices with these arguments.

The PCN informed its membership of the Supreme Court outcome in the February/March edition of its newsletter. As opposed to the front-page billing that past injunction-related court news had garnered, the story was tucked away on the third page under the headline "US Supreme Court Upholds PCN's Preliminary Injunction." As the placement suggests, the Supreme Court news, especially in relation to the loss of the floating buffer, was downplayed.

Reading the decision by the Supreme Court, issued January 19, 1997, it is hard to understand how the media could describe it as a huge "victory" for the anti-abortion protesters. . . . In short, the preliminary injunction that has been in place for the last five years is effectively still in place, with practical consequences of the lack of a "floating buffer zone" falling primarily on those patients who must take public transportation to and from the clinic.

. . . [The floating buffer] was a concept only *alluded* to in the preliminary injunction and *ignored* in the decision by the court of appeals. It has rarely been challenged in a court trial.[117]

Reflecting the views published in the newsletter, Lucinda Finley also dismissed the relevance of the floating buffer zone.

We never had any occasion or need to enforce or worry about what subsequently became known as the floating bubble. And I had concluded that it was sort of unnecessary and unenforceable. And at one point, when the Spring of Life was happening and the big, big, massive Operation Rescue protests in the Spring of '91, or of '92, we were preparing for it and trying to get some changes and tightening up of the injunction, and I had asked, and actually had a motion before the District Court to modify the preliminary injunction. And one of the modifications was to get rid of the stupid floating bubble, and expand slightly the fixed buffer. The case was pending in the Second Circuit, and Judge Arcara said that as long as it was on appeal, he wasn't going to entertain any motions to modify. So, I was extremely frustrated when I was having to defend in the Supreme Court this thing that I was trying to get rid of for two years and didn't want.

But then, I, you know, other people were saying that other clinics might need it and want it, and you kind of have to defend it for the sake of others. *But we don't want it*! So, Sekulow may think that he won a great victory by getting rid of the floating bubble, but he may not realize that I'd been trying to get rid of it for two years [Laughs]. . . and the cease and desist was held up [which was a clear PCN victory].

See, I thought that the cease and desist was the, one of the most important things in that litigation . . . and I knew that they were going to uphold the fixed buffer because of *Madsen*. So I knew that the only things that were in doubt were the two different provisions—the so-called floating bubble and the cease and desist. So, as I said to others, the floating bubble is useless. I could care less whether that goes, but what is *really* important is that we keep the cease and desist. So I consider the outcome like, about 100% of what I wanted.[118]

The PCN newsletter article on the case concludes by quoting the Court majority's rationale for upholding the cease and desist provision in an effort to both underscore the anti-abortion activists' wrongdoings and vindicate the Network's efforts to preserve First Amendment rights. "These counselors remain free to espouse their message outside the 15-foot buffer zone, and *the condition on their freedom to espouse it within the buffer zone is the result of their own previous harassment and intimidation of patients. . . .* We can be proud to have played a part in the drama."[119]

The same mixture of pride in defending the First Amendment and the need to find hope in the face of a partial victory was present on the other side of the case. By the time the case had been heard by the U.S. Supreme Court, many of those who were involved at all levels of the Buffalo-area anti-abortion movement had retired from activism. In the words of Doug Mueller, a street-level activist and not a leader in the movement, "what we were doing was effective for a season," but that season had passed.[120] As a result of this commonly shared feeling and the affirmation of most of the injunction, the response to the case's conclusion was subdued if the decision was even noticed.

Paul Schenck, by then well-settled into his job at the ACLJ, acknowledged the recession of the movement that he was once at the helm of, but he also found purpose in the drawn-out court case.

By that time it was a moral victory. The price that had been paid was so high, by the protesters—imprisonment, fines—that uh, eventually led to . . . some people in bankruptcy. By then it had so instated, discouraged the uh, that it didn't really have a, that it didn't result in larger numbers of people turning out.

I think what it did do was secured the place of the sort of day-to-day protesters. So the people praying the Rosary outside of the clinic; the people handing out Scripture; sidewalk counselors offering women alternatives. It gave them a sense of some security. Where they could go ahead and continue their work without being put in jail.[121]

The decision by the U.S. Supreme Court did not end the legal skirmishes between the Buffalo clinics and the protesters. Disputes over increasing the buffer zones' area, making the preliminary injunction permanent, and other related issues continued. The Supreme Court decision also could not prevent the most disturbing outcome of the fight over abortion in Buffalo. On October 23, 1998, Dr. Barnett Slepian, a party to the *Schenck v. Pro-Choice Network* case, was shot and killed at home by James Kopp. This was an event that shocked and understandably still deeply upsets many on both sides of the conflict.

Along with the diminished ranks of the protesters, the Pro-Choice Network of Western New York is no longer the thriving activist group that it once was. Some of the clinics have since shut down or have moved to sites where they can more easily limit the area available for protesters— a preventive mechanism that does not depend upon court decisions. Many of the PCN members have drifted off to tend to other causes and concerns, but there are still some who continue to escort women in and out of the clinics.

Along with the escorts, the painted lines demarcating the buffer zones are still on the sidewalk in front of Marilyn Buckham's clinic, and small groups of protesters still come to carry signs and attempt to counsel those going in and out. Occasionally, passing drivers honk their support or yell their disapproval. These and other smaller signs still exist around Buffalo, revealing to the aware observer hints of the area's troubled past. It is clear, though, that the "season" of the large-scale rescues has passed.

4

From Litigation to Legislation
Hill v. Colorado

Colorado Democrats were hopeful, but reserved, in the march leading up to the 1992 general election. Bill Clinton was on his way to defeating both George H. W. Bush and Ross Perot to become the first Democratic president in 12 years. At the state level, it looked as if the Democratic Party might be able to make some headway in the legislative bodies that Republicans had controlled since 1976. With eight days until Election Day, the Denver *Rocky Mountain News* took stock of four Senate and nine House "races to watch."[1] Among the listed races were those in Senate District 21 and House District 6.

In the Denver suburb District 21, Michael Feeley, a 39-year-old lawyer, was locked in a heated race for the Senate seat with an older conservative lawyer, Lynn Watwood. Watwood, having "used strong anti-abortion support and anti-tax sentiment to knock off [fellow Republican] Sen. Bonnie Allison" in the primaries, failed to gain her support in the general race.[2] Instead, the deposed Senator Allison supported the Democratic, pro-choice Michael Feeley.

In the more traditional, but still heavily contested, race in State House District 6, an even younger lawyer, Diana DeGette, was facing off against Clarke Houston, an "independent insurance agent," for the recently vacated Denver seat.[3] Having worked on and managed various Democratic campaigns since 1982, this was the first time that DeGette had been the focal point of a campaign. After November 3, both she and Michael Feeley found themselves as members of the minority party in Colorado's newest legislative class.

Diana DeGette started her first session in the Colorado House of Representatives with short-lived timidity and discretion. Wanting to learn the basic mechanics of crafting legislation, Rep. DeGette began by drafting "a reviser's bill, so [one addressing] all the mistakes in the statutes. That bill, that bill was designed to fix those mistakes. So I learned how to do a bill by doing a pretty easy bill."[4] Getting the rudimentary mechanics of legislation out of the way, DeGette set out to attempt to accomplish some of the goals that prompted her to run for the Denver House seat.

I had . . . been involved in pro-choice issues. I was active with Planned Parenthood, and I decided that Colorado had not had any Choice legislation since . . . the 1960s when we were one of the first states to liberalize the abortion laws. . . .

I really wanted to do some pro-choice legislation . . . [and so] I called the pro-choice groups and they told me that . . . right at that time [they] were having all these protests at clinics where . . . protesters would actually block patients and healthcare workers from going in and out of the clinics. And it was getting to a . . .dangerous tension, and it was preventing people from getting healthcare. So . . . the pro-choice groups told me what they really needed right then was, was legislation to help access the clinics.[5]

The substantive area, abortion, was one that she cared about, and the specific topic, clinic access, did not initially appear overly controversial. At first glance the combination of the two seemed to make for a good transition from her starter reviser bill to more significant legislation.

DeGette may have been unaware at the time, but she was launching a process that was anything but uncontroversial. What would begin with a freshman legislator in the Colorado House of Representatives in 1993 would conclude in the United States Supreme Court in 2000. "I was a little naïve, I will admit, because I thought, 'Well, OK, now I want to do this. It's really not a *big* abortion bill, because it's not *Roe v. Wade*. It's just this clinic access bill.' And I must say I think I really, um, I was naïve when I didn't think that it would be a big deal, because it turned out to be the biggest deal of the session."[6]

DeGette's next step in this progression was seeking out a legislator in the Senate to work with her on crafting and passing a clinic access bill. She chose a fellow freshman, Mike Feeley from Senate District 21. Unlike DeGette, Sen. Feeley did not have abortion politics dog-eared as an issue to champion in the Senate. "[Was I] very concerned [with abortion politics]? No. Attentive? Yes. You know, I knew what was going on."[7] During the recent election he had been forced, quite publicly, to "be attentive" and deal with the issue of abortion because of both the presence of a clinic in his district and his opponent's conservative, anti-abortion campaign. "The question of abortion, pro-life, pro-choice, was a significant debate in my campaign. *I won.* In fact I won reasonably handily that year."[8]

Possibly drawn to him as a result of the high-profile electoral abortion dispute, DeGette extended an invitation to Feeley to work on, and sponsor in the Senate, her clinic access bill that would come to be known as the "Bubble Bill."

I saw a problem, and it was obvious to pretty much everybody, and even though I actually didn't carry a lot of legislation that year purposefully to try and learn the system and learn how to work in the legislature, I said, "What am I here for? I am here to try and make a difference. This is something that I think will help to make a positive difference. Let's go for it." So that's why I didn't think of it as a risk at all. I thought of it as a challenge.[9]

Feeley's enthusiasm, however, was kept in check by what he saw as the political realities that he and DeGette faced.

Frankly we did not think we could pass it when we started. . . . This was the time when the Christian Right was starting to have its impact on politics . . . and there was quite a few of that ilk of Republican— Christian legislators who had been elected.

Choice was always a difficult issue. We knew that it would be clearly characterized as pro-choice legislation. . . . We also were two freshmen, I mean brand new elected freshmen both in the minority party in both houses. And we thought, "What the heck, we'll take our best shot at it. But you know, if we don't pass it we'll go down swinging, but we won't be shocked if we go down."[10]

Starting with the problem of access, the duo began searching for options. Conscious of both local and national surges in anti-abortion activity, and knowing that they were not alone in the fight to regulate protests and blockades, DeGette put her legal training to use and began searching for existing regulatory models. "There had been some . . . injunctions that were issued that had a bubble concept and there had also been some municipal ordinances. [The city of] Boulder [Colorado] had a municipal ordinance that had sort of a bubble concept."[11] As lawyers with experience seeking injunctions, both saw the problems with leaving the issue of access solely with the courts via ad-hoc injunctions. They did, however, see value and potential in the emerging buffer- or bubble-zone concept.

Both Diana and I are attorneys. We've both been through temporary restraining orders, injunction processes. It is a fairly complicated process and you get sporadic results. In fact, that's what was happening. When we looked at the cases all around the country, if they were successful, they usually involved some sort of buffer . . . sometimes it was this, sometimes it was that . . . quite often there was a determination that there was not a sufficient showing to obtain injunctive relief. It was sort of hit or miss. It was incumbent upon often very poor plaintiffs to bring the action. Planned Parenthood responded now and again, and they did, if I remember. But it was sort of hit or miss and we wanted to try something a little novel.[12]

A clinic can only get an injunction if it is an individual situation and they go to court and they are under an imminent threat, and they go to court and get a court to issue an injunction. What I wanted to do was get a bright line law in Colorado that would give both patients and protesters notice as to what kind of conduct was appropriate, and legal, and what kind was not. So it seemed to me that a statute was the only way to go.[13]

Fixed bubble zones that clearly demarcated distance-based rules were attractive for the two legislators since the bubbles were seen as effective in promoting both civility and access when protests were occurring in front of clinics. They would also help establish the "bright line" that DeGette sought.

We wanted to do something; we wanted to do a bubble concept. Something that would set up a radius around people because the techniques of the protesters were to get right up in people's faces and spit on them, and to yell at them, and to shout at them, and intimidate them from going in. So it was a physical intimidation. So we thought that if we got a little range around the person, then they could at least have a zone of comfort to get ingress and egress, and not the psychological effect of that person right up in our face an inch away.[14]

Once the buffer zone or bubble style of regulation was selected, the details needed to be worked out. How big of a bubble would be created? What objects would the bubble be in reference to (e.g., entrances, people, cars, driveways)? Where would the bubble exist (at abortion clinics only, or at a range of places)? To whom would the bubble apply? All of these became important matters and potential sticking points.

The final legislative decision in response to these questions was that no one could "knowingly approach another person within eight feet of such person, unless such other person consents, for the purpose of passing a leaflet or handbill to, displaying a sign to, or engaging in

oral protest, education, or counseling with such other person in the public way or sidewalk area within a radius of one hundred feet from any
entrance door to a health care facility."[15] In other words, if an activist
is within 100 feet from the entrance of a health care clinic, that activist needs permission from her intended audience in order to approach
within eight feet and pass out a leaflet, display a sign, protest to, educate, or counsel. If the intended audience does not give consent, but the
activist persists in approaching, she is in violation of the law and has
committed a criminal misdemeanor punishable by fines up to $750 and
6 months in jail. In addition, she is also subject to civil liability. If the
protester is more than 100 feet from the entrance to the clinic, or if she
is standing in a fixed spot and the targeted audience approaches within
8 feet of her, the law does not apply and the protester does not need consent in order to engage in her activities.[16]

The Bubble Bill's primary sponsors selected the regulatory distances
through a practical, hands-on manner.

We literally stood there and put our arms out and said, "How far away is that?" And
then we thought, "Well, what if someone is trying to hand you a piece of literature?
Then could you take it, and how far away would that be?" Some people wanted us
to do 30 feet, but we said that was too far away. You can't communicate in a normal
tone of voice 30 feet away, so we finally settled on eight feet.[17]

Diana and I and a couple of other people were down in the basement of the—this
is when we were drafting this thing—we were down in the basement of the state
capitol trying to figure out, you know, how big should we make this thing? And
we literally stood on opposite sides of the room and tried to talk in a normal tone
of voice. Then we got closer together. We went back and forth until, we were sort of
making it up as we were going along, until we were standing about eight feet apart
and realized that we could carry on a normal conversation, but neither of us could
reach out and smack the other one in the face. That's how the eight-feet came about.[18]

While the greater 100-foot applicable area could not be determined
within the capitol basement, it was still determined in a similarly practical
manner.

That [the 100-foot range] was, actually, that was pretty much the distance from
the front door of the clinic at 20th and Vine [in Denver], to the entrance to the
parking lot. That was our best guess, but that is exactly the measure we used. We
said, "How far do you think it is from there to here? About 100 feet?" "Yeah, sure.
100 feet."[19]

With the details worked out, DeGette proposed her second bill to the House on January 28, 1993, approximately three months after Election Day.

News of the bill, and the almost simultaneous opposition to it by Operation Rescue, reached the public the next day under the *Rocky Mountain News* headline "Bill Would Shield Women Entering Abortion Clinics." The brief article allowed DeGette to frame the bill as one meant to preserve the meaning of the "unrestricted right to reproductive choice" through clinic access; it let Operation Rescue frame the bill as an attack on the First Amendment rights of protesters as well as a move by "pro-abortion people . . . to keep women ignorant"; and it also enabled Planned Parenthood to argue for the necessity of the bill, brought on by constant protests that involved verbal abuse and obstruction of traffic.[20] In less than two weeks House Bill 1209 faced its first formal challenges in the House Judicial Committee hearings.

In room LSB-A at quarter to eight in the morning on February 12, the meeting of the House Judicial Committee was called to order, roll was taken, and DeGette was called by the committee chair to give an opening statement on House Bill 1209. DeGette launched into the introduction of the Bubble Bill, consisting of three elements. First, DeGette anticipated the criticism that this bill was an example of the improper use of state power by the abortion-rights movement to attack the anti-abortion movement. In an attempt to deflect this claim, the opening statement worked to broaden the bill—from being seen as one brought on behalf of those seeking abortions to one brought on behalf of all those who sought health care at clinics that may have provided abortions. DeGette argued that since the protesters had no way of discerning abortion patients from others entering these clinics, all those who were entering were forced to run the gauntlet.

The second element of the introduction focused on what DeGette characterized as the "atrocities" taking place in front of these clinics and how the state had the power to regulate such behavior.[21] In discussing the state's authority, she observed that House Bill 1209 involved the regulation of speech rights, but argued that it was an acceptable time, place, and manner regulation of those rights. The final component of the introduction simultaneously underlined the state's power to regulate and showed the modesty of this particular regulation. This was done by alluding to other states that had ordinances and statutes regulating protests that were much more stringent than the proposed House Bill.

Following DeGette's introduction, four witnesses associated with Planned Parenthood gave emotional testimony in relation to the first two elements of the bill's introduction. This testimony included illustrating the harassment alleged against Colorado's anti-abortion activists, arguing the need to create both literal and emotional space between these activists and their audience, and stating that only about 7 percent of Planned Parenthood's patients were there for abortions. In addition to the emotional recounting of conflicts in front of Colorado clinics, the Planned Parenthood speakers attested to the benefits derived from a Denver ordinance similar to the Bubble Bill. Witnesses acknowledged that the local ordinance had not stopped protesters from pouring acid onto clinic floors, calling clinic volunteers "guards from Dachau," and yelling at arriving patients that another patient had died in the clinic the previous day. However, Ruth Hofenbeck, a clinic volunteer, recounted specific instances where protesters were forced back by the Denver ordinance. She argued that while "prior to the Denver Ordinance we had no recourse," the Denver clinics now had a nonphysical means of making the protesters back away. The House Committee was largely silent during the approximate 25 minutes of testimony except for the occasional question asking for clarification.[22]

The same cannot be said for the committee's response to the countertestimony of Phillip Faustin, a spokesman for Operation Rescue Colorado. The committee members were no longer content to largely listen. Instead, the committee hearing turned into a prolonged question-and-answer period with Faustin standing in as a spokesman for all anti-abortion activism in Colorado. In an attempt to lift the veil that he saw covering the bill and the hearing thus far, Faustin began his testimony by directly addressing, and opposing, the assumptions underlying the bill and the narrative created by its supporters.

It seems to me what this Bill is really talking about is not being dealt with. A lot of the things that have been said so far seem to be things that are trying to create a hysteria that there's all these poor women who are being, the image that is being given is you cannot walk into one of these places without someone right up in your face. That's just not true. That probably happens on occasion, but as far as being the norm, it wouldn't be.

The talk of healthcare facilities, and the, all these other um, people going in for all these other reasons, in some of the places that's true . . . [but] some places it's just abortions. But we are not talking about women going in for cancer screenings and pap smears. That's not why pro-lifers are outside these places. And it's not those people they are trying to speak to. . . . We are trying to give correct medical information. Information that is being denied inside of those places. . . . So we are not there just to harass people. Does harassment happen sometimes? Sure it does. There's people who do not behave as they should. But that is the exception rather than the rule. That is not why people are there.

. . . "Healthcare facilities" is really a euphemism here. We are talking about the legislature being prodded to protect the abortion industry. To legislate uninformed women. And that is what is being talked about in section three [of the Bill]. . . . What is going on in section three is a chipping away of First Amendment Rights. You can't speak or even hold a sign to someone unless they give consent. Which, of course, there is the big question—What does that mean, consent?[23]

The question of what consent meant in relation to House Bill 1209 was not one the committee wanted to directly debate with Faustin. Rather, the committee was interested in a range of other questions related to his disputing the claims made by those in support of the bill. How could or did anti-abortion activists discern their target audience from the other patients that he said were not of interest? How does Operation Rescue train its members, and how do they select which clinics to target? Why would the bill actually infringe on one's right to stand in one place and hold a sign or offer a leaflet? How could he believe that the protests were not meant to harass, and that the portraits drawn by the bill's supporters were mischaracterizations meant to create an image of hysteria, when the committee members themselves had been receiving harassing, "irrational . . . and hysterical" phone calls in the "last two or three days"?[24] Faced with this barrage of questioning, none of the other witnesses present were able to speak. The hearing concluded with the speakers' list being closed and moved to a final hour of testimony that would be heard after the President's Day holiday.

Leila Jeanne Hill was one of those waiting in the audience and on the speaker's list of the February 12 hearing. Called "Jeannie" by her friends, she moved to Colorado when she was young, after her father sold their farm in Texas and bought a ranch in Colorado. In the early to mid-1970s she became a registered nurse, joined the U.S. Air Force, and met and married her husband, an air force doctor. After leaving military service, the couple decided to move to the Denver suburb of Wheat Ridge and start a family.

Jeannie Hill became active in the anti-abortion movement in the late 1970s when she found out that abortion was legal through all nine months of pregnancy.

It wouldn't have made any difference if it was all nine months or not, but it just kind of horrified me to think that that would be legal . . . I don't remember what made me say "Oh my gosh. You are kidding," but I do know that it was not right away. It was not in '73 [shortly after the *Roe* decision]. . . . [It was in the late 70s when] I became aware of it and became an activist soon after.[25]

She wrote her first letter to the editor in 1982 and started to go to clinics "as soon as I found out that's what people were doing."[26]

Initially, you know, it was, I knew the babies would die if I weren't there . . . I would feel guilty if I didn't do anything about it. And so initially . . . when I became an activist it was to save the babies going in, not to protest it [abortion as a political issue]. I wasn't there to protest it to the women going in, I was there to help them. . . .

I carried literature that was short and to the point and told each one of them . . . that we would be glad to help them. And if they continued on in I would say, "You know, that's fine, but come out here afterwards and talk to us too" because a lot of times it was not their day to have an abortion. They were just going in for, you know, to talk about if they could get one. . . . And that's when I picked up a lot of literature from Planned Parenthood and other clinics that they [the women leaving the clinics] would give to me. . . . And then that's when I discovered the powerful lies in that literature. Telling them that their baby is not a baby. Not to worry about it. No big deal.[27]

By 1984 she formed the group Sidewalk Counselors for Life, Inc. to organize volunteers to sidewalk counsel at clinics. "It was very difficult to get two [volunteers] a day. And it was usually the same two people on their day every week. And then it started to grow somewhat. And then Operation Rescue came into being. And when that happened, it really got a lot of people activated. Which was a good thing. Then we [Sidewalk Counselors for Life] could pull back a little bit. Then we didn't feel like we needed to do it all."[28]

Continuing her activism, Jeannie increased her message's range by writing and widely distributing the booklet *Sidewalk Counseling Workbook*. The book, which has been updated numerous times since it was first written in 1985, provides encouragement, information about fetal development and abortion procedures, and practical advice for those who want to do sidewalk counseling. Among the topics covered are: "Our Rules and Responsibilities", which includes advice as mundane as "Arrive on time," and as experientially rooted as "Beware of remaining at the abortuary by yourself. Abortion personnel do not hesitate to call the police or to press charges on a whim. To be without witnesses in a court of law will jeopardize your freedom to [sidewalk] counsel and assure your defeat in court";[29] "Use of Signs," which discusses the place of signs in sidewalk counseling as well as weighing the pros and cons of various types of signs;[30] and "Abortion and Our Free Speech Rights," which informs readers,

The sidewalk constitutes a traditional public forum from which cherished First Amendment freedoms may not be prohibited. . . .

Only "fighting words," obscenity, and speech that incites imminent lawless action may be prohibited by government action.

Where particular words such as "killing" or "murder" are used in regard to protest, the use of the word murder may or may not be protected. . . . You would be advised to seek legal advice from an attorney familiar with local and national case law regarding slander before using the word "murder" in a personally accusing manner.

You may experience threat of arrest for "disturbance" or "harassment," or for things you may say or write on your signs. Use good judgment but do not let these acts of intimidation have a "chilling effect" upon your work. When in doubt, ask an attorney.[31]

Another section, titled "When the Patient Says 'No, Thank You,'" suggests possible last-minute statements to patients that might explain the risk of being perceived as harassment:

If the patient says "No thanks," or you are unable to walk with her to the front door, all is not lost. You may have time to say just one sentence to her so the message you relay must be brief and meaningful. At times you may feel that silence and prayer are your best response.

Ex-Abortion clinic staff workers say that two questions which patients ask most frequently after entering the clinic are, "*Will it hurt?*" and "*Does it look like a baby?*" Keep these questions in mind as two significant concerns of the patient.

Here are some suggestions:

. . . "Happy Birthday, Precious Baby! Today is your baby's birthday!"

. . . "You don't want to be the mother of a dead baby!"

. . . "This isn't Disneyland! They kill kids here!"

. . . "I know you don't want a baby, but you Already Have One!"

. . . "Take your baby to McDonald's instead."

. . . "Are you sure you want to give them your baby? Are they selling his body for transplants? What *will* they do with him?"

There are many other things that you can think of to say. Keep talking to the patient until she is out of your sight. You will be competing verbally with the escorts as they will often talk to the patient until she enters the building.[32]

Jeannie Hill's confidence in knowing the limits of acceptable activism and her conscious decision not to get arrested as part of Operation Rescue did not keep her from experiencing conflicts with clinics and the law.

From the get-go they [Rocky Mountain Planned Parenthood] opposed us. And they called in people from their other clinics to come and help, help oppose us. . . . Trying to get to these girls first. And then, from then on it was nothing but trouble.

They bought the house behind their clinic so that they could make their parking lot bigger. They put a big wall around, you know, on the street, on the two street sides, they put a big wall, I don't know, 4, 4 feet high probably. They closed the front door and it became a true back alley abortion clinic—they only had the one door open in the back. They did everything in their power to keep us from reaching those girls.

. . . They locked their trash because we got in their trash and found all kinds of bad stuff. . . . And they, they were calling the cops on almost a daily basis. Complain about one thing or another. And I don't think ever, in about the 150, 200 times that they charged people with offenses, I don't think that they ever won in court because it was a form of harassment. It was to intimidate us.[33]

Jeannie was included at least two times in what she estimated as the 150 to 200 times that the clinic charged people with an offense. First, in 1987, she was arrested for trespassing and assaulting a patient in front of Rocky Mountain Planned Parenthood. Second, Jeannie was involved in the case of *Cannon v. City and County of Denver*.[34] This case is important because it gave Hill her first experience with the federal appeals process as well as valuable, lasting political and legal connections.

In late January 1988, Jeannie Hill and Joan Cannon were arrested for disturbing the peace for refusing to cover the words "The Killing Place" on the signs that they carried in front of Rocky Mountain Planned Parenthood. The two arresting police officers, one of whom was off-duty but at the clinic in uniform as privately hired security, had apparently misunderstood a Denver County Court judge's advice in relation to determining the limits of the right to protest. Believing that the phrase "The Killing Place" was an example of fighting words, and that the judge had previously made a ruling to that effect, the two women were arrested, charged, and held in detention for about eight hours. While the charges against Hill and Cannon were dropped, the two brought suit against the City and County of Denver and sought:

Damages under 42 U.S.C. §1983 for violation of their First Amendment rights and declaratory and injunctive relief under 28 U.S.C. §2201. The complaint also averred state tort claims of false arrest, false imprisonment, assault and battery, tortious violation of state constitutional rights, intentional infliction of emotional distress, and malicious prosecution.[35]

Citing the difficulty of on-site determinations of whether the First Amendment protects certain behavior, the District Court summarily dismissed the claims made against the officers and determined that the Police Department and the City and County of Denver could not be held liable. The lower court's determinations were reversed and the case remanded on appeal to the Federal 10th Circuit Court, where the determination was made that there were triable issues in relation to a possible policy of discrimination against anti-abortion activists.

Although these incidents do not conclusively prove the existence of a general municipal practice of First Amendment violations against antiabortion protesters, when seen in the light most favorable to the plaintiffs we agree that they are evidence from which the trier of fact could reasonably infer the existence of such a policy. The evidence submitted by plaintiffs would support an inference of considerably more than one instance of conduct, which alone may not prove a custom or policy.[36]

In addition to being victorious on appeal, one of the most significant products of the case was that it introduced Jeannie Hill to James Henderson, Jay Alan Sekulow, Thomas Patrick Monaghan, and Walter M. Weber. All of these lawyers would eventually be members or affiliates of the American Center for Law and Justice—the same conservative public-interest law firm that was active in both the *Williams* and *Schenck* cases.[37]

When House Bill 1209 became an issue, Colorado Right to Life, the state branch of the anti-abortion activist organization National Right to Life, contacted Hill and informed her about the committee hearings. In light of her claims in *Cannon* that the City and County of Denver were systematically discriminating against anti-abortion activists, House Bill 1209 could not help but look to her like a statewide continuation of that discrimination.

Well I knew it was just another attempt to shut us up. Because the truth, you have to shut it up or, or you are going to lose money as far as Planned Parenthood and abortion clinics go. . . . Our information is so powerful that we did change minds.[38]

Determined to speak at the next hearing, Jeannie Hill braved the bad weather and returned to Room LSB-A on the morning of February 16 with the hope that her name would be reached on the speakers' list.

The testimony during the final House committee hearing unfolded along largely predictable lines. Those against the bill said that it was an attempt to secure the ability of the abortion industry to increase profits and continue to misinform patients. Those in support of the bill said that it would help to preserve privacy and ensure that the proper respect was given to the wide range of patients going to medical clinics. Anti-abortion activists countered that the lack of patients filing suits against activists in Colorado was proof that patients welcomed, or at least tolerated, the activists' counseling message. Abortion-rights proponents retorted that patients are disinclined to file suit, and that it is hard for the clinics to use existing law against the protesters. Employing an increasingly familiar tactic, the anti-abortion activists went on to argue that the proposed bill violated speech rights and that its effect would be to intimidate and stop those who would like to counsel. The bill's supporters highlighted both their concern with preserving speech rights and specific cases of the acceptable regulation of protests. As the names on the speakers' list were checked off and the debate volleyed back and forth, the committee members were largely content to stay quiet.

Mixed in among the other statements during the hearing, the seventh speaker to address the committee—Jeannie Hill—announced what was to come.

I have discussed this matter with attorneys who believe that this Bill poses a substantial threat to the Colorado Constitution and the United States Constitution. I am advised that if this Bill is adopted as law, a cause of action will be available to me to challenge the constitutionality of the law. And like *Roe v. Wade*, I won't need to wait for a denial of my rights to challenge this law because the law itself will be a threat to me each time I go out onto the street near a medical facility.[39]

When the committee members began to speak it became apparent that their concerns lay with the potential constitutional problems referred to by Hill. The bulk of DeGette's closing statement focused on her attention to protecting the right to speech when drafting Bill 1209, and her belief that the courts had upheld similar types of regulations. When the floor opened to the rest of the committee members, she continued mounting the defense of the bill's constitutionality and fought against the threat of a court challenge as a significant deterrent to passing the bill out of committee.

Chair: I understand what, where the initiation comes from in the Denver Ordinance. I don't understand the same thing when I read, particularly, section 3 of this Bill. Can you address that please?

Rep. DeGette: Thank you Madame Chair, I will. I considered a section of that nature in my Bill. My concern was, if you define in the legislation what consent is—in other words, "stop," "get away," "back off," [and] so on—you may actually be restricting someone's free expression rights who wants to give a leaflet and the person wants to consent in a different way other than using words. And so what I did was I put the burden on them to stay away unless some kind of consent was given. Either verbal consent, or nonverbal consent.[40]

Chair: I guess I have fewer problems personally with civil damages . . . but section three gives me a lot of problems because of the potential chilling effect you have there. Money does indeed, and the threat of huge monetary damages does indeed have a chilling effect on free speech.

Rep. DeGette: Madame Chair, as you know, we discussed this yesterday and I know an amendment will be offered . . . to avoid that chilling effect, and I have no objection to that amendment.[41]

Chair: I am really struggling with the balancing of the rights here. I don't have a problem creating the misdemeanor portion of this. The bubble concept, I am still troubled about how we are going to enforce this.[42]

Rep. Freednash: To get back to Rep. George's initial question, in my view, if the bubble is challenged constitutionally, and the court finds that it is unconstitutional, I think that we are left with . . . the crimes of menacing and harassment as described here are still, in my view, prosecutable. So I think that you are still left with this in the law. And based upon what we have, I think that it's worthwhile to at least, if there is concern, if it is tested constitutionally, at least we've had a ruling on it and know whether or not it's constitutional and provides more protection and safe access to clinics.[43]

Rep. DeGette: I'm sure it's been your experience, as well as mine, Rep. George, that we never try and second guess what a court is going to tell us about what we're doing. And that the best we can do is really do the research and give our best educated guess.[44]

When the period for amendments and comments concluded, the House Judiciary Committee unanimously voted to send the bill to the House floor.

A little over a week later, on the afternoon of February 24, House Bill 1209 reached the House floor. While relatively brief, the 32 minutes of the full House debate were spirited. Against the wishes of the chairwoman, who asked that "the committee not discuss whether it's constitutional or not [since] we could debate that all day because we are of different opinions," the House Chamber debate focused squarely on the constitutionality of the bill.[45] Minutes into the introduction of the House Committee Report, Rep. Bill Jerke offered the first amendment to House Bill 1209.

> *Rep. Jerke*:   At this time I want to move the first and only Jerke amendment to the Judiciary Committee report. Members, what this does is on page two of the Bill strikes paragraph number three. This is the portion that deals with, I guess the bubble, the eight-foot section. . . . I don't think that . . . paragraph three which gives people this invisible eight-foot bubble out there I guess makes any sense from the point of view of enforceability and of course, once again, that great constitutional question. . . .

> *Rep. DeGette*:   . . . I would urge a no vote on the Jerke Amendment. It is clear that the, an eight foot bubble around people entering a clinic is constitutional. I've practiced Constitutional Law for 10 years. I've researched it and I believe it's constitutional. Furthermore, the Bar Association has researched this. They believe it's constitutional . . . I think it's just clear that it's constitutional.[46]

From here the debate split between those who did not see any constitutional issue involved, and those who saw a constitutional violation in the existing form of the bill. Rep. Maryanne Keller argued that, "This is not a matter of free speech. This is abuse. This is verbal abuse. This legislation wouldn't even be before us today if there had been respect from one person to another."[47] Rep. Martha Kreutz felt that the bill needed to be expanded to include groups like the KKK, while Rep. Drew Clark saw the bill as being too broad, unenforceable, and an unconstitutional prior restraint on speech. Reps. Jerke and Penn Pfiffner argued that the bill was unconstitutional because it regulated speech on the grounds that some people found the message to be offensive. Rep. Charles Duke sympathized with the bill's supporters (sympathy that they likely did not want), but added that because of a mixture of support for the anti-abortion movement, a desire to not create "special" rights, and fidelity to his oath to uphold the Constitution, he could not support the bill.

> *Rep. Duke*: I feel many of the same frustrations when other classes of people are in my face, such as the homosexuals, as they frequently do. I feel the same disgust for that and I feel the same need for protection from that. But I don't want to live where we start excluding specific classes of people from [speaking]. . . . The General Assembly shall not pass local or special laws . . . granting to any . . . individual any special or exclusive privilege.
>
> . . . I further remind you we all swore an oath, every one of us, to uphold that constitution. You cannot do both. You cannot vote for this Bill and maintain your oath to the people of Colorado.
>
> . . . Well, obviously I am going to ask for a no vote. I wish I could take credit for the following phrase, but it comes to mind when we consider issues like this . . . "We kill them before they are born. We kill them when they are infirm. We kill them when they are old. My God, what kind of place is this?" I encourage a no vote.[48]

After those final words by Rep. Duke, House Bill 1209 passed the Republican-dominated Colorado House with only 12 of the 65 members voting against it.

Having been passed by the House, the Bill moved to the Senate Judiciary Committee under the guidance of Feeley. Learning from the House Judiciary Committee hearings, the Senate Judiciary Committee set aside ample time to hear what turned out to be largely the same testimony. From 3:04 to 5:30 p.m. on March 3, room SCR 356 hosted the testimony of 21 speakers, of whom nearly two-thirds were opposed to the bill.

The hearing began with the introduction of the bill to the committee by its Senate sponsor. Again learning from the House hearing and floor debate, Feeley attempted to draw attention away from the bill's more controversial elements. "This is not about abortion. This is not a Bill about infringing on First Amendment rights of any individual. . . . This Bill involves common courtesy."[49] In order to illustrate that the bill was about civility and not limiting speech, Feeley made sure to sit eight feet away from the committee chairwoman to demonstrate the distance that the bill aimed to put between speakers and their unwilling audiences.

The first five witnesses tried to support Feeley's reframing of the issue by labeling the protests and sidewalk counseling as subtle acts of cruelty and harassment, and not as speech or aid. This line of argument ended after roughly 20 minutes, when the sixth speaker, Jeannie Hill, discussed what she saw as the bill's false premises. This began the long line of speakers who objected to the proposed legislation.

While the bill's opponents dominated the audience microphone, the committee members did not remain silent. In a move mirroring, but quite different from, Hill's approach, the majority of the committee's comments and questions were targeted at what they saw as the false premise underlying the opposition's main argument—that the bill was offensive to free speech generally, and that it stifled the speech of anti-abortion protesters specifically.

Sen. Groff:	Don't you become a harasser after they say "I don't want to talk to you?"
Mr. Faustin:	I don't think so. . . . What if we have what that woman wants and after a few seconds, or a few minutes of conversation she changes her mind? . . . Was that harassment? Was that wrong to persist? . . . If you are there for honest, genuine help to that person, then that's not harassment.
Sen. Groff:	Except that it's their choice to either accept what you have to offer, or reject it upon which time you are then required to leave them alone and not bother them. . . . That should be all that they have to do to get you away. . . . You are saying that you should have a right to continue to harass someone once they've told you they are not interested. . . .
Mr. Faustin:	Then why don't we pass a law against Kirby vacuum salesmen that after the first time the customer says "I don't think I'm interested in this" the guy has to leave?
Chorus of Senators:	He does.
Sen. Groff:	That's why I only sold two vacuums [as a Kirby vacuum salesman].[50]
Sen. Feeley:	I just want to clarify one thing since I think there was a blatant misstatement by the witness here. There is absolutely nothing in this Bill that requires oral consent. It was specifically omitted and the witness is, uh, if he can point

	to it in the Bill, I would be very surprised. . . .
Mr. Harrison:	It is very evident that it does require oral consent. Maybe not in a specific word that is in that legislation, but the intent of the legislation is there.[51]

A telling moment in the two-and-a-half hours of testimony was the misfiring of a move calculated to sway the committee to vote against the bill. Laura Lee Gorton, a soft-spoken anti-abortion demonstrator testifying as to the peaceful nature of the protests, distributed a pamphlet to the committee with the words "Woe unto them that call evil good and good evil: Isaiah 5:20. What do you call this?" printed on one side and the "photograph of a 7-month aborted fetus with its head missing" on the other.[52]

Sen. Lacy:	I um, I guess your picture here I do find offensive. I ah, I happen to know what an aborted fetus looks like. I happen to have my own ideas about that. And it's because of situations like this to where you feel like we have to be told, we have to be shown on a regular basis. You say you have not heard of anybody being, pushing, shoving, or hateful in their comments? Well that's not . . . .
L. L. Gorton:	I said I never saw any violence.
Sen. Lacy:	I consider . . . some of [your] comments having to do with . . .an aborted fetus [violence]. I happen to be a pro-choice individual. And I do that because I was able to make a decision having to do with my own child. And I had her, and she is a beautiful child, and I am very glad that I did that. But what I did not appreciate is the phone calls that I received [before the committee hearing]. Because you, nor anyone else, knows [my stance on abortion], unless I've told you where I stand on abortion. But you choose to constantly put this type of thing [this pamphlet] in front of my face, which I do not appreciate. And I, I apologize Madam Chairwoman, because I came in here not knowing where I was going to be on this particular [bill], but unless we deal with the extremes on both sides of this issue, I happen to think that our society is going to be in great danger.[53]

After a five-minute recess following Feeley's concluding statements, which mirrored DeGette's closing in front of the House committee, three senators felt compelled to make appeals to the audience both to find other means of protesting and to police their own side of the debate.

In the words of Sen. Lacy, who began by apologizing to the committee for:

Getting a little intense earlier. . . . When 1209 came out, as the sponsor knows, I was in opposition to it. As I stated earlier, the uh, the pro-life, pro-choice, pro-abortion issue is something that is really, really starting to wear on me. I have a great deal of respect for those of you who are sidewalk counselors. I think that the job that you are doing is very well. The problem is, it's the type of people that are not in the audience today that is causing the problem. . . .

I don't know that I will get anywhere with you, and it's probably a useless cause, but I guess I just need to try to do it. Because the people that have called me during my campaign once they found out that I was a pro-choice candidate, and what I went through *not* being pregnant, *not* looking to have an abortion, and winding up having to hang up on people, winding up having to have other people drag me out of the middle of a group that had surrounded me and just hammering me with just comment after comment, I wasn't physically abused, this is true, but I considered it harassment. And moving around, trying to keep an objective viewpoint—and that's the one thing with 1209 that I have tried to do, is keep an objective viewpoint.

I don't know that this Bill has anything to do with abortion. Unfortunately, we have all interjected it into this. I um, when you look at the people that are going to these clinics—and it's not the pro-lifers, it's the pro-choice people too . . . I would just ask you to think about it in another vein. And you may not be the ones that are doing the harassing, but if you are wanting to carry on your cause, you need to identify some of those people that are so we can pull them back and let some of the jobs need to be done because we wouldn't be here today if there wasn't harassment going on in front of these clinics.[54]

After the final senator encouraged both sides to find another way to get their messages out, and to find a way to come together, the committee voted 9–0 to move the bill to the entire Senate.

Just over one week after Senate committee members pleaded with the activists in room SCR 356 to rein in the extremists among them, an extremist who was far beyond their reach ended any remaining possibility that House Bill 1209 would be defeated. On May 11, 1993, in Pensacola, Florida, Michael Griffin shot and killed Dr. David Gunn as he entered the clinic that he had founded. While clinics had been bombed before, this was the first time that an abortion provider was shot and killed. Seven days later, the Bubble Bill was placed in front of the Colorado Senate.

Stepping up to the microphone to introduce the second reading of Bill 1209 to the Senate as a whole, Feeley was asked by the chairwoman to "see if we can keep it faster here."[55] Feeley opened by repeating his belief that this was not a bill dealing with abortion or speech rights, but rather one about the courtesy owed to others. He then briefly reminded the Senate of the recent shooting death of Dr. Gunn and of the mass demonstrations in neighboring Wichita, Kansas a few years prior. While he did not claim that a similar bill in Florida could have prevented Dr. Gunn's murder, he did state that "it might prevent . . . something from escalating into that kind of situation."[56]

Once his introduction was completed, only one senator, Jim Roberts of Loveland, spoke against the bill. Sen. Roberts's warnings that the bill stood on shaky constitutional ground, and that its definition of consent was unclear, fell on deaf ears. The Senate was in no mood to debate. After a little over 10 minutes had passed, the Republican-dominated Senate voted 32–3 to make the Bubble Bill Colorado State Law. On April 19, 1993, less than three months after DeGette introduced it, Colorado Republican Governor Roy Romer signed the Bubble Bill into law, calling it "a very important piece of legislation."[57]

A feeling of being on the defensive seemed to descend on Colorado's anti-abortion ranks. The House Judiciary Committee unanimously voted down a bill by Rep. Clark that "would have defined a fetus as a human being protected by criminal law in all cases except for legal abortions."[58] Sen. Roberts also announced that he was no longer going to propose a parental-notification bill or any other abortion legislation for the remainder of the year. "There isn't any sense in banging your head against a wall . . . I don't think it's likely that anything would be done by this legislature."[59] At the activist level, Operation Rescue spokeswoman Wendy Faustin noted, "It's going to be an uphill battle from here. . . . We're getting no support."[60] The string of defeats did not cause pro-life activists to concede, however. As Hill had told both the House and the Senate Judiciary Committees, anti-abortion activists could still seek to overturn the Bubble Bill, which was now state law, in the courts. Within five months such a courtroom challenge of the law would begin.

Thinking that the lawyers representing her in *Cannon v. City and County of Denver* might be interested in the Bubble Bill, Hill contacted James Henderson, then at the American Center for Law and Justice in

Washington, D.C. As she had predicted, Henderson and the ACLJ were quite interested in challenging the law.

She called me up and asked "Could we assist her?" And so frankly, I drafted the original complaint filed in that case. I drafted every discovery instrument used in that case on our side. The summary judgment briefs. The appellate briefs. The petition to the Supreme Court that was granted. . . . The Supreme Court briefs in the Colorado Supreme Court. And then the briefs with the petition the second time around with the Supreme Court, and the Supreme Court briefs in that case. So I was very deeply intimately involved in that case.[61]

I never heard about the Bubble Zone statute until she contacted us. We did work with her to find folks that were doing the other activities. The provision in the statute that we challenged prohibited oral counseling, protest, and education. We felt fairly confident with Jeannie that we had counseling and education. And it also prohibited leafleting and sign displays. And with Jeannie we also had leafleting. But we didn't have protesting or sign displays. Yet we felt that those were both completely eminently subject to challenge if there were additional parties that could be brought into the case. And she, uh, worked with us to find Audrey Himmelmann and Bo Simpson. . . . Bo used to, if memory serves me correct, used to walk with a sandwich sign and Audrey was involved with both protest and with signs and then just verbal protesting—chants and the like.[62]

The ACLJ wanted not only additional litigants who could represent these other aspects of anti-abortion activism affected by this law but also individuals who had not been involved in acts of civil disobedience that led to arrest. As Audrey Himmelmann recalls, "Jeannie Hill . . . recruited me and Bo Simpson to be plaintiffs with her. . . . What they were looking for was people who had never been arrested. We weren't out there with Operation Rescue blocking doors or anything like that. We were just protesters."[63] By selecting plaintiffs with clean arrest records, the ACLJ made it harder to claim that the Bubble Bill only targeted the "extremists" that so concerned the Senate Judiciary Committee members.

The final element required before the case could move to court was to find local counsel. Jim Henderson secured Roger Westlund, a sole practitioner in Colorado who had the right credentials for the case. Along with his more typical work in family law and other areas of general practice, Westlund had experience representing "probably 100 to 150 different defendants on charges stemming from Operation Rescue activity."[64] He also had been involved in challenging the Boulder ordinance that the

Bubble Bill had been roughly modeled on, and he had previous experience working with the ACLJ.

With the team assembled, the lawyers were able to file suit in Jefferson County Court without having to wait until someone was arrested for violating the law. They submitted a facial challenge to the constitutionality of the eight-foot bubble, "Because the statute was effective. It was in place and it was intimidating . . . [and] spectacularly chilling" for potential anti-abortion activists.[65] The lawyers' strategy was to both obtain an injunction against the law's enforcement and get the bubble provision of the law overturned as an unconstitutional violation of speech rights.

Among the lawyers chosen to defend the state of Colorado was Carol Angel. Angel came to the Colorado attorney general's office shortly after graduating from law school. "I was not interested in big firms particularly, and then I, there were openings here and I had a friend here who alerted me. . . . I was drawn to the public sector by my own interests and then it was just kind of luck that I knew someone who told me to apply."[66] Once in the attorney general's office, Carol Angel's work had little or nothing to do with First Amendment issues. "I was doing water cases primarily involving Federal reserved water rights claims."[67]

When First Amendment issues would come to the State, Gale Norton, the Attorney General at the time, would seek out Ms. Angel's boss, Trish Bakert, who formerly worked for the National Parks Service in Washington D.C. Like Carol Angel, Trish Bakert's legal experience primarily consisted of work in relation to natural resources issues. However, the National Park Service also managed the National Mall in Washington D.C. As a result, the Park Service faced First Amendment issues regarding the regulation of speech related activities by various groups who asked to use the Mall to stage protests and other events.

The Attorney General turned to her [Trish Bakert] . . . for very specific advice on some tricky First Amendment issues. And since I worked with Trish, and I was at a point where our work was not overwhelming, I ended up helping Trish on some preliminary First Amendment issues. . . . We worked on, there weren't any regulations on our State Capitol Grounds, and so we worked on, you know, regulations there.

And then when the Hill case came up, the law was passed and they filed their, you know, their facial challenge to it, the people in the general government section that would have been working on it were all, all tied up with a major reapportionment case. And so Trish sort of volunteered me, you know, and I was happy to do it.[68]

Joined by other members of the attorney general's office on the official listings of lawyers representing the State, Carol Angel was the only lawyer present at all stages of the case—from the opening district court appearance, to the final U.S. Supreme Court argument.

At its start, the *Hill* case did not appear to be one that would make it very far in the court system. The district court judge who first heard the case issued a summary judgment that the statute did not violate the First Amendment of the Constitution. Undeterred, the plaintiffs appealed to the Colorado court of appeals. In July 1995, this court, like the lower court, found no First Amendment violations. Under Judge Edwin Ruland's pen, the Colorado court of appeals said that the statute's consent language was not vague and the bubble zone was not a prior restraint on speech. Rather, together these two elements formed an acceptable content-neutral regulation of the time, place, and manner of speech.[69]

Seven months later, in February 1996, the Colorado Supreme Court refused to hear the case. Persistent in their cause, the ACLJ submitted their first *Hill* appeal to the U.S. Supreme Court. Almost four years after the Bubble Bill became law, and one year after the Colorado Supreme Court denied certiorari in the case, the petitioners got their first, and only, ray of hope for their case. In the briefest of statements, the U.S. Supreme Court announced, "Petition for writ of-certiorari granted. Judgment vacated, and case remanded to the Court of Appeals of Colorado for further consideration in light of *Schenck v. Pro-Choice Network of Western New York*, 519 U.S. 357, 117 S.Ct. 855, 137 L.Ed.2d 1 (1997)."[70]

On remand to the Colorado court of appeals, Judge Ruland again wrote for the court and again affirmed that the Colorado law was constitutional. In light of the recently decided *Schenck* case, the question in *Hill* became "whether the restrictions in the form of an eight-foot floating buffer zone are narrowly tailored to serve . . . [the] governmental interest."[71] While the floating buffer zones in *Schenck* were struck down, the Colorado court of appeals let the Bubble Bill's eight-foot buffer stand since it, unlike *Schenck*'s 15-foot buffer, allowed ample opportunity for speech to take place.

Initially, we reject plaintiffs' claim that the statute is unconstitutional because of the determination in *Schenck* that a 15-foot floating buffer precluded protesters from expressing their views from a normal conversational distance. In our view, a lesser distance of eight feet is sufficient to protect that type of speech on a public sidewalk— even for the insulting and outrageous language protected by the First Amendment.

Further, under the statute a protester is permitted to approach to a distance of less than eight feet with consent of the patient or staff member.[72]

In addition, the court responded to the petitioner's claims that leafleting is stifled by the statute's 100-foot application area by stating that

we view the significant governmental interest here as sufficient to warrant the requirements of the statute. . . . [I]n our view the governmental interest of ensuring easy access to those with physical disabilities by creating an eight-foot buffer zone within a 100-foot area is amply sufficient to justify the statute.[73]

The next judicial stop for Hill and the ACLJ was at the Colorado State Supreme Court, which chose to now hear the case. Largely repeating what the lower courts had said, the Colorado Supreme Court affirmed that the Colorado law was intended to protect a significant government interest and was constitutionally sound. "Here, the fundamental right balanced against the First Amendment rights of petitioners is the right that the General Assembly determined was 'imperative,' a citizen's right of access to 'counseling and treatment' at Colorado medical facilities."[74] This right to access counseling and treatment at a medical facility was found to be part of the constitutionally recognized right to privacy.

In moving on to consider the relevance of *Schenck* to *Hill*, the Colorado Supreme Court found that there was none since *Schenck* dealt with an injunction, whereas *Hill* dealt with legislation. The fact that the Colorado regulation found its beginnings in the legislature was then grounds to give greater deference to the regulation.

As explained by the Supreme Court in Madsen, 512 U.S. at 763, 114 S.Ct. 2516, one of the differences between judge-drawn injunctions and statutes crafted in the political process is that, "[i]njunctions . . . carry greater risks of censorship and discriminatory application than do general ordinances." As such, the General Assembly's enactment of section 18-9- 122(3) [the Colorado Bubble Bill], which is not premised upon an evidentiary record for identifiable parties to litigation, but, instead intended for general application reaching all citizens, is entitled to greater deference than the judge-made injunction in *Schenck*.[75]

Clear of *Schenck*, the Colorado Supreme Court's final step was to determine if the regulation was a content-neutral time, place, and manner regulation—a determination that it did not have trouble making.

First, section 18-9-122(3) is sufficiently and narrowly drawn to further a significant government interest. The statute mandates that an individual can only be convicted of criminal conduct under specified circumstances. Specifically, section 18-9-122(3) prohibits an individual from knowingly approaching another person within eight feet: (1) for the purpose of oral protest, counseling, education, leafleting, or displaying a sign to that person; (2) within 100 feet of a health care facility entrance; (3) without that person's consent.[76]

Second, we also hold that the statute furthers a significant government interest. After open public hearings that provide support for its public policy action we review today, the General Assembly declared in section 18- 9-122(1) that "access to health care facilities for the purpose of obtaining medical counseling and treatment is imperative for the citizens of this state." Indeed, the statute was enacted, in part, through the General Assembly's police power, and by a General Assembly that was concerned with the safety of individuals seeking wide-ranging health care services, not merely abortion counseling and procedures.[77]

Finally, turning to the last requirement under *Ward,* that ample alternative channels of communication be left open, we similarly conclude that section 18-9-122(3) passes muster. Section 18-9-122(3) does not prohibit verbal communication, as petitioners contend. While the authority to regulate in some instances may include the power to deny, here petitioners' argument is not persuasive. Petitioners, indeed, everyone, are still able to protest, counsel, shout, implore, dissuade, persuade, educate, inform, and distribute literature regarding abortion. They just cannot knowingly approach within eight feet of an individual who is within 100 feet of a health care facility entrance without that individual's consent.[78]

Faced with a unanimous Colorado Supreme Court, the U.S. Supreme Court was the final option remaining for the petitioners. On September 28, 1999, over six-and-a-half years after House Bill 1209 was introduced, the Court agreed to hear the case of *Hill v. Colorado.* Jay Sekulow argued the case on January 19, 2000 for the ACLJ, and Michael McLachlan, the Colorado solicitor general, and Barbara Underwood, the deputy solicitor general for the United States, argued in defense of the statute. In the Court's audience that day was Diana DeGette, now a first-term member of the U.S. House of Representatives.

Two issues dominated the ACLJ's time in front of the Court. Moments into his opening statements, Jay Sekulow was interrupted by the Justices in order to introduce him to his first, and most significant, problem. The Court needed him to convince them that the statute actually posed a problem for speech rights. In the words of Justice Breyer, "[If] this is a speech case, what's the restriction on speech?" "What's exactly the problem? I'm not just saying [that you should cite] another case. I am trying to understand what the problem is [in this case]."[79] The crux of the issue was that Justice Breyer and the Court could not see how it was an infringement on speech rights if one was able to remain in a self-selected spot and offer a pamphlet, or say whatever one wanted to, so long as she did not approach those who did not want to be approached.

Sekulow's attempts to inform the Court as to the problem—that it was caused by putting eight feet between speakers and their audience—led to the second flaw that the Court found with his argument: "You just don't acknowledge that there is any distance at which you can talk to somebody which is inherently intimidating." Since Sekulow would not concede this point, a wide range of Justices, including Justice Scalia, were taken aback. The Court eventually took Sekulow's uncompromising interpretation of the First Amendment to mean that there were *no* grounds on which one could regulate the delivery of speech. Sekulow's position seemed to create a regulatory Catch-22. Regulations were either narrowly tailored and therefore unconstitutionally content-specific, or they were *not* content-specific and therefore unconstitutionally overbroad.

Oral arguments were not much easier for the Bubble Bill's supporters. The attorneys who defended the law's constitutionality faced two main issues put forward by members of the Court. The Justices' primary concern when addressing McLachlan was the statute's potential overbreadth. The hypothetical used to illustrate this problem concerned a doctor's office on the top floor of a high-rise building. If only one floor, or one office on one floor, of this building were a health care facility, would the statute still apply to the sidewalk in front of the building? If this were the case, the argument that the law was justified by the need to protect the "sick, disabled, and vulnerable" who go into health care facilities would not be strong enough to justify the broad range of all those covered by its regulation—that is, all those who would be going into this building for nonmedical reasons. Since the issue was not addressed in either the legislative record or the case briefs, it provided a substantial stumbling block for the defense of the law. As a result, the Court spent a significant amount of time trying to nail down an answer to the question.

The second major concern voiced by a member of the Court was that the statute was content-based. "I just wonder whether this statute is, although facially applicable to anybody who approaches this kind of facility, I think we know what it's aimed at—which is abortion protests. And I wonder what justification there is for singling them out as particularly intimidating as opposed to labor picketing."[80] This argument was under-lined by the fact that the statute, Colo. Rev. Stat. 1999, § 18-9-122(3), spe-cifically addressed "engaging in oral protest, education, or counseling." Justices who were not concerned by this joined the State attorneys by attempting to draw the focus away from the undeniable reality that the statute's roots lay in anti-abortion protesting and toward what they saw as the law's content-neutral language.

When the final ruling and opinion were issued at the end of June 2000, the State of Colorado's string of victories held. Justice Stevens's majority opinion, joined by Justices Rehnquist, O'Connor, Souter, Gins-burg, and Breyer, echoed the points from the case's oral argument.

Although the statute prohibits speakers from approaching unwilling listeners, it does not require a standing speaker to move away from anyone passing by. Nor does it place any restriction on the content of any message that anyone may wish to com-municate to anyone else, either inside or outside the regulated areas. It does, however, make it more difficult to give unwanted advice, particularly in the form of a handbill or leaflet, to persons entering or leaving medical facilities.[81]

While acknowledging that "a brief review of both sides of the dispute reveals that each has legitimate and important concerns," and that public forum and leafleting rights are lessened by this law, the Court recognized the State's power, need, and careful construction taken in protecting the health and safety of its citizens—especially when those citizens are held as a captive audience.[82]

The Colorado statute passes that test [the time, place, and manner test] for three independent reasons. First, it is not a "regulation of speech." Rather, it is a regu-lation of the places where some speech may occur. Second, it was not adopted "because of disagreement with the message it conveys." This conclusion is sup-ported not just by the Colorado courts' interpretation of legislative history, but more importantly by the State Supreme Court's unequivocal holding that the statute's "restrictions apply equally to all demonstrators, regardless of viewpoint, and the statutory language makes no reference to the content of the speech." Third, the State's interests in protecting access and privacy, and providing the police with clear guidelines, are unrelated to the content of the demonstrators' speech.[83]

Furthermore, although the statute specifies a prohibition on oral protest, education, or counseling, this is not a form of content-based regulation.

It places no restrictions on—and clearly does not prohibit—either a particular viewpoint or any subject matter that may be discussed by a speaker. Rather, it simply establishes a minor place restriction on an extremely broad category of communications with unwilling listeners. Instead of drawing distinctions based on the subject that the approaching speaker may wish to address, the statute applies equally to used car salesmen, animal rights activists, fundraisers, environmentalists, and missionaries. Each can attempt to educate unwilling listeners on any subject, but without consent may not approach within eight feet to do so.[84]

In addition to Stevens's majority opinion, Justice Souter penned a concurring opinion that was joined by O'Connor, Ginsburg, and Breyer. Directly addressing the abortion politics aspect of this case, the concurrence clarified that "there is always a correlation with subject and viewpoint when the law regulates conduct that has become the signature of one side of a controversy. But that does not mean that every regulation of such distinctive behavior is content based as First Amendment doctrine."[85] While relying on the ability of the stationary figure to say or distribute whatever he may, the concurring opinion also notes that there is still an effect on speech, but that it is acceptable since the message is allowed to survive.

This is not to say that enforcement of the approach restriction will have no effect on speech; of course it will make some difference. The effect of speech is a product of ideas and circumstances, and time, place, and manner are circumstances. The question is simply whether the ostensible reason for regulating the circumstances is really something about the ideas. Here, the evidence indicates that the ostensible reason is the true reason. The fact that speech by a stationary speaker is untouched by this statute shows that the reason for its restriction on approaches goes to the approaches, not to the content of the speech of those approaching. What is prohibited is a close encounter when the person addressed does not want to get close. So, the intended recipient can stay far enough away to prevent the whispered argument, mitigate some of the physical shock of the shouted denunciation, and avoid the unwanted handbill. But the content of the message will survive on any sign readable at eight feet and in any statement audible from that slight distance. Hence the implausibility of any claim that an anti-abortion message, not the behavior of protesters, is what is being singled out.[86]

These arguments, however, did not satisfy Justices Scalia, Thomas, and Kennedy. Rather, Scalia called out his colleagues as being politically biased in their approach to this and other related abortion cases. That is to say, Justice Scalia accused the Justices in the majority of being subject to the "abortion distortion" that anti-abortion activists see as plaguing the nation's elite institutions.

Having deprived abortion opponents of the political right to persuade the electorate that abortion should be restricted by law, the Court today continues and expands its assault upon their individual right to persuade women contemplating abortion that what they are doing is wrong. Because, like the rest of our abortion jurisprudence, today's decision is in stark contradiction of the constitutional principles we apply in all other contexts, I dissent.[87]

Moving beyond statutory language and highlighting the effect of a law in determining if it is a regulation of content, Scalia, joined by Justice Thomas, reached back to his *Madsen* opinion.

"The vice of content-based legislation—what renders it deserving of the high standard of strict scrutiny—is not that it is always used for invidious, thought-control purposes, but that it lends itself to use for those purposes." *Madsen, supra,* at 794, 114 S.Ct. 2516 (opinion of SCALIA, J.) (emphasis deleted). A restriction that operates only on speech that communicates a message of protest, education, or counseling presents exactly this risk. When applied, as it is here, at the entrance to medical facilities, it is a means of impeding speech against abortion. The Court's confident assurance that the statute poses no special threat to First Amendment freedoms because it applies alike to 'used car salesmen, animal rights activists, fundraisers, environmentalists, and missionaries,' *ante,* at 2493, is a wonderful replication (except for its lack of sarcasm) of Anatole France's observation that "[t]he law, in its majestic equality, forbids the rich as well as the poor to sleep under bridges. . . . " J. Bartlett, Familiar Quotations 550 (16th ed.1992). This Colorado law is no more targeted at used car salesmen, animal rights activists, fundraisers, environmentalists, and missionaries than French vagrancy law was targeted at the rich.[88]

Justice Scalia, in finding the regulation to be content-based, stated state interest used by the Court to be different from the one used by the State, that an eight-foot buffer is the opposite of a narrowly tailored regulation, and also that there were no alternative means of communication left open to protesters since there were no other places than clinic entrances to make their appeals, condemned the majority opinion and made the grand step to declare that "the First Amendment is a dead letter."[89]

While not going so far as to say that the First Amendment had just died, Justice Kennedy's separate dissent did diagnose a potential fatal condition contracted by the public forum doctrine. "If from this time forward the Court repeats its grave errors of analysis, we shall have no longer the proud tradition of free and open discourse in a public forum."[90]

The Court uses the [public forum doctrine] framework of *Ward v. Rock Against Racism* (1989), for resolution of the case. The Court wields the categories of *Ward* so that what once were rules to protect speech now become rules to restrict it. This is twice unfortunate. The rules of *Ward* are diminished in value for later cases; and the *Ward* analysis ought not have been undertaken at all. To employ *Ward*'s complete framework is a mistake at the outset, for *Ward* applies only if a statute is content neutral. Colorado's statute is a textbook example of a law which is content based.

. . . The law imposes content-based restrictions on speech by reason of the terms it uses, the categories it employs, and the conditions for its enforcement. It is content based, too, by its predictable and intended operation.[91]

Following much of the same reasoning as Scalia's dissent, Justice Kennedy likewise ends his in similar, but less grandiose, fashion.

It [the majority opinion] in effect tells us the moral debate is not so important after all and can be conducted just as well through a bullhorn from an eight-foot distance as it can through a peaceful, face-to-face exchange of a leaflet. . . . So committed is the Court to its course that it denies these protesters, in the face of what they consider to be one of life's gravest moral crises, even the opportunity to try to offer a fellow citizen a little pamphlet, a handheld paper seeking to reach a higher law.[92]

Seven years after the Bubble Bill became law it survived its last constitutional challenge. After her involvement with two prolonged court cases and years of sidewalk counseling, Jeannie Hill stepped off of abortion politics' front lines. "I am not a quitter, but I have pulled back because of my age."[93] Audrey Himmelmann, now retired, continued to picket daily at her local clinic, but she worried about the Bubble Bill.

One of the women that protests with me, she violates it every day . . . I am really afraid to do that. I don't want to go to jail. Now the woman . . . she says "Now Audrey, they are not gonna report you. They're not gonna want to go to court and admit that they were there to have an abortion. They are not going to do that." And so far she's been right. Nobody's been arrested or anything like that. But I just don't want to risk it.

. . . I am afraid to run down the block with the girl the way [she] does. I am afraid that one of these days we are gonna be set up. . . . I feel that it is quite within the realm of possibility that some abortion activists will plant somebody down there that will press charges and I don't want to go to jail.

. . . I make sure that I go down there and stand beyond that [100-foot] mark so that I can say that I was beyond 100 feet. . . . Sometimes, if I am caught by surprise, if I am down there within 100 feet, I will stand absolutely still and I will not speak to the girl until she's past me because I think any kind of movement I might make might be considered I was approaching her. . . . And I often carry a sign around my neck, and I think that I cannot do that within 100 feet either.[94]

In spite of this fear, she has not sought out legal advice about how to safely protest within the 100-foot bubble. "We pretty much went through it at the time [of the case] . . . I just don't feel the need [to seek out legal help]. I pretty much know what the law says. I have to be 100-feet from the entrance if I am going to do anything."[95]

With the law remaining on the books, and Himmelmann's overly cautious interpretation of it presumably held by others, anti-abortion protests and counseling in Colorado declined and never reached a level that was seen in places like Buffalo or Wichita. But while the Colorado legislature avoided what they feared, they did not exactly gain what many hoped the law would bring. Instead of becoming a catalyst for a change in the rhetoric of each side of the debate, the Colorado Bubble Bill was and remains a divisive law that can be used by either side to illustrate the corruption of their opponents in the abortion debate.

Abortion rights activists and lawmakers around the country quickly recognized the value of Colorado's statutory approach to regulating anti-abortion activism. The federal government accelerated the wave of regulatory change that Colorado helped initiate by enacting the Freedom of Access to Clinic Entrances (FACE) Act one year after the Bubble Bill was signed into law. The national effect was immediate and astounding. As the National Abortion Federation's count of clinic blockades shows, there was a sharp drop in blockades in 1994, the year that the FACE act was signed into law, and the anti-abortion tactic has since largely disappeared.[96] While one can still find groups of protesters in front of the offices of abortion providers, clinic employees interviewed for this project have noted that the remaining handful of stalwart anti-abortion activists largely obey the established regulations and are thus quite manageable for the clinics.

Considering this, and read in conjunction with the chapters on *Williams* and *Schenck*, the Bubble Bill's story stands as a convenient signpost marking significant changes in the realities on the ground and, correspondingly, the dominant strategies employed by the competing movements.

The abortion-rights movement's innovative use of law in all three of the above cases increased the risks associated with clinic-front activism. As the previous chapters have shown, anti-abortion activists clearly recognized these changes. One-time rescuers, counselors, and picketers were demobilized, and potential future members of their ranks were presumably kept from mobilizing due to the very real fear of hefty fines, bankruptcy, and imprisonment. The stories from these cases also show that other factors, like the strategic placement of clinics so as to preclude protest space and the lethal violence indirectly associated with *Schenck* and *Hill*, further contributed to driving existing and possible members away from popular activism in the anti-abortion movement.

The resulting street-level demobilization is captured in the image of Audrey Himmelmann standing stock-still and silent. This picture is a far cry from that of the rescuers who had become the public face of abortion politics through conflicts in Western New York, Atlanta, Wichita, and elsewhere. Himmelmann's post–Bubble Bill behavior even stands in contrast to the aspirations of the Solano Citizens for Life and others who employed far less aggressive tactics than Operation Rescue and its followers. Her stationary silence thus represents the effective end of the street politics of abortion at the hands of the abortion-rights movement's strategic innovations.

The successful regulation of direct-action tactics through instruments initially won in court, and later modified, refined, codified, and spread in statutory law, may have effectively eliminated this marque of abortion politics, but it did not do away with the anti-abortion movement itself. Rather, the anti-abortion movement learned from and responded to these measures by internalizing the value of controlling the law. Anti-abortion activists have correspondingly relocated the main abortion politics battlefield from the visible, participatory, and volatile streets to the more private, elite, and staid state legislative halls. This strategic shift to institutional politics is encapsulated in the Schenck brothers' transition—from leading rescues in Western New York to working at the American Center for Law and Justice and cultivating a network of government connections.

Today's abortion politics, as dictated by the anti-abortion movement, is concentrated on limiting abortion rights and access through regulatory provisions passed at the state level.[97] This strategy did not start suddenly after the waning of the street politics of abortion. As many significant political and social movements do, the anti-abortion movement had been attempting to use any and all means available to it. The difference in eras is more a matter of the degree of organization, professionalization, commitment of resources, and success.

The institutional state politics of abortion began to emerge in its new, more productive form at the height of the street politics era. In 1989 the Supreme Court's ruling in *Webster v. Reproductive Health Services* upheld a Missouri abortion regulation that required physicians to perform viability tests upon women in their twentieth week or more of pregnancy; it also prohibited public employees and public facilities from being used in encouraging, counseling, performing, or assisting abortions unnecessary to save the woman's life.[98] In light of this dual legislative and judicial anti-abortion victory, Marshall Medoff, citing the NARAL Foundation, notes that "in the first year after the *Webster* decision, nearly 400 bills were introduced in state legislatures about abortion policy."[99]

The sign pointing anti-abortion activists to state legislatures grew larger in 1992 when the U.S. Supreme Court upheld the majority ruling on a Pennsylvania abortion regulation in *Planned Parenthood of Southeastern Pennsylvania v. Casey.*[100] The Pennsylvania law required informed consent and a 24-hour waiting period prior to receiving an abortion, parental consent for minors, and spousal notification for married women seeking abortions. The Court upheld all but the spousal notification requirement and in doing so replaced the previous trimester framework of regulatory constitutionality with the "undue burden" test. In the words of the Court:

It must be stated at the outset and with clarity that *Roe*'s essential holding, the holding we reaffirm, has three parts. First is a recognition of the right of the woman to choose to have an abortion before viability and to obtain it without undue interference from the State. Before viability, the State's interests are not strong enough to support a prohibition of abortion or the imposition of a substantial obstacle to the woman's effective right to elect the procedure. Second is a confirmation of the State's power to restrict abortions after fetal viability, if the law contains exceptions for pregnancies which endanger the woman's life or health. And third is the principle that the State has legitimate interests from the outset of the pregnancy in protecting the health of the woman and the life of the fetus that may become a child.[101]

While the Court upheld the right to abortion in *Casey*, they also established the lines along which anti-abortion advocates could now seek to restrict abortion.

Most obviously, the Court's opinion invited anti-abortion legislators to restrict abortions after fetal viability. The opinion, however, also opened a space for legislative experimentation and conflict before fetal viability. While the Court insisted that "[t]hese principles do not contradict one another," the dual recognitions that (1) women have the right to obtain an abortion before fetal viability without undue interference from the State, and (2) that the "State has legitimate interests *from the outset of the pregnancy* in protecting the health of the woman and the life of the fetus," can be seen as unclear, if not in conflict.[102] The post-*Casey* mission for anti-abortion advocates became creating legislation that limited or discouraged abortion via the state's interests in women's and fetal health but that would not be perceived as unduly interfering with the previability right to abortion. States across the country responded to the *Casey* ruling by passing over 200 regulations in the following 13 years.[103]

Anti-abortion activists have since used sympathetic state legislatures to directly target abortion by outlawing "partial birth" abortions and creating gestational caps on when abortions can be performed. They have also attempted to use, but have been less successful with, direct appeals to the voting public. For example, in what the *New York Times* reported as "an intentional provocation meant to set up a direct legal challenge to *Roe v. Wade*," South Dakota Governor Mike Rounds signed a bill in 2006 that banned nearly all abortions in the state.[104] The law, known as the "Women's Health and Human Life Protection Act," was rejected by South Dakota voters eight months later. A similar South Dakota ban resurfaced in 2008 and was again defeated at the polls. That same year, Colorado voters rejected a measure that would have amended their state constitution to grant rights to fertilized eggs. More recently, in 2011, Mississippians were asked to vote on, and ultimately rejected, a state constitutional amendment granting personhood to fertilized eggs. Like the Colorado amendment, this measure would have effectively banned all abortions in the state.[105]

Anti-abortion activists have had more success using indirect legislative routes to limit abortion access. For example, following *Casey*'s lead, as of the start of 2013, 9 states require ultrasounds before getting an abortion, 11 states have mandatory counseling requirements on fetal pain, 26 have obligatory waiting periods, and 37 possess parental consent or notification laws.[106] Other tactics have expanded on those seen in *Webster*, including limiting state funding and insurance coverage for various abortions, as well as allowing institutional and/or individual providers' rights of refusal. In a more novel and indirect route to the goal of limiting abortion, state legislatures have passed physician, clinic, and hospital controls sometimes referred to as "Targeted Regulation of Abortion Providers" (TRAP) laws. These laws, for example, create physical specifications for clinics as well as staffing and licensing requirements. Both are seen in a 2013 bill signed by Alabama's governor requiring doctors performing abortions to have admitting privileges at local hospitals and that abortion clinics needed to meet the building, equipment, and staffing standards of ambulatory surgery centers. Such TRAP laws, as well as many of the other above-listed regulations, increase both the institutional and personal financial costs of abortion. They therefore decrease the number of clinics providing abortion as well as the abilities of women to access them.[107]

Other states have been more direct in their efforts to effectively ban abortion. In the spring of 2013 Arkansas and North Dakota passed the most restrictive abortion laws in the nation by prohibiting abortion based on fetal heartbeat. Arkansas, citing the time when a heartbeat can typically be detected when using an abdominal ultrasound, outlawed abortions at 12 weeks of pregnancy. Alternatively, North Dakota's prohibition is determined on the case-by-case basis of detectability. Using a transvaginal ultrasound, this places the limit as early as six weeks into a pregnancy. At the same time that North Dakota passed its heartbeat ban, the state also prohibited abortions performed due to fetal genetic abnormalities and instituted a TRAP law requiring doctors providing abortions to have admitting privileges at local hospitals. A few weeks after passing these regulations, North Dakota also banned abortions performed after 20 weeks citing fetal pain. According to the Guttmacher Institute, legislators in Kansas, Kentucky, Mississippi, and Wyoming have recently introduced bills similar to those passed by Arkansas and North Dakota. Given their clear conflicts with current Supreme Court rulings, and in North Dakota's case, their redundancy, such laws seek to provoke the Court to reconsider the abortion's absolute or effective legality. Taken as a whole, the new state law-based fight over abortion policy is a slow, incremental, less participatory, and underpublicized one, and it is proving far more effective for the anti-abortion movement.[108]

The anti-abortion movement's shift from street-level to more conventional institutional politics reflects—and is a part of—the broader trend seen in the political development of the New Christian Right.

Christian conservatives generally, and anti-abortion advocates specifically, have dedicated increasing resources not only to the legislative means outlined above but also to the defense of the gains made in these areas. The second step in this process is realized by cultivating cadres of conservative lawyers. Christian conservatives have opened new conservative law schools, created public-interest law firms, and become actively involved in the processes of stocking the judicial bench.[109] By building up these legal resources, social conservatives are creating the means to defend their legislative achievements in the inevitable court challenges that they will face. They are also increasing their potential to further develop novel strategies that will enhance their offensive capabilities and move them closer to their ultimate goals.[110] These moves therefore speak to Christian conservatives' high levels of organization and foresight.

The anti-abortion movement's new state institutional approaches and innovations have again forced the abortion-rights movement into a tactical defensive stance. As the Center for Reproductive Rights (CRR) states, "TRAP laws have proven extremely difficult to challenge in court. Nonetheless, in a number of cases, the Center has sought creative and compelling ways to fight these laws, and we continue to use litigation as a means of trying to block this growing threat to reproductive rights."[111] The CRR and likeminded organizations' problems, however, are not limited to TRAP laws. In the immediate term, they are burdened with finding effective responses to the range of legislative approaches taken by the anti-abortion movement. In the long term, they are also faced with matching their opponents' mounting legal and institutional resources. If the abortion-rights movement is going to continue to be effectual it will have to creatively adapt to the changing conditions dictated by its rivals and develop new tactical strategies, and potentially new institutions, to match them. That is to say, the abortion-rights movement will have to perform as the anti-abortion movement did when it faced the dual court and legislative strategies that defeated the street politics of abortion.

5

Limited in Victory, Enabled in Defeat

The preceding chapters have told the story of how three conflicts developed; how competing social-movement groups organized; and how the ensuing court cases proceeded, were decided, and affected those involved. The focus now turns to exploring how the differently situated actors involved in these events simultaneously created, were constrained by, and used the law when recounting their experiences. The interest here is in determining if and how law mattered for those involved in these disputes; how their stories may or may not reproduce, challenge, or amend legal power and state authority; what conditions contributed to evident variations between differently situated groups of actors; and how their conceptions of law affect the ongoing politics of abortion. In turning attention from the larger picture of how the movements interacted with one another to how individual actors constructed law in their stories, the focus, in one way, is narrowing. In another way, though, it is broadening. It is through the patterns within and across individuals' stories that larger questions of law's relationship to power can be approached.

It is natural to first point to the state's use of coercive force when thinking about the relationship between law and power. State-sanctioned violence is a highly visible and obvious form of power. We are reminded of its close relationship with the law when we see a policeman's gun, hear about a prisoner being executed, or watch a ubiquitous police drama. In spite of this, one should not overestimate the importance of coercive force in terms of understanding legal power. A range of academic and popular sources—from Foucault's discussion of the Panopticon in *Discipline and Punish*, to *The Godfather*'s Don Corleone—inform us that greater, lasting power is not found in violence.[1] Rather, it is found in the ability to persuade, to win willing consent, and to have authority internalized and assumed by subjects.

This, of course, does not mean that violence cannot or does not play a part in establishing authority. Rather, it is to highlight that violence cannot be the sole pillar of power if that power is meant to be stable and enduring. Don Corleone is a good example of this. While the Godfather's empire is steeped in blood and coercion, his lasting power is rooted not in his capacity for violence but in his status as a "man of respect" and a "man of reasonableness."[2] He thus eschews violence whenever possible in favor of working other means of leverage. Turning from the illicit to the formal political world, Murray Edelman's statement that "force signals weakness in politics, as rape does in sex" also applies to the place of overt coercion in a legal system.[3] Strong rule-of-law societies are those where the symbols of the state's coercive power are not obviously paraded. They are instead places where the legal system's authority enjoys a tacit legitimacy and acceptance that reduces the need for visible signs of force.

Law's stability and power is tested whenever the system fails to produce the results that people desire. Returning to *The Godfather*, this is the reason why Amerigo Bonasera appeals to the Don for "justice" at the book's start. While the court found in favor of Bonasera's interests, the state's legal system failed to significantly punish the two college students that brutally assaulted his daughter. Thus, Amerigo, who in "all his years in America . . . had trusted in law and order. And . . . had prospered thereby," lost faith in that system and resolved to appeal to the Godfather's extrastate authority.[4]

Amerigo Bonasera's story represents an individualized version of a standing threat to law's enduring power. However, the problem of obedience and continued fidelity to the system is compounded when the state finds against or otherwise fails to satisfy organized groups of actors like those belonging to a social movement. In these cases it is not just an individual or a family that stands to abandon, and therefore weaken, the state. Rather, it is potentially a mass of people who can go on to convince others to follow their lead. It is at these moments of heightened stakes that one can learn about the state's power. Do spurned actors challenge or defy the system like Amerigo Bonasera, threatening its stability and revealing the state's partial or even precarious grasp on true power, or do they accept the ruling and move on? If they do the latter, do they accept the adverse outcome out of fear of reprisals, because of a respect for the state's legitimacy, or because they recognize other values in compliance? With these questions in mind we can revisit the disputes that surround the *Williams, Schenck,* and *Hill* cases. We know how the actors in these disputes have behaved, but in order to fully understand the nature of legal power, we need to explore how they understand their behavior and construct law in their stories.

By largely upholding the various anti-abortion protest regulations in court cases, and reproducing the regulations in statutes, the state has declared that anti-abortion activists have committed acts of violence and intimidation that do not warrant First Amendment protection. More bluntly, the state has announced that elements of the anti-abortion movement present a standing threat to public safety and are therefore legitimately open to regulation. By doing so, the courts have labeled these actors as existing outside of state law. Anti-abortion activists therefore face three options in their lives and in the stories that they tell: they can accept state law as seen in the rulings, they can reject it but accede to the state's overwhelming force, or they can resist. The first option requires these activists to recognize that their previous conceptions of law were fatally flawed and needed to be abandoned in favor of the state's understanding of law.[5] This is an example of what Robert Cover termed complete "jurispathic" regulation where the state successfully eliminates competing conceptions of the law.[6] It also severely limits, and effectively eliminates, the storyteller's ability to use law in a self-affirming or advantageous way. If these stories unfold in this form they will clearly sustain and reproduce the state's conception of law, thereby reaffirming its power in the strongest sense.

The second option, to reject the rulings and the standing laws, but accede to the state's force, involves a degree of resistance. It also allows storytellers access to extrastate law to legitimate their actions during these disputes. The speaker's version of extrastate law, however, would be weak because it would not be backed by the speaker's continued actions.[7] Rather than constructing a vigorous, alternative conception of law that substantially challenges the state, the activists would at best be attempting to amend, but would ultimately still be reaffirming, the state's formulation of law. While such stories effectively affirm the state's legal authority, they suggest that obedience is linked to the speaker's fear of facing the state's coercive force. As a result, the affirmation, like the level of resistance, is weak and subject to continued challenge.

Constructing a strong version of extrastate law requires these activists to move toward coupling their stories with more open, lived resistance. Anti-abortion activists engaged in resistance would need to cultivate, according to Cover, "a new elaboration of 'law'—the development of an understanding of what is right and just in the violent contexts that the group will encounter" at the hands of the defied state.[8] Backing narrative with action preserves anti-abortion activists' abilities to affirmatively and authoritatively cite law—albeit an extrastate version—in their retelling of events. It also clarifies the place of such stories in the construction of legality since these narratives would clearly be part of "a new elaboration of 'law'" that competes and contrasts with the state's conception, directly threatening the state's desire to monopolize legal authority.

When considering how litigants will respond to state authority, the initial concern is rightly with those who lose cases. The state, however, must also be concerned with how the other parties to these cases respond. The court, after all, did side with Amerigo Bonasera by finding the boys that assaulted his daughter guilty. In spite of this, Amerigo still abandoned the state because he was insulted by the details of the ruling.

By taking sides and largely declaring the anti-abortion activists' conception of law void, the state has supplied abortion-rights advocates and clinic members with the ability to authoritatively invoke state law in their accounts. This grant, however, is not limitless. In mostly upholding the regulations, the courts have reaffirmed that obstructionist and harassing tactics are clearly outlawed, but so too are measures that target content or excessively impede activism. By drawing this line, the courts have presumably narrowed abortion-rights advocates' abilities to legitimately regulate opponents and also to authoritatively appeal to certain conceptions of law in their personal narratives. Abortion-rights interviewees, like their opponents, are therefore in the position of either affirming state law by constructing narratives that fall within these stated boundaries or challenging state law by creating, and possibly attempting to act on, competing elaborations of the law.

The rulings thus provide different rhetorical possibilities and challenges for both abortion-rights and anti-abortion activists. Questions remain, however, as to how law actually comes to matter in these personal postlitigation narratives. What do these stories specifically tell us about how these activists construct and relate to law, how does it affect their political actions, and how does it affect state power?

Abortion-Rights Activists' Narratives

Given their courtroom victories, one would expect abortion-rights activists to have easy access to the law as an affirming symbolic, normative resource when constructing their postlitigation narratives.[9] A close reading of these stories, however, reveals that in spite of the clinics' courtroom victories, abortion-rights activists still faced significant challenges in fully and effectively utilizing state law. Applying McCann's description of the "dynamics of consciousness raising," abortion-rights activists employed law in order to describe how their expectations rose concerning the possibilities of exploiting state power as a coercive force, but they were not able to succinctly and effectively harness law to name injustice and claim rights.[10] In short, the primary rights associated with these cases— First Amendment rights—interfered with, but did not eliminate, these activists' abilities to fully employ law's normative force. Specifically, the actors' First Amendment principles and their access to the limitations, as opposed to the expansionist, free speech arguments hobbled the effective use of rights language to crystallize issues in their postlitigation narratives. Abortion-rights activists simply lacked uncomplicated, familiar, and resonant rights claims that fittingly and powerfully described their experiences. Their stories therefore included a scattershot collection of somewhat vague rights claims that clustered around broadly defined property rights and a continuum of other harms. Surprisingly, an appeal to reproductive rights—the traditional source of rights talk for these activists—was conspicuously absent from these narratives. This section will proceed by first addressing how law raised expectations and was used in reference to accessing state power, and it will conclude by describing some of the limiting effects of the First Amendment on the activists' narratives.

Many of the abortion-rights activists' stories referred to the problems that they had in accessing state law prior to winning their respective injunctions. State law in the pre-injunction sections of these narratives is controlled by institutions or, more accurately, by individuals who either could not, or more often would not, extend help to the clinics. As a result, while these activists hoped that the injunctions would have some effect, these hopes came laced with a healthy degree of skepticism.

We went to the state court before Lucinda [Finley, the PCN member and the group's lead attorney] came on. It didn't go well. [Laugh] We just quickly ran out of state court and said, "This isn't going to work." I mean, I was in state court talking to the

Catholic, Irish Judge while they were blockading the clinic and I couldn't even get back into the clinic that day, and he's going, "Well, what do you want me to do?" He wasn't going to do a thing. Nothing. Nothing.[11]

I think we, we thought we hadn't been very effective in the old ways [pursuing individual trespassing cases in state court]. And it was so frustrating not to have law on our side . . . the local folks didn't seem to be doing their jobs. . . . [I]t just felt like we were on a track that was going to last forever and this [the injunction] was the next step.[12]

It [law] wasn't being enforced at the local level. These [trespassing] laws are not being enforced and we felt we needed something more. And that was the Federal Government Marshals. It just wasn't being enforced. I don't mean the police did nothing. Some of them were very good. But it was just not enough. . . . We just felt we needed something stronger.[13]

We called the police, and the police, you know, got squirmy about, I don't know, you know? And they wanted us to get an injunction. That was how they covered themselves. So they weren't willing [to enforce the law]. And what's so hard sometimes for my staff sometimes in our ten different centers and ten different sets of picketers at different times, the response from the police can really vary. They [the staff] can say, "Why? Here they keep them there. There they let them come here," and it's like well, what the police are willing to do makes a big difference about both safety and how quickly will the police come.[14]

In spite of these past experiences, these actors came to present state law as a very effective tool. Law, via the injunctions, morphed from being a source of frustration to functioning as the means to three strategic gains. First, it became the mechanism by which activists could control previously inaccessible or ineffective state institutions and actors like the police. Second, it became a practical way to help ensure clinic access. Third, it became a method for inflicting wounds upon adversaries. In short, law mattered to these activists and entered their stories because it raised the groups' expectations regarding their effective tactical options.

Lucinda [the PCN lead lawyer] took us beyond what I ever thought we could . . . I mean, she did things that I thought were never going to be possible.[15]

[The injunction is] partly about helping the police feel comfortable to be able to be firm to say, "Sorry you can't be here. I have a piece of paper that makes it really clear you can't be here." . . . They like clarity.[16]

Crowd control . . . I wanted to make it possible for people to reach my practice.[17]

Having the injunction was being able to have the police, or the federal government, or the marshal, or whatever, read the injunction to these people. . . . They [the protesters] know that they had to hire a lawyer and pay for it. They could be arrested and then they'd have to pay a fine or they'd go to jail. And that's what I hoped to accomplish, to make it more severe for them just to constantly be in our personal space.[18]

Law's positive transformation and portrayal is also seen in many sources from the time of the actual conflict. For example, one can look to touting the power of fines in the Planned Parenthood Shasta-Diablo newsletter *Planned Parenthood*; tallying arrests, fines, and court actions in the PCN's newsletter *SPEAK OUT!*; strategic planning conversations recorded in the PCN's board meeting minutes; and, finally, media coverage of the high-profile conflict in Western New York.[19]

The injunctions also represent, in the words of one PCN interviewee, winning the "imprimatur . . . of our national federal legal system." The federal license that they gained, however, appears to be limited. While state law supplied coercive force that was effective against the opposition, it did not provide an unambiguous and equally effective "discourse that clarified divisions between right and wrong, and between supporters and opponents of a good cause."[20] That is, the clinics' courtroom victories did not translate into a consistent, clear, and resonant set of rights claims that allowed abortion-rights activists to fully wield law's symbolic power.

Normative labeling is somewhat assumed when activists revel in the ability to harness state law, and it was definitely part of these postlitigation narratives. Abortion-rights activists employed legal language to argue that they were in the right and that anti-abortion activists were in the wrong by drawing a line between what they saw as harassment and free speech.

This is not counseling. This is harassment, just plain harassment. I sort of saw that as not physically violent behavior, but verbally violent behavior.[21]

I'm not distressed by someone saying, "Excuse me, would you like some brochures?" . . . But they weren't doing that. They were being aggressive, and weird, and nasty, and scary—making patients cry.[22]

The protesting we had then, they would be blocking one driveway or the other. And being able to like—corner is a strong word—they were able to some degree to have a captive audience of the people either trying to get in or trying to get out.[23]

I think there's a difference between harassment and free speech. That's sort of the way I used to figure it out. You might draw the line differently.[24]

The invocation of harassment and captive audience doctrine shows that state law underlies labeling who was right and who was not. However, statements like "You might draw the line differently" and "corner is a strong word"; the differentiation of physical and verbal violence; and the vagueness of the description of behavior as "aggressive, and weird, and nasty, and scary" begin to show the lack of confidence in unambiguously claiming the law to apply normative statuses. This inability to succinctly crystallize and convey the conflicts' normative meaning was particularly due to the First Amendment's centrality in these cases.

The majority of abortion-rights activists' narratives reveal that these actors identify with the center-left end of the political spectrum and highly prize free speech rights. For example, one of the PCN members said that many of those involved with the Network were "the old warhorses from the Vietnam War protests."[25] A California clinic manager gave her liberal and free speech bona fides by stating, "I went to [the University of California,] Berkeley. I am all for free speech." [26] However, in these cases, instead of defending free speech and being in a position to harness familiar rights language, these activists had to align themselves with the arguments for *limiting* speech rights. This put the abortion-rights activists in an unfamiliar and uncomfortable position, and produced significant disadvantages that undermined the value of their courtroom victories.

The limitations side of the free speech debate is built on a claim to safety. While this appears to be rhetorically attractive, and abortion-rights advocates did appeal to it, safety justifications have distinct shortcomings. Much modern First Amendment jurisprudence has unmasked various safety claims as illegitimate, or has at least significantly challenged and weakened them. In the process of doing so, this jurisprudence has helped construct speech rights that are lionized in our political culture, and it has contributed to an environment where immediate suspicion is cast on those who are seen as trying to restrict our nation's "first right." This is especially true for liberals who praise the Court's defense of antiwar activists and others who have protested state power and traditional cultural institutions. When clinics use speech regulations, then, they are asking their liberal members and supporters to go against a fundamental political, even personal, principle. Furthermore, the proregulation side of the speech debate simply lacks the culturally resonant constitutional rights talk that is found on the free speech side. As a result, the abortion-rights activists are deprived of a comfortable and compelling rights lexicon. While there is still an ability to claim a right to safety, these shortcomings make this right's claim less accessible for liberals, lace it with suspicion, and therefore limit its value.

Both of these limitations were evident in the abortion-rights activists' postlitigation narratives. These activists noted being restricted, or at least being made particularly sensitive, by their free speech principles.

[W]e don't go for injunctions every time we think we could get them, and we don't do it needlessly. Not because it's a whole lot of trouble and in some cases money, but because of some of those [First Amendment] concerns.[27]

I have been working for 20 years on . . . what is free speech. I mean it's like burned into my brain. What I think we could accomplish if we had to do another court case. People calling and asking "Do you think this will fly?" . . . It has made me keenly aware of what is possible. . . . [And] I do think it has heightened my awareness of how important free speech is . . . because I want to be able to go out and demonstrate . . . I want to make sure that I, that the right is still there for me.[28]

Well I think there's a recognition that they had a right to speak. . . . But we didn't like what they were doing to the patients. And so the compromise I think was to get some distance between the two. Nothing ever stops the signs . . . and they got grislier and grislier as it went on. . . . But you can't do anything about that. And I think that's legitimate.[29]

[I]t was about [pause] making it so that protesting could still happen, using the Time, Place, and Manner basis in deciding what worked in a particular scenario of how people could protest, or precisely how they could protest. . . . So I would say it was much more, it was more about restricting the locations of where protesting could happen vis-à-vis that specific building [as opposed to a speech regulation with broader impact].[30]

I have a somewhat unusual background as an abortion provider in that I have both parents who are holocaust survivors. . . . I am very sensitive to the notion of living in a totalitarian state where free speech isn't a protected right. I think it comes naturally for me to consider free speech in this kind of setting. I would not want to live in a society that didn't—that took away a free speech right to protect a private interest such as reproductive choice. [long pause] . . . If, God forbid, that it should ever be an either or, it had to be an either or, I would side with free speech first. . . . Again, I think we've reached . . . a fairly good solution. . . . It's a pretty good balance.[31]

As all of the above quotes show, the concern with fidelity to principle led to a common theme of portraying the injunctions as balanced, or as compromises between protesters and clinics. Since the clinics were conscious of matters of principle they made sure to note that they did not endanger speech rights. This introduced a more nuanced view of the conflicts and the regulations—a view that limited their ability to fully access law's potential. Rights and rights talk are most powerful when they present a situation in absolutist terms. The rights that these activists could claim in order to "clarif[y] divisions between right and wrong" were anything but absolute.[32]

The interviews show these activists searching for legal language that never seemed sufficient to capture the harms perpetrated by the protesters. Law was invoked in a list of harms that ranged from property violations, to captive audience, to assault, to counseling without a license. The range and inconsistency of these harms, their frequent sweeping or vague qualities, and finally the common resort to effectively saying that the harms lay beyond description—that no legal category adequately captured them, and that they had to be witnessed to be understood—made the frustration with the lack of sufficient language evident. Almost all of these elements are seen in one extended quote from a California clinic manager:

Manager: This case wasn't about speech, quite. It's about, well, anyway.

Interviewer: No, actually, how would you categorize what is going on?

Manager: Well, again, when you're, *it felt like a personal assault* going on. I mean no one was clubbing them [the patients], but . . . it was such that *they couldn't get away* from them [the protesters] and they [the patients] weren't sure what was going on and they were forced to take those little, those baby plastic fetuses and stuff. You know, I just don't think you should. That to me, that not only is *a whole safety thing* which I'm about, *but it's also invasion, a personal invasion of the space* and their *expectation of being able to have a reasonable, a healthy medical experience* without getting, you know, trampled by people who were, who hated them. And you weren't sure what they [the protesters] were going to do to you the next second. And I do think, I'm, *the property rights are kind of an interesting one*, the fact that, O.K., you know, *this is our property*, and there's some responsibility to where you get to do what. I think it certainly made it more complex. Confused.[33]

This quote is unique in that it addresses so many issues at once, but it is common in terms of what is listed. The patients are harmed by not being able to easily escape the protesters, by being forced to take "those baby plastic fetuses and stuff," by not being able to maintain personal space, and by not being able to have a "reasonable, healthy medical experience."[34] Clinic staff is also harmed by this harassment, as well as by the inability to control clinic property.[35] Finally, the perceived unpredictability of the protesters posed a general threat to all.

This collage of offenses, however, was not sufficient to capture and convey the full extent of the perceived and experienced harm. The problem was "complex" and "confused" and really came down to the experience— "it *felt* like a personal assault." In short, what was missing was a language that could powerfully and succinctly convey the harm. Since the First Amendment case frames did not seem to provide such rights talk, and liberal principles encouraged the speakers to develop more nuanced portrayals of the events and the law, the activists were not able to effectively translate their courtroom victories into symbolic and rhetorical resources.

Beyond the First Amendment, it is interesting to note that only two of the interviewees directly, and briefly, mentioned the right to reproductive choice as a relevant right in these conflicts. This may underlie part of the activists' frustrations. In short, the movement's master frame lay outside of the reasonable range of possibilities imposed by the First Amendment's centrality in these conflicts.[36] These activists are typically able to express themselves using the rhetorical force provided by the established "pro-choice" rights talk. The evolving movement-countermovement dynamics represented in these cases, however, alter the context and present a unique set of possibilities and limitations that make this rhetoric inappropriate.

These interviews show that, consciously or not, external factors (i.e., the cases' legal frame and the lack of compelling alternate rights language) interacted with internalized First Amendment principles to significantly affect the construction of these stories. Speakers were unable to easily use the pro-choice, abortion-rights master frame. The case's legal frame forced them to appeal to the weaker limitations side of the free speech argument. Finally, internalized principles encouraged them to present a nuanced view of the conflicts and the regulations. As a result, these actors were not able to effectively utilize the full rhetorical power of the law. Law thus mattered and was constructed by their narratives as a tangible, coercive instrument controlled by the state, rather than as a symbolic resource at their disposal that succinctly crystallized and conveyed the conflicts' normative meaning. Ironically, while the victors in these cases were unable to fully and effectively utilize legal discourse, their opponents were not similarly constrained.

Anti-Abortion Activists' Narratives

The first thing to notice about law in the collection of anti-abortion activists' narratives is that it is defined and employed in two somewhat distinct ways. For the majority of these activists, law is primarily constructed as state law. It is closely bound to official state documents, institutions, actors, and decisions, and its power is seen in both normative rights claims and the state's coercive muscle. For an important minority of the interviewees, however, law is partially freed from the state, revealing the creation of extrastate law as discussed in Cover's work.[37] The resulting extrastate formulation sees some law as created and controlled by the state, but other, more fundamental law as created and controlled by God. In the words of one rescuer, "Judges should use the word of God, first and foremost, as their standard."[38]

While all of the anti-abortion activists suggested or explicitly referred to this hierarchical differentiation, the two conceptions of law were primarily employed by two largely discrete groups. Extrastate law dominated in the postlitigation narratives of those who engaged in the more aggressive forms of activism—a group of actors here referred to as "rescuers." Anti-abortion activists who saw themselves as "sidewalk counselors" or who took part in other less confrontational forms of protest—a group collectively referred to here as "picketers"—overwhelmingly invoked a state-based conception of law in their narratives.[39]

McCann's work has consistently argued that people do not necessarily lose the ability to access and advantageously use the law when they lose in the courtroom.[40] Given this, it is not surprising that in both anti-abortion activist groups' accounts, law operated as a normative resource—providing a "discourse that clarified divisions between right and wrong."[41] More surprisingly, given their losses and the presence of extrastate law, both sets of narratives also ultimately bolster, rather than significantly challenge, the state's conception of law. This section will proceed by first looking at the place of law in the rescuers' stories, and then move to examine the picketers' construction and use of state law.

Given the rescuers' strong hierarchical differentiation of God's law and man's law, and the fact that the rescuers were directly subject to the state's coercive force, one would expect their postlitigation narratives to be, in Cover's words, "texts of resistance." This expectation is met by the stories' inclusion of the requisite "development of an understanding of what is right and just in the violent contexts that the group will encounter."[42] For example, all of the rescuers articulated some version of the following statement:

I understand that these people have this right [to an abortion] because the government gave them that right in what, 1970? What was it '72? . . . But God is the one who institutes government. The government is not above God. God is above the government. And I felt since He was the one that, that creates human life that I was going to obey Him in this and have to say, "Well, I'd always been a law abiding citizen, but I'm sorry at this point—I have to say this is where the line was drawn." So I was willing to step beyond that line.[43]

As this quote demonstrates, the rescuers come to terms with the state's violent response to their actions by constructing and appealing to a different conception of law. Because this extrastate understanding conflicts with state law, and because the speakers live (or have lived) in accordance with this alternate conception of law, one can accurately see this as a strong form of resistance and extrastate law. It is important, however, to note precisely how the narratives construct resistance and law.

Resistance narratives of this sort have the ability to generate norma tive and rhetorical force by reframing conflict. The logic of civil disobedience, for example, is that one breaks state law and faces punishment in part to delegitimize the state. If the extrastate understanding of law is persuasive, people will see the state's violent response to it as fundamentally unjust, thus undermining the state's normative authority. Interestingly, the rescuers' stories are restrained in this regard. Rather than using extrastate law as a device to attack and delegitimize the state's normative authority to regulate, the rescuers' narratives largely supported, or at least did not oppose, the state's response to their tactics.

I don't believe that what we did should have been protected. We obviously trespassed. . . . I never felt I had a legal right to do that. I didn't think I was being protected by the Constitution and it didn't offend me that a police officer came and took me away.[44]

I don't [think that] . . . those injunctions are wrong. I understand again why they would want to do that.[45]

I didn't want to fight the restrictions to the entrances and exits, and precisely because in fairness. . . . I didn't want a judge saying, "Well, it's perfectly fine for an atheist and the Satanists to gather in the entrance and exits of the church on Sunday."[46]

The rescuers see themselves as acting in accordance with higher law and outside of state law, but they do so in a way that does not conflict with the enforcement of state law in these cases. The rescuers do this by rejecting the belief that these regulations and rulings violated their First Amendment rights. That is, the rescuers are denying the central claim of both the legal arguments mounted on their behalf and their fellow anti-abortion activists' narratives. The rescuer's quotes reveal that they never expected, nor would they want, their actions to be protected by the First Amendment. They see value in the state's ability to regulate aggressive protest and, as the last of the above quotes shows, possibly even undesirable speech. Similar to interviewees from the clinics that they opposed, the rescuers' preexisting First Amendment beliefs significantly affected the construction of their stories, eclipsing the possibility of invoking resonant speech rights in their defense.

Given these responses, the rescuers' narratives cannot be wholly or broadly read as texts of resistance. The rescuers justify their actions via an appeal to an extrastate conception of higher law—but higher law as it relates to abortion, not free speech. Rescuers can accept the state's rulings as just and even desirable because their higher law does not lead them to a competing understanding of the law at issue in these specific cases (i.e., the First Amendment). The point where the two conceptions of law do conflict, and thus where the portrayal of higher law becomes an actual form of resistance, is limited to the separate point of abortion's legality. The rescuers therefore not only fail to frame their stories in terms of injustice and resistance to these rulings, they actually reaffirm and legitimate the state's authority to regulate the rescuers and other disruptive activists.

Those who rejected or did not participate in the more aggressive forms of protest faced a different set of limitations or, more correctly, challenges when constructing their stories and the law. While many of the picketers expressed admiration for the rescuers, they fixed their own identities to acting within state law and not being confrontational or aggressive.

Really, all of us are law-abiding citizens. We believe in law. We believe in right. And so we didn't want to violate the law to do what we were doing.[47]

First of all, we are not causing harm to anybody. We are trying to help them. And we are trying at least to advise the girl that there are alternatives—that they don't have to do this—and I don't see how that could possibly harm anyone.[48]

I don't bring any harm into their life. I will tell them that there are consequences to abortion. And all they have to do is to read the studies and they'll know what the possibilities really are. . . . So I'm not speaking fear into them . . . if there's any fear, it's probably a fear that's already there. But I'm out here to help the moms. I don't want to hurt them.[49]

The degree of their investment in state law is reflected in the conflation of the legality of their actions and their Christian identities. To paraphrase an earlier quote, they believe in law and they believe in right because in the United States, which Christian conservatives see as a "Christian Nation," the two are inseparable. To be a good Christian is, largely, to be a law-abiding citizen.

There was no one threatened. No one would have ever gotten hurt at Planned Parenthood because as Christians we never would have hurt anyone, including the Planned Parenthood employees.[50]

[W]e were all Christians so there was no one out there screaming or harassing people or anything.[51]

As these quotes show, the picketers' identities and stories orbit around the belief that they were not only permissibly helping others but, as Christians, they are wholly incapable of causing harm. To say that they were breaking the law (i.e., that they were harming others) was therefore tantamount to saying they were acting in an unchristian way. As a result, the rulings struck at the core of their identities and posed a significant problem.

Somewhat surprisingly, the severity of the conflict between the law as pronounced in the judicial rulings and the picketers' core beliefs about both the law and themselves did not prompt them to craft Coverian resistance texts. Their stories, unlike the rescuers' narratives, simply lacked a strong, competing legal construction that justified their being labeled as acting outside of state law. Instead, these actors took careful steps to create narratives that appeared to preserve their unity with state law by defusing the adverse rulings and accompanying state coercion. While this process of amending the state's articulation of law is a form of resistance, picketers, like rescuers, ultimately reaffirm rather than significantly challenge the state's authority.

The cases' First Amendment legal frame and accompanying opportunities for rights talk initially enabled picketers to go on the offensive
against the clinics. Seeing themselves as acting within state law, they were
able to dramatize the injustice of the clinics' actions via the resonant right
to free expression.

My mother was raised in Nazi Germany and I've always been so thankful to live
in America, and I've always thought that freedom came at such a cost and so I just
always thought we had the freedom to do those kinds of things [that we were doing
as activists].[52]

[T]he plaintiffs began this action. . . . But to turn it around, my legal defense was to
protect my and all Pro-Life protesters' First Amendment rights in the public square.[53]

If we keep silencing groups . . . if we silence one, why don't we silence all? And if we
start silencing one, then pretty soon we will silence all, and pretty soon we'll just be
robotic.[54]

[I]f they can make a law like this then I can see how China came to be what it was.
You just lose your rights a little bit at a time, until you don't have any anymore and
the powers that be—whoever is controlling the country at the time—tells you what
you can do and what you can't.[55]

These activists were able to access and use free speech rights language to
articulate the wrong that was done to them specifically and to generalize
it into a public harm. As seen, many of the picketers made statements
that followed the logic of, "It may be me today, but if you let this happen
and this precedent to stand, it could be you tomorrow." The references to
China, Nazi Germany, and becoming robots also illustrate the degree to
which the right to free speech is bound up with American conceptions of
national identity and individuality, and thus is powerful. Given this, these
quotes are archetypal uses of rights talk to apply normative labels and
communicate an issue's importance and relevance to others.

The eventual judicial rulings, however, threatened both the picketers' abilities to continue freely using the law in this way and their law-
abiding Christian self-image. This placed them in the awkward position
of having to construct stories that simultaneously rejected and elevated
state law. They had to neutralize state law as articulated in the ruling
because failing to do so would be to accept that they posed a substantial
threat to others, broke the law, and acted against their Christian principles. However, they also had to preserve state law because it was a valuable

normative resource—both politically and personally. They were able to accomplish both ends by targeting the context in which state law rulings were reached. This process took two forms.

First, a significant amount of time was spent discrediting the factuality of the clinics' arguments, as well as outlining their motivations to lie.

Well, first of all, a lot of the arguments that were brought up in favor of it [the Bubble Bill] were based on lies. We were accused of spitting on people and pushing and shoving them and things like that. None of that ever goes on. We're trying to get that girl to change her mind. We're not going to change her mind if we spit on her.[56]

They were lying. They were just lying. I mean literally.[57]

We weren't endangering anyone. To me that's totally false and just an excuse to get us off the premises. . . . We were speaking the truth and the main money making of Planned Parenthood is from doing abortion. So if we were telling people the truth and they believed it and left, there's several hundred dollars out the window.[58]

I think the abortion industry is very, very powerful and it has a lot of money, and every time we get a girl to change her mind, they lose $400. And, so, there's a real incentive for them to keep us away from those girls.[59]

Presenting the clinics and their supporters as liars who prize financial gain over all else fits nicely with the familiar abortion politics master frame of demonizing the clinics. It also conveniently incorporates the conflict-specific free speech frame. Together, the clinics were wrong not only because they valued their financial interest over life but also because they valued it over our collective First Amendment values (i.e., disseminating truth, allowing people to make informed decisions, seeking change through persuasion rather than coercion, etc.).

This frame also has a third benefit of preserving state law by placing the blame for the decision on the clinics' greed and duplicity rather than on the state and its law. The state is insulated from wrongdoing because they were deceived. The judicial rulings and existing regulations are voided because they are presented as the products of greedy, duplicitous clinics. By framing their stories to discredit the clinics and not the state, these activists defuse the normative implications of the state's rulings and coercive measures; harm the clinics; preserve their own self-image; reaffirm the state law's sanctity, authority, and power; and salvage the legitimate ability to appeal to state law in their narratives.

A collection of these activists also insulated state law and themselves by discrediting specific judges.

[G]rossly exaggerated claims were made, more often by a third party that is not the aggrieved party. They were made by clinic personnel who were allowed to testify hearsay under *a spurious ruling of the judge in my case*, that privacy rights trumped the right to face your accuser.[60]

I want to know who paid the judge . . . I am serious. I really do think that there is something very, very seriously wrong with the judgment that came out of the Solano Courts. It's too weird. It's too weird. And I feel deep down inside that something happened to cause him to do it the way that he did that had nothing to do with the facts. And nothing to do with his intelligence.[61]

That was the beginning of judicial activism there. It's a sad thing. If you lived through it like I've lived through it you understand how detrimental and ugly it can be. . . . I remember when the Supreme Court asked the California Supreme Court to revisit their issue. And I remember the attitude of the judges on the California Supreme Court. . . . I remember several of the judges and their attitude was, "We don't even let the United States Supreme Court tell us how to think." That was judicial activism. I saw that firsthand, I lived that, it angers me that they would do that—that they would literally just mock the United States Supreme Court. That was not justice. That was tyranny.[62]

These quotes amend the construction of law as presented in the judicial opinions, but they do not attack the state's fundamental authority. As a result, these anti-judge arguments actually work to preserve, rather than reject, state law's power and the picketers' abilities to invoke it. Like the previous narrative technique of discrediting the clinics, this is achieved by both articulating a positivist procedural understanding of legitimacy and limiting the scope of narrative resistance to specific bad actors.

While judges typically create state law via their verdicts, the picketers' argument assumes that certain judges fail to create legitimate state law because they violated the basic tenets of positivism—they disobeyed the rules of the office that gives them authority. Said in the common conservative refrain, these judges became "activists." They handed down "spurious" rulings, violated judicial hierarchy, and were corrupted by outside sources. Worse yet, these violations were seen as the product of conscious and, in one claim, malevolent action rather than mistake. These decisions are therefore not seen as actual state law, and the regulations that they uphold are discredited. However, pegging these judges and rulings as *aberrations* preserves the state's general authority by tacitly affirming that the judicial institution is typically defined by procedural fairness.

Although it is inconsistent with their accounts, the picketers further affirm state law's authority through their actions. Simply put, all of these interviewees obeyed the rulings.[63] Cover would see such acquiescence as a "weakness of commitment in the original interpretive act"—lowering their narratives' status from creating law to mere "literature."[64] However, the significant work the activists have performed in their stories to keep state law accessible illustrates both state law's importance to these speakers as well as how state power can be reproduced by dissatisfied subjects. Picketers can disagree with the rulings, be unable to use law as an instrument to dictate clinic action, and be subject to the threat of the state's coercive force. They are, however, still able to advantageously employ a version of state law as a normative device. This allows picketers to maintain a certain self-conception, as well as continue to use these conflicts specifically, and state law more generally, as normative resources in the continuing movement-countermovement struggle of abortion politics.[65] It also enables the state to remain as the legitimate source of legal authority. These narratives thus illustrate how "the stories and accounts that are told to and by litigants . . . are not simply reflective of or determined by those dominant meanings and power relations. They are implicated in the very production of those meanings and power relations."[66]

Conclusion

In spite of their reasons to challenge the state, the street-level activists on both sides of these conflicts overwhelmingly affirm state legal authority even when they have to perform significant work to do so. For example, the activists most invested in an extrastate conception of law (i.e., rescuers) tell stories that exemplify how extrastate law can be constructed and acted upon but still allow the state's institutional power and legitimacy to be affirmed. Alternately, anti-abortion picketers who shared the religious conception of extrastate law, but who did not follow it to the point of intentionally breaking state law, actually engaged in meaning-making processes that amend, and therefore resist, state law. This resistance, however, is carefully limited, and the overwhelming weight of their stories is so dependent upon state law that they reify the state's legal authority.

The above analysis also reveals the converse of a well-established argument concerning law and social movements. Michael McCann and Douglas NeJaime's work informs us that losing in the courtroom does not necessarily lead to surrendering the ability to appeal to law.[67] The anti-abortion activists illustrate this via their continued ability to effectively harness both extrastate and state law's symbolic power in their stories. A surprise comes, however, from noting the symbolic and rhetorical resources available to the clinics and their supporters.

Although the clinics won these cases, abortion-rights advocates' narratives exhibit that these actors experienced significant difficulty accessing state law as a normative device. Victory in the court provided coercive power on the street that changed the way these actors viewed law. It did not, however, provide an unambiguous and equally effective "discourse that clarified divisions between right and wrong, and between supporters and opponents of a good cause."[68] The actors' access to law's symbolic power was inhibited by the lack of familiar rights talk but also, more significantly, by a concern with or impulse to preserve a liberal conception of speech rights. These activist litigants were thus ironically limited in and by their victory, while their opponents were enabled in their defeat.

6

Degrees of Separation

By shifting the focus away from traditional sources of legal meaning (e.g., judicial opinions) and toward individual stories, legal consciousness scholars make an overt attempt to understand legal power outside of the formal state. When selecting storytellers, then, these scholars gravitate toward those who are outside of the official legal apparatus. The previous chapter strayed slightly from this mold by targeting activists who were directly involved in court cases. In spite of this deviation, it returned to the traditional purview of legal consciousness research by focusing on the ways individuals, movements, and the formal legal system interact in the process of constructing and, in these cases, ultimately sustaining state law.

The current chapter maintains this connection with the traditional objectives of legal consciousness research, but it uses a starting point that directly assaults the approach's norms. This chapter begins from the premise that legal consciousness research should *not* be limited to institutional outsiders. Building from this belief, the chapter examines how law is constructed in the stories told by three different types of state legal insiders, or elites.[1] Specifically, this chapter looks at the stories told by legislative members, initial litigation and appellate lawyers, and amicus brief authors involved in *Williams*, *Schenck*, and *Hill*.

These actors all formally participate in the official creation and sustaining of state law through their institutional capacities. As a result, their role in the process of maintaining law's authority seems obvious. This, however, oversimplifies matters. While they may be institutional insiders, these actors are still individuals who have the potential to think and behave independently and thus to challenge official state law. This is especially true within the United States' decentralized governmental and adversarial legal systems. The potential for these elites to challenge the hegemonic conception of law that they also directly help to create is further heightened when competing social movements use these systems and employ these actors in their causes.

Legal insiders may arrive late to the movements that call on them, but they can play important roles not only in dictating movement strategy—a typical way in which they are examined in the law and social movements literature—but in forming activists' perceptions, beliefs, and the vocabulary that they use to describe the events that they experience. For example, this is evident in chapter 5 when a clinic manager referenced time, place, and manner regulations. There is also no reason to assume that the road of influence is a one-way street. These elites are potentially susceptible to having their perceptions, beliefs, and language affected by their interactions with the activists. When this happens, it shows that there are bottom-up, not just top-down, effects when movements enlist elites. The range of possibilities for legal insiders to become part of challenging state legal authority, or alternatively to protect and impose this authority, complicates their position in relation to law. The stories that elites tell are therefore worth studying to see whether and how they, as Susan Silbey put it, "create, sustain, reproduce, or amend the circulating . . . structures of meaning concerning law."[2]

Movement Language and Frames in Elite Narratives

Elites' stories are in part interesting for what they can tell us about the relationship between a movement's primary, or initial, actors and the elites that they appeal to as they employ legislative or litigation-based strategies. In this context, elites can be thought of as resources that social movements are trying to possess in order to access new tactical capabilities. This way of viewing elites raises the question of how safe and reliable these elites are as resources.[3]

Researchers who study the interaction between movements and elites have often argued that elites can have a detrimental effect on movements. Among the elites, lawyers are particularly singled out as being problematic for social movements. They are thought to be true believers in the "Myth of Rights" who pacify movements by taking them away from direct action strategies and pushing them into litigation strategies.[4] Litigation is then subsequently thought to limit or eliminate grassroots participation, disproportionately absorb resources, discourage alliance building and the use of more radical movement tactics, and move lawyers—as opposed to traditional activists—into leadership roles.[5]

One of the specific concerns that researchers have regarding the relationships among elites, law, and movements is how law and lawyers affect movement framing.[6] The worry here is that lawyers will impose legalistic frames for the problems that social movements organize to change. In doing so, lawyers are thought to set off a chain of negative events as described above. The previous chapter presented examples of street-level movement actors using legal language and frames in their stories, so the first step in the chain is found. The secondary nature of these cases, however, contains many of the problems that researchers then warn against.

The cases are still costly, they can divert movement resources, and they pose their own internal consistency and self-image problems. They do not, however, encourage the street-level activists to see the larger movement goals in legalistic terms. The legal frames in such secondary movement litigation are too far removed from these goals to pose such a risk. The same is true for the fear that involving lawyers will, on its own, prompt the movements to exchange disruptive and participatory tactics for more passive elitist institutional strategies. It is true that the politics of abortion have made such a transition, and that these cases are clearly part of that move, but the simple inclusion of lawyers is not the cause. Rather, upheld protest regulations raised the costs of disruptive direct-action strategies, and so they died off.[7] The need to continue to respond, innovate, and open new fronts in the ongoing movement-countermovement struggle also strongly encouraged the anti-abortion movements to develop more elite legal resources. As will be developed in the concluding chapter, this is not a problem of including elites as discussed in the law and social movements literature.

The more interesting question regarding framing and elites is one that is far less common in the literature. There is much to gain from reversing the causal arrow and noting the degree to which the lawyers and other elites that work with movements adopt the street-level activists' frames and rhetoric.[8] Do these legal institutional insiders discuss the conflicts in the dispassionate and technical language of removed elites or with the normatively charged rhetoric of embroiled activists? Answering this question provides one measure of the degree to which elites internalize aspects of the causes they represent and thus become committed and incorporated into these movements. The more that the lawyers and other elites are like the activists, the safer and more reliable they become as movement resources.

In order to understand how the elites in *Williams*, *Schenck*, and *Hill* discuss these cases, one must first have a general understanding of the rhetorical styles employed by street-level activists. As seen in the previous chapters, demonizing the opposition and situating these cases, as well as one's actions, within a larger movement context defines activist rhetoric on both sides of these conflicts. Each side, however, has its own individual nuances and vocabularies.

The abortion-rights activists have a less pronounced rhetorical style than their opponents, but it is still identifiable. Clinic members and their supporters demonized anti-abortion activists by wholly defining them through the language of violence and religious fanaticism, as well as overtly questioning the sincerity of their motives—both generally and in relation to the legal claims made in these cases. They also tended to refer to their opponents in terms that clumped all anti-abortion activists into one coordinated movement. Reflecting the latter trait, these cases were not seen as discrete or local events. Rather, the cases, and the events leading up to them, were part of a highly coordinated effort aimed at not only ending abortion but also imposing conservative religious ideals on the general public.

On the other side of the conflicts, anti-abortion activists have a distinct rhetorical style marked by normative absolutism. They present these conflicts as being part of a wider war between good and evil. This binary framing largely justifies their own actions and demonizes the clinics and their supporters. This style reflects the general observation that Christian conservatives "wish to construct a conception of the world that is secure, unambiguous, where there are good people and bad people, and where they themselves are clearly on the side of the good and true."[9] Specific examples of this can be seen in the assumption that anti-abortion activists are incapable of causing harm to others and also the belief that the clinics, portrayed as wholly motivated by greed, will indiscriminately use whatever means are available to them in order to protect their financial interests. More generally, anti-abortion activists also employ a distinct vocabulary. For example, they commonly use the words "abortuary" and "abortionist" in place of "clinic" and "doctor." Finally, because of their use of morally charged civil disobedience, these activists often present themselves as being the present-day descendants of the abolitionist or civil rights movements.

Turning to the elites, movement rhetoric and frames are best seen in the stories told by the competing lawyers for each side. Eleven of the 13 lawyers interviewed for this project clearly used movement-style rhetoric in the discussion of these cases—seven to a high degree, and the remaining four with significant, but more tempered, use of movement language. The passion that marks anti-abortion-movement rhetoric is clearly seen in the following litigator interviewee quotes:

I think the most valid thing would be to weld up the doors of places like this [abortion clinic] so that nobody could go in and out of them. That would be the most valid thing. It could be done. There are lives being destroyed. Mothers' lives, and human lives . . . babies being killed. . . . [10]

The admission is made that, "Well, no, no one was hurt. Well no, no one was assaulted. No one was battered." You boil it on down to . . . what it boils down to is, "We're Planned Parenthood and we don't like people standing out front of our clinic on the days when we have abortions scheduled to tell women that they should rethink the whole subject. We just don't like it. And why don't we like it? Well, because that's what they're in business to do." I mean, abortion, doing abortions is a high profit margin for any abortion provider. Because it's quick and easy money. [11]

The same passion is seen in the following quotes from clinic lawyers:

And I felt that first of all 15 feet was an incredibly mild restriction that really did not impair anybody's ability to get their message across. . . . And anyone who insisted that they had to get closer than 15 feet simply wanted to obstruct, impede, interfere, and harass. [12]

Generally speaking, their object was to cause economic harm. Their object was to close the clinics. Their object was not to be just talking about abortion. And uh, their object was not just expression of their fundamental right to say "Don't do that." Their object was to make people upset, make people sick from the stress they were causing, and cause physical damage to the clinic and to the various doctors who performed procedures. They were bent on closing the clinics. . . . It wasn't a pro life message. That wasn't so much that was important. [13]

As one might predict, the interviewees that tended to use the strongest movement-style rhetoric were also those that are most clearly seen as classic "cause lawyers." [14] These lawyers have spent the most time with, and have the strongest connections to, their clients and the wider movement so in some ways they are easily seen as specialized extensions of the street-level activists. It is interesting to note, though, that the lawyers for the State of Colorado also used language similar to the more traditional cause lawyers and ground-level activists interviewed.

For example, the state lawyers framed the case as being, in part or in whole, about abortion politics. Like the street-level activists, the state law-yers saw the case and the Bubble Bill as being directed at protesters who were "trying to impose their religious views on people."[15] Their opponents, and the targets of the Bubble Bill more generally, were seen as "absolutely over the top aggressive protesters. People who were sometimes physi-cally violent, who were . . . part of the movement that had expressed the avowed intention of shutting down abortion providers."[16] They also saw anti-abortion activists as disingenuous, "in my opinion they fabricated the chilling thing . . . none of them were willing—I mean unlike just about any other protest in the history of the human race—none of them were willing to even try and violate [the Bill] and get arrested."[17]

The use of movement language reveals a connection between the state lawyers and the abortion-rights activists that could benefit the latter. Movements employ state-based strategies in part to merge the movement's and the state's interests. If a movement succeeds in getting the state to formally adopt its agenda through precedent and/or legislation, the move-ment has entrusted the state with the duty of defending the movement's interests. In some ways, state lawyers are a relatively successful movement's ultimate lawyers, because they are specialists that allow movements to reap the benefits of litigation without directly incurring many of the usual associated costs.

Entrusting the state with protecting one's interests in court, how-ever, comes with its own costs. Movements already risk losing control of the lawyers that they hire directly. This problem increases when move-ments have no direct connections to the state's lawyers. When state law-yers use movement rhetoric, though, it can help put the movement at ease by suggesting that the state actors and the movement share perspectives and interests.[18]

That said, these same lawyers were also conflicted about what their work on the *Hill* case meant in terms of activism. The two lawyers for the state who were interviewed were both supportive of the abortion-rights movement, which increased the desire to win the case. As one of the lawyers said, "I didn't want to be the one who screwed up and allowed women to, you know, continue to be intimidated."[19] These lawyers, however, also recognized that the state was formally protecting "the people's" interests and that they were not directly working on behalf of or with the abortion-rights movement. As a result, their use of movement language should likely be seen more as a testament to the success of the movement's public frames and language than as a sign of the state lawyers being fully incorporated into the movement. Regardless, the use of movement language should be encouraging for the movement.

While the state lawyers have distance from the movement that keeps them from being directly incorporated, the same explanation cannot be used to the same degree for the large-firm appellate lawyers from the clinic side of the *Williams* case. In their study of cause lawyers, McCann and Silverstein found that "a hired gun closely situated within movement organizations over sustained periods of time tended to be a broader movement activist."[20] The two large-firm appellate lawyers for the clinics who were interviewed had ongoing relationships with the activists via related cases and they stated that these cases significantly affected their understanding of abortion politics. In spite of this, they did not identify as movement actors or employ movement rhetoric. Rather, these cases remained like any other and were discussed in dispassionate, detached professional terms.

The interesting thing of being involved in a case like this, as a lawyer, you have to do your best job regardless of your own personal views as to the merits of the cause.[21]

[M]y job was to establish that there was sufficient evidence at the trial level. At the appellate stage we really didn't get into arguments over First Amendment principles so much as the sufficiency of the evidence to sustain the trial court injunction. So it really focused immediately on the adequacy of the evidence as opposed to who's right and who's wrong in this particular case. So it was more, much more, immediately it was much more of a technical debate over who testified as to what. What was the nature of their testimony? Did the trial court have enough evidence to support certain findings that they made? So it really became technical and going through the record and finding what was said.[22]

These quotes reflect a dedication to the view of the lawyer as a neutral professional and cases as dispassionate technical affairs. It is worth noting that a dedication to this view can not only effectively block one from embracing the movement's rhetoric but also obscure the wider political implications of a case, and thus distance a lawyer from the movement that is being served. For example, one lawyer flatly stated, "I was just doing my job of representing a client in a unique fact situation, and really, frankly, wasn't concerned with the precedential values that I was establishing."[23]

These two hired-gun appellate lawyers for the clinics mark the significant drop-off in movement rhetoric in the remaining legal elites interviewed. The legislators who voted in favor of the Bubble Bill, as well as the two amicus brief authors who wrote in favor of the clinics, showed some use of movement language and frames but not to the same level as the street-level activists or even the state lawyers. As a whole, they recognized and referred to violence that was believed to be occurring at the clinics, but they did not dwell on it. In fact, only one of these elites referred to violence at the clinics more than one time. Even she, though, ended up expressing a nuanced view of anti-abortion protesters. In talking about present-day picketers, a Colorado state legislator stated that their activism is "done in such a thoughtful way that you can't help but think, 'who can those people be?' They are out there on a cold Saturday morning with their signs and their prayer books, or they're standing in a circle praying, and it's very effective."[24] This almost admiring view of the protesters is a far cry from the vehemence seen in the street-level narratives.

Switching to the elites who supported the anti-abortion protesters, only one employed strong movement rhetoric and frames. In a discussion of his opponents' portrayal of the harms that women faced in front of the clinics, this legislator responded with classic activist language. "The purpose of going to an abortion clinic is to harm the child. . . . The child is ripped to shreds. . . . You know, what the debate is about, presumably what protesters are there to accomplish, is to provide protection for and encourage mothers to consider their children."[25]

This language revealed that this legislator was the only vehement supporter of anti-abortion activism in the remaining elites. With the exception of the anti-abortion protesters' litigation lawyers, the elites who ostensibly supported the anti-abortion activists (or at least opposed the protest regulations) did not use any language resembling that employed by the street-level activists. In fact, five of these elites explicitly stated that they were either pro-choice, that they recognized the problem of real violence at the clinics, or both.

Taken collectively, two conclusions emerge from the above. First, the more pervasive acceptance of abortion-rights activists' accounts of the events at clinics suggests that they have been successful in controlling the national narrative for these conflicts.[26] Second, even though abortion-rights activists have been successful in controlling the general conflict narrative, its internalization does not necessarily translate to complete support. As will be discussed more fully below, these elite narratives suggest that the further one is from the events in the street or from the movements themselves, the less sway this narrative holds. In fact, as the pro-choice no-vote legislators and amici show, the further one moves away from each movement, the more that other values can overshadow the power of the abortion-rights account of violence in the streets.

The above is both promising and concerning for movements that are striving not only to control public opinion but also to convert legal elites into stable, effective, and safe movement resources. The elite narratives show that movements can have an effect on how these elites discuss, and thus presumably think about, these conflicts. This in turn possibly limits some of the risks of bringing elites into a movement. However, these narratives also show that the effect of the movement's language diminishes the further one moves from direct contact with the movement.

The discussion of the adoption of movement rhetoric and frames is the first means of looking at what these narratives can tell us about elite-movement interaction. The second is to examine the ways that one's position affects their construction of law. As with the above, an analysis of elites' constructions of law needs to be seen in light of street level activists' constructions.

Constructing Law in Abortion-Rights Elite Narratives

There are three main themes in how law was constructed, and how it mattered, in the narratives of abortion-rights street-level activists. First, law was presented as an ultimately effective coercive force that regulated the anti-abortion activists and largely stopped their most aggressive tactics. Second, law was seen as binding principle in the form of their attested fidelity to an expansive reading of the First Amendment. Third, because of this belief in a permissive reading of the First Amendment, law was a constraint that interfered with their ability to employ the strongly symbolic normative force of law.

Variations of the first two constructions of law were seen in differing degrees in the narratives of legal elites that sided with abortion-rights activists. The third way that law mattered in activist narratives, however, was not seen in the legal elites' accounts. Instead of being constrained by their fidelity to a reading of the First Amendment, legal elites were able to use their institutional positions to avoid the issues that the activists encountered. In addition, many of the elite narratives also take a realist political view toward law that is not seen as strongly in the street-level narratives. The portrayal of law as subject to individual preferences and manipulation distances it from the insulated and principled view that the street-level activists forwarded, which helps to legitimate state law. Taken together, the ways that law is constructed in these elite narratives both affirms the power of the state and presents unique reasons to question the legitimacy of law and legal institutions.

By describing how their expectations rose concerning the possibilities of exploiting state power as a coercive force, the first presentation of law by street-level activists reified the power and authority of state law. Given the involvement of legal elites in securing the power of the state for the clinics, and the success of the regulations in moderating anti-abortion protesters, it is not surprising that this view of law was also prevalent—though somewhat modified—in the lawyers' and legislative members' stories. The portrayal of law was modified in that while many elites presented law as an *effective* response to the protesters, others emphasized that it was an *appropriate* one. While the distinction can appear to be minor—just an issue of semantics—it points to important situational differences between the elites and street-level activists in these conflicts.

The initial litigators in *Schenck* and *Williams* all highlighted the efficacy of injunctions and therefore most closely reflected the street-level activists. For example, a PCN attorney stated, "[W]e didn't have problems with blockades anymore. . . . We were able to enforce our injunction, and actually have some of their leadership arrested, which kind of put the wind out of their sails." In California, the clinic's lawyer noted that the injunction "had the effect of moving most of the true people—the people who were truly expressing their opinions. They realized . . . there was some legal restrictions on them and they backed off. So that's where the major change occurred. . . . It was clearly the injunction. There was nothing [else] that was going to stop this. We tried." Like the street-level advocates, these lawyers had witnessed the clinic-front conflicts over long spans of time and saw the effects of the introduction of state law. Correspondingly, the law in the initial litigation lawyers' stories goes through a process of redemption similar to that seen in the activists' accounts and is ultimately proven to be effective, thus reifying the power of state law.

Moving further from the elites closest to the street-level action, the emphasis switches from efficacy to appropriateness. The appropriateness and efficacy of legal action are different, but they are also related. They are first related in that appropriateness typically assumes effectiveness.[27] Second, in the context of this project, they are also related in that both ultimately affirm state law's authority. The terms are also distinct in at least two ways that highlight the gap between activists and some of the elites they recruited. The language of appropriateness that the appellate lawyers and legislative members used shows that they were removed from the events and actors at the clinics—they did not experience the drastic changes in life before and after the law's intervention, and so it was not emphasized.

More importantly, the distinction is noteworthy because of what it reveals about what was possible for each group. In short, the street-level activists were not in a position to emphasize appropriateness. The language used in street-level stories revealed that the activists were not completely comfortable with their use of state law, and thus its effectiveness far outshone its appropriateness. The elites, however, did not have this problem.

The transition away from emphasizing effectiveness begins with the state lawyers whose stories assume, rather than directly address, the Bubble Bill's effect. One state lawyer's concern that she didn't want to be the one who lost the case and "allowed women to . . . be intimidated," as well as the other's criticism that none of the anti-abortion activists were "willing to even try and violate it [the Bubble Bill] and get arrested," both suggest that the bill effectively checked activist behavior. However, because these lawyers were not closely associated with clinic members who had directly experienced protesting, they did not emphasize the Bubble Bill's efficacy. Their stated personal investment in the abortion-rights movement, however, appears to differentiate them from the appellate lawyers and the amici who *never* mentioned—directly or indirectly—either the effectiveness or the appropriateness of the regulations.

The legislators who voted in favor of the Bubble Bill were similarly removed from the events at the clinics and so they too lacked cause to stress state law's efficacy. Instead, the legislators approached the events from the standpoint of being asked to decide if the clinics' problems warranted introducing the state's coercive force. As a result, all of the legislators in favor of the bill concentrated on the appropriateness of legal intervention. One legislator, for example, stated, "I think the purpose is to protect those being harassed to an unacceptable level. . . . If those people would have been treating police officers like that, it probably would have been harassment." Another, borrowing from the street-level narratives, said, "I just felt like, obviously other things have been tried, and they weren't working, and people were still being harassed. And I just felt like this was the solution." Both of the above quotes justify state action by pointing to the clinics' exceptional circumstances, but neither speaks directly to whether the bill worked. Like the Colorado state lawyers' stories, though, the legislative members' statements assume its efficacy—"this was the solution"—and thus affirm state law.

The legislators' emphasis on the appropriateness of state law was something uniquely available to elites. Street-level activists' fidelity to a liberal self-image and to a permissive reading of the First Amendment interfered with their ability to fully use rights language to crystallize issues concerning why they legitimately sought the state's help. As a result, they could not convincingly discuss the appropriateness of using state law. A small collection of elites that sided with the abortion-rights activists also expressed how their First Amendment beliefs functioned as a constraint, but they were not ultimately constrained to the same degree. Many elites, though, never suggest that law was ever a significant constraint on their actions.

At first look, the initial litigation lawyers are again most like their clients in terms of presenting law as a constraint. These lawyers were joined by one of the appellate lawyers, the two amicus brief authors, and the Bubble Bill's two sponsors. Like the street-level protesters and the majority of the elites that sided with the clinics, these actors noted their liberal, free-speech bona fides during their stories:

My father was a general counsel for a labor union.[28]

I was perhaps more liberal than some of my clients.[29]

I . . . have become a feminist liberal Jew.[30]

There were not any greater First Amendment absolutists or left-wing Democrats than either Diana or me.[31]

In general, I am probably more protective of speech than the organization is.[32]

After this, many transitioned to stating how their understanding of law limited their, and the activists', actions:

My clients are saying, "Can't we push them all the way across the street?" Right from the get-go I always said, "No, we can't because of the First Amendment."[33]

We didn't want to make bad law for subsequent protests of a more liberal nature.[34]

I would not have advocated justifications and restrictions that I did not feel were justified in the record, in the facts of the case, in the environment of that particular context.[35]

If the goal is . . . to suppress the speech itself, then I think the, it's an illegitimate use of judicial power.[36]

The story I just told you about crafting it [the Bubble Bill]. I mean, we were very concerned about the free speech rights.[37]

Some people wanted us to do, like, 30 feet. And we said that's too far away.[38]

At this point in the course of the typical street-level activist narrative, the interviewee would turn to arguing that the clinics' legal actions were balanced or were compromises between protesters and clinics. The talk of compromise and balance introduced a more nuanced view of the conflicts and the regulations that undermined their rhetorical power, but in doing so it showed how these activists were constrained by legal principle. While the above-mentioned collection of elites said that they were similarly constrained by legal principle, their stories did not show it in the same way. The themes of balance and compromise, for example, were muted and almost completely absent in the elite narratives. When elites did refer to balance and compromise, these themes did not play the exact same role or have the same effect in their stories. In the street-level activists' stories, the themes of compromise and balance were included to show that they were not disregarding the rights of the anti-abortion protesters. They also often took a defensive tone. In the elites' cases, balance and compromise were simply referred to as the product of political and legal realities.

And so I think it was really the reasonable approach that we took, both trying to protect the patients and trying to protect the First Amendment rights of the protesters. I think that's why the bill was upheld.[39]

The general configuration [of the clinic grounds] and the few options available to try to strike the appropriate balance between the rights of the protesters and the rights of the patients inside [made the case challenging].[40]

I think that [the 60-foot buffer in one injunction] was reflective of the particular configuration of trying to strike that balance between the protesters. They can still stand across the street.[41]

For the quote from the first speaker, a legislator, the Bubble Bill was balanced in part to ensure its passage and legal survival. For the latter two quotes, both of which are from lawyers, the injunctions' particulars were largely the products of real-estate limitations. None of the quotes present balance or compromise in a strong or principled sense. It is, for example, hard to objectively view a 60-foot buffer between speaker and audience as being balanced or a compromise.

The initial clinic lawyer in the *Williams* case makes the most extreme distinction between the ways that balance and compromise are referred to by elites versus street-level activists.

To be totally candid, in most cases, I was able to balance fairly well. I do, I believe in the First Amendment to an extraordinary degree and in fact, *the picketers at some point actually had good points. And the most good point was that they were a little too far away from the clinic. This was their best point—they wouldn't be heard. From a fundamental, pure First Amendment position, they were right.* . . . [But] as applied to the clinic, I thought that was a good solution, [to] put them on the sidewalk so they couldn't be heard. And that's what I tried to do, but in fact, I see that [the anti-abortion activists' objections] as a very good point.[42]

The reference to "balance" in an affirming admission that the injunction silenced the anti-abortion activists stands in stark contrast to the abortion-rights activists' use of the term. The fact that the quote also begins with the statement that "I believe in the First Amendment to an extraordinary degree" only sharpens the question that the contrasting uses raise—that is, why are liberal legal elites not constrained in the same ways as the street-level activists?

The answer to this question lies in the different roles that elites and street-level activists played in these conflicts. When they did appear, the themes of compromise and balance did not occupy the same space in elite narratives because they held institutional positions that altered their relationship to volition. Elites had the ability to reference their legal institutional roles in order to distance themselves from the belief or accusations that their actions were undermining their attested fidelity to legal principle. As a result, they were not required to justify their actions in the same ways as the street-level activists and show that they were respecting the protesters' rights. For example, the lawyer's quote above ends with her saying, "*as applied to the clinic*, I thought that was a good solution."[43] Like the other quoted lawyers, this lawyer is not putting herself in the place of volition. Rather, they are responding to the clinics' particulars. Their actions are dictated by the configuration of the clinics and so they are not full and free instigators of action.

Similar moves to distance oneself from action are seen in every lawyer's story—including the amici. For example, the lawyers, among other things, cited the police as requiring them to act: "The cops are telling me that I need 100 feet for traffic safety. So that's why we got the bigger buffer zone";[44] "The clinic had been told to get an injunction . . . by the police."[45] Most commonly, though, volition and responsibility were placed with the clients:

Well, I'm an advocate, so I do what my client wants.[46]

I was there representing a client in this particular fact pattern.[47]

I mean, as a lawyer if your client says "this is what I want and need" and you think you have legal grounds to get them that, you try to get them.[48]

Lawyers of all levels that are dealing with advocacy are really fighter pilots . . . you have a mission, you have an objective, you have a goal, you have a plan, you have a strategy. . . . It's my job to do everything within my power to have the court uphold the statute.[49]

I am a lawyer for an agency. Like any other lawyer that works for a client . . . my views are not terribly relevant.[50]

In these final quotes, we are told that it is the lawyer's role and professional responsibility, even duty, to execute the clients' desires. This shifts the duty of weighing questions of principle to the clients. Lawyers are presented simply as conduits—tools, and not necessarily advisers, for their clients. When professional roles are viewed this way it is not surprising that these lawyers were unencumbered by their attested fidelity to a principled understanding of law.

This view of lawyers does not affirm the conception of state law as being wedded to principle. In fact, it portrays state law as the opposite. Law is seen as an aggressive, ends-motivated game that one plays strategically like a "fighter pilot." The construction of law freed from principle was repeated, and thus underscored, in other ways throughout these lawyers' stories. The state lawyers elsewhere emphasized the "theatrical" and storytelling aspects of law. A PCN lawyer echoes this sentiment by stating, "Even if they [the judges] don't buy the legal argument, it's more about which *picture* they buy . . . I knew that it was my task as a lawyer to push that picture of purely peaceful protesters on the public sidewalk out of their head." When law is theater, it is about image and not substance or principle. Lawyers from all of the cases also raise the possibility that judges' personal preferences, not law, dictate rulings. One state lawyer expressed this by saying, "You always worry that . . . a judge would decide it on the basis of support for abortion versus opposition to abortion rather than the First Amendment." These views of law as unmoored from principle may be realistic, but they work to undermine state law's legitimacy.

Citing one's institutional role and attributing volition and responsibility to others are also seen in the legislators' stories. Of the interviewees who voted in favor of the Bubble Bill, the legislation's two lead sponsors were the only ones to cite personal, principled First Amendment concerns with the legislation. This does not mean that the other legislators were unaware of the potential constitutional problems with the law. The bill's constitutionality, remember, was the central topic in committee and floor debates. In addition, all of the legislative interviewees stated that they knew that the bill's constitutionality would be challenged in court. Surprisingly, this was not a significant concern in their accounts. The reasons for this are rooted not in a belief in the frivolity of the potential constitutional challenges but in the legislators' understanding of their institutional roles.

First, legislative members dispensed with the Bubble Bill's potential problems by citing their legislative role and the duty to act even if their actions might be unconstitutional.

I think there is no doubt that it [the Bubble Bill] would probably be challenged . . . [but] you always vote what you believe.[51]

You don't think about that [the constitutional issues] at the time. You vote the way you think. You vote your conscience.[52]

Sometimes you stand up for something even when you know it may be thrown out. It's just a personal, deep conviction that you have. And I am sure the other side would say the same thing.[53]

The second appeal to institutional roles in downplaying the importance of the bill's possible constitutional problems was to note that the individual legislator does not have a duty to judge constitutionality.

You have three branches of government. The third branch is there to test constitutionality. We are not all constitutional scholars. . . . Every bill we do could have a constitutional challenge to it.[54]

That [questions regarding constitutionality] really goes into details that the prime sponsor of the bill would have to [address].[55]

I knew there was no laws like that law . . . and [it was] one that somebody would have to determine if it was an appropriate time, place, and manner restriction.[56]

This sentiment was even articulated in the Bubble Bill's legislative hearings when the committee chairwoman asked that "the committee not discuss whether it's constitutional or not. We could debate that all day because we are of different opinions."[57]

Where the lawyers place responsibility with the clients and other actors, the legislators place it with the bill's sponsors and the courts rather than with themselves or the full legislative body. The dedication to deferring to colleagues, the separation of powers, and voting one's conscience may initially appear noble and therefore affirm state law. The sum effect of it, though, can be argued as the opposite. When the legislative members are told or volunteer that it is not their place to consider a bill's constitutionality, they are harming the source of state law's legitimacy. They are, in effect, ultimately saying that they are not directly bound to or by the Constitution.

As a whole, the elites who sided with the clinics simultaneously constructed two ultimately conflicting versions of state law. The first affirms state law by showing it to be both effective and/or appropriate for use. The second shows it to be unprincipled, or at least undisciplined. Legislators are not seen as being duty-bound to seriously consider issues of constitutionality with bills where constitutionality is legitimately in question. Lawyers are presented as needing to serve and not challenge their clients' desires even when these desires may be in tension with established understandings of constitutional principle. This second construction of law not only conflicts with the law as portrayed by the street-level activists but also attacks the source of state law's legitimacy. As a result, it contributes to undermining state law's authority.

Constructing Law in the Narratives of Elites Aligned with Anti-Abortion Activists

Switching to the other side of these conflicts, the street-level anti-abortion activists constructed versions of law that allowed them to challenge the protest regulations. The state, however, overwhelmingly announced that these conceptions of law were fatally flawed. These actors were therefore on the receiving end of state law's jurispathic regulation. In spite of this, they were still able to access the symbolic power of law and, more surprisingly, they ultimately validated state law in their postlitigation stories. They accomplished this by first narrowing what the court cases were about. Second, they controlled the scope of their criticisms of the state so as not to harm or significantly challenge state law.

Briefly, rescuers accepted that their behavior exceeded the First Amendment's scope of protection and so they did not challenge the rulings. They did this because they saw the regulations and the rulings as targeting their more extreme tactics and not their extrastate understanding of God's law. As a result, they were able to preserve their extrastate conception of law while still helping to sustain state law. The picketers were in a more difficult position in relation to the rulings because they had self-consciously avoided the rescuers' aggressive tactics, but they were still affected by the regulations and the rulings. As a result, they could not as easily cordon off the cases' scope and accept the rulings. Instead, these actors amended state law by flagging the cases as anomalies produced by illegitimate litigant and judicial behavior. This delegitimized the rulings in their minds, but preserved the state-law system as a whole. Because of this the picketers were still able to align themselves with state law and use law as a normative device in their stories.

Like the abortion-rights legal insiders, there is a division here between the anti-abortion lawyers and the remaining elites. Also like those quoted in the previous section, the lawyers here have similarities with the street-level activists, but they construct an elite-specific version of the law that initially affirms, but also significantly challenges, state law. Unlike in the previous section, though, all but one of the legislators and amici tell radically different stories from the lawyers and the street-level activists that they ostensibly ally with. As a result they have a unique construction of law that wholly affirms state law in a way that is not available to the activists and initial lawyers on either side of these cases.

Starting with the lawyers that represented the anti-abortion activists, there is a collection of elites who, like the activists, distinguish between rescuers and picketers.

Operation Rescue–style blockage wasn't at-risk with the portion of the statute that we were challenging. There was a provision of the statute which addressed that, but frankly we weren't representing Operation Rescue in that lawsuit and nobody that we were representing would have had standing to challenge the provisions on Rescues because they weren't involved in Rescues.[58]

Well, I've got to be careful about this . . . making a generalization. . . . We're talking about different people, different dates . . . different cities when you're talking Western New York.[59]

Well, Grayson, who chained himself to an abortion clinic doorway . . . can be prosecuted. . . . They [the activists] have to, you know, permit ingress and egress or they'll risk legal consequences.[60]

These quotes limit the regulations' legitimate scope to the rescuers' behavior just as the rescuers themselves did in their narratives. This does some work to validate the regulations and therefore to also validate state law and the clinics' use of it. This work is, however, quite limited. The distinction between rescuers and picketers does not lead the lawyers to accept the regulations and the rulings as the rescuers did. Rather, the lawyers are drawing the distinction to highlight the inappropriateness of applying the regulations to picketers. The distinction thus sets up the lawyers' largely negative construction of state law.

The most common construction of law in these lawyers' stories is of state law as a coercive bludgeon. State law's jurispathic role is succinctly presented by one attorney's story about a judge in Colorado.

I will never forget I was in front of a judge in Boulder. . . . The judge, after hearing all the evidence on one of these Operation Rescue cases, found all my clients guilty. . . . All those hundreds of people, they all did what they were accused of and they were all found guilty. And even after finding them guilty, he was sentencing them and he stopped and he looked at all of them and he said, "You are the most frightening people I have ever had in my court." And he said, "I'd love to have any of you as my neighbors and yet you're willing to take the law into your own hands and make these decisions, completely contrary to what the law is currently and that is terrifying." Yeah, and I'll never forget it was one of the first opportunities that I realized he was absolutely right because it was people that would normally not be any type of trouble. You know, they probably never jaywalked.[61]

This story nicely summarizes the state's view of the situation and of the court's role. The anti-abortion activists held a rival conception of law that prompted otherwise peaceable people to break with the state. In calling this "terrifying," the judge articulates the threat that this alternate conception poses and justifies why the state must use its coercive force to crush it.

While this story establishes a legitimate reason for the use of coercive force, the majority of the lawyers' stories—the previous lawyer included—convey that the use of force, while effective, was illegitimate.

People became afraid to even go [to clinics] because people feel contempted—it became a verb here . . . cited for contempt for *quasi violations, fabricated incidents.* They're very interested, escorts and pro-choice sympathizers, in lying about things that happened and getting people subjected to contempt proceedings. So the injunction just by itself, even though on its face right now, is not terribly impressive, it chills.

. . . I recognize the inevitability of the injunction. I think the most valid thing would be to weld up the doors to places like that [clinics], so that nobody can go in and out of them. It would be the most valid thing that could be done. . . . It's indefensible [the clinics' actions]. . . . Legally valid, yes, the injunctions are legally valid. . . . Until the law has changed.[62]

You know, [they were] essentially trying to crush a social movement, which they effectively did.[63]

The abortion providers seek relief in court because it's intimidating. And they are fairly certain they can get it. And it immediately, *whether you're right or wrong,* it immediately puts the defendants, at least momentarily, on their heels, before they can respond to what's done and, you know, brings to light or show whatever it is that the defendants are doing or not doing. And generally it's what they are *not* doing.[64]

Like their clients, these lawyers suggest that state law's "hammer" was brought down on the activists because the clinics lied to the courts. This makes the use of coercive force illegitimate.

If the narratives ended here state law would be blemished, but not significantly harmed. The blame for the misuse of force is primarily attached to the clinics and not the state. This is largely the pattern and conclusion seen in the picketers' stories. They dealt with facing the state's coercive force by carefully labeling who the bad actors were—lying clinics and a few rogue judges—and how they caused what the picketers saw as flawed and invalid rulings. Their sparing and precise attacks bruised, but ultimately preserved, state law's overall legitimacy.

The lawyers that represented the picketers, however, do not exercise such restraint. Instead, they broadened the attack and directly challenged state law's authority. The expansion of the criticism starts with the above quoted lawyer's distinction between what is "legally valid" and what is defensible. The slights directed at state law become less abstract as the lawyers repeatedly doubt and deride the judiciary as a whole, and the Supreme Court in particular.

I mean judges are human beings like everybody else. . . . Maybe it's easier to issue the restraining order, make sure nothing happens out there, that way I am insured that I won't have to, not that I won't have to deal with this again, but I won't be getting complaints in my court room from Planned Parenthood in the future.[65]

Oh, I think [the regulations were upheld] because it was convenient as a way of deciding the case. . . . If this were not an abortion protest case it wouldn't have come out the way that it did. I think that it was tassoled reasoning to go around and say "Well, in these legislative cases we're going to apply a different standard than we do in the injunction cases."

. . . [This was the] simplest, frankly, the simplest of First Amendment cases and somewhere there is a dunce cap with Justice Stevens's name on it.[66]

So the state of Connecticut passed a law that said it is illegal to harass hunters and that is the same word they used. The Second Circuit Court of Appeals held that this anti-hunter harassment pitch was unconstitutional. . . . I showed it to Judge Arcara and I showed it to Lucinda Finley and I said, "How can you distinguish this?" . . . The crucial language that was held to be unconstitutional in that case was in the injunction she [Finley] wanted. . . . And they couldn't distinguish it. They couldn't withstand the argument. They pretended it hadn't been made. They wouldn't even dignify it with a response . . . I mention this because I thought it was my most—my first acquaintance with something called the "abortion distortion."[67]

The people should be paramount in what they want. And there should be a democracy in that regard. And they made it into a tyranny of the Supreme Court. . . . My color's rising as I speak about this.[68]

The frustration that these lawyers are expressing was conveniently summed up by the term "abortion distortion." This term was shorthand used by all of the anti-abortion lawyers to refer to abortion politics causing these cases to be treated differently from what they saw as similar First Amendment cases. This frustration contributed to the reasons why one lawyer ultimately left the movement, but for the rest of these lawyers, they accepted the judicial bias as part of the larger challenge that they faced.

Because this problem was presented as systemically plaguing the judiciary—from the trial courts up to the Supreme Court—condemnation in the elites' narratives is far less contained than in the picketers'. As a result, the lawyers' stories directly assault state law's legitimacy. The clinics are presented as bearing responsibility for dishonestly using the state's coercive force, but this behavior was seen as expected from them. As one lawyer said, "If you anticipate that the court is going to drop the hammer on them, why not let the court use its hammer? I mean, it's not like neighbors that have kind of a friendly dispute over a property line. I mean, what you have are two sides that are so far apart that there is no middle ground."[69] The lawyers' bigger problem is with the state law system. Its supposedly neutral institutions are portrayed as cutting corners and being deeply biased.

Like the realist position taken by the abortion-rights lawyers, state law cannot directly combat the corrupted portrait that these lawyers are drawing.[70] Also like the clinic lawyers' narratives, it is again interesting to see that the broader condemnation of the system is limited to the elites. It would have been easy for the street-level anti-abortion activists to share in this large-scale denunciation. The criticism fits neatly with staples in conservative and Christian Right rhetoric about the "war on Christianity," "activist judges," and the general failure of government institutions. Rather than adopting the views of their lawyers, though, the anti-abortion activists perform significant work in their stories to preserve a more pure, principled conception of law.

The remaining elites that sided with the anti-abortion activists also present a pure and principled version of state law, but they do not need to perform significant work to do so. These legislators and amici are unique among all of the interviewees for the political distance they maintained from the activists they ostensibly supported. The distance thus insulated them from the politics of the larger dispute and the sting of the final judicial rulings, which in turn enabled them to construct law in their stories as pure principle.

The political distance between these elites and the other actors involved in these cases comes from the fact that only one of these elites was strongly anti-abortion. In contrast, the three amici and one of the legislators overtly expressed their support for abortion rights. The other two legislators said that they had little interest in social issues generally, and abortion politics specifically, and that they considered themselves to be social issue moderates. For example, one of these self-stated moderates said that he chose to vote against the Bubble Bill, but he "wasn't going to support a constitutional amendment" banning abortion.[71]

In addition to this political distinction, four of these six unique elites conceded that the clinic protests posed a significant problem.

It [the Bubble Bill] was there to prevent fairly serious forms of intimidation from going on.[72]

Oh, do I think that there was a problem with people protesting out in front of clinics? . . . Oh, absolutely. Absolutely. . . . It was incredible.[73]

I thought in this case, it was a close case, in that there certainly were, there was need for government intervention to stop violence at clinics. . . . I thought government had a legitimate interest in making sure that people had access to the clinics.[74]

I am not discounting what's happening at some of these protest situations. It is not pretty. What is on the placards is not pretty. What people yell out to women entering the clinic is not pretty.[75]

It is almost impossible to imagine any of the anti-abortion lawyers, and certainly any of the activists, making similar statements.

Since all but one of these remaining elites started from a position that was in some way sympathetic to the clinics, but they still actively resisted permitting the clinics' chosen regulations, one can begin to see why they constructed law as pure principle.[76] In order for these elites to not act on one of their political preferences, another significant interest had to be present, conflicting, and more compelling.

The minute that we say we can make an exception here, or an exception there, we allow the government or private parties to use the government to restrict speech, that's the minute that we lose freedom, or some measure of it.[77]

It [the arguments for the injunction] would give the government way too much power to regulate speech. . . . People can be cruel, but we don't want the government to be able to squelch that message.[78]

As long as you regulate around the fringe, you are probably in good shape. And that's really the problem they ran into in *Schenck*. The government, the local government, didn't regulate around the fringe. Instead they deemed the protesters' speech actionable based upon the reactions of the listener and the physical position of the listener.[79]

So that's why the vote is very, very serious, as far as whether or not enforceability would be possible, whether the . . . law will pass Constitutional muster.[80]

I would say that because I apply those concerns [with First Amendment principles, and] you have people highly motivated to change the world.[81]

Unlike the anti-abortion activists and their lawyers, these elites do not attack or blame the clinics in their stories. Rather, they concede that there was a legitimate problem, but that the chosen solution was itself problematic because it ran afoul of what they saw as established, and stronger, constitutional principles. In fact, their stories show that there was little to no contest between the competing interests. The choice of how they should act seemed obvious. In the words of one of the amici, "These are neutral principles that should apply no matter what the political climate, or the issues, or the people who are advocating issues." This faith in law's neutrality and the resulting ease in choosing legal principle over political preference strongly affirm state law's authority.

While it does not necessarily bolster state law, these elites continue to differentiate themselves by not attacking the courts. As a group they were overwhelmingly silent when it came to the judiciary. For example, none of the legislative members that voted against the Bubble Bill said that they followed the case. It was just not of interest to them. As one legislator stated, "Certainly, it was not high on my list. When you are in the legislature you have so much that you are trying to do within the branch of government, you don't spend a lot of time worrying about it [subsequent court cases]." Another added, "No [I didn't follow the case] . . . I mean, a lot of the laws we give passes on are in the courts. It wasn't one of my bills [so I did not follow it]." Similarly, one of the amici authors said that he never read the eventual Supreme Court opinion because he was not that invested in the case. The amici's ambivalence for the underlying politics is emphasized by the fact that their brief was filed in support of neither party. "The idea [of the filing] was just to remind the court that we have a position . . . that is driven more by the First Amendment than by . . . the plaintiff's support for abortion, or the protester's, defendant's opposition to abortion."

This lack of attention given to the court cases is not due to a belief in the insignificance of the court's work. Rather, it is further testament to the interviewees' separation from the activists and initial lawyers on both sides of these cases. When the issue went to court, the legislators did not have to worry about the negative ruling because they did not couple their understanding of law or their vote with either strong support for the protesters or actual anti-abortion activism. The same was true for the amici. While their brief ultimately supported the anti-abortion activists' First Amendment argument, it did not directly support the extreme tactics that prompted the regulations. In fact, as their stories and neutral brief filing underscore, they made an effort to distance themselves from the anti-abortion activists and "to point out to the court . . . [that] you can't completely dismiss the interests of the people going inside the clinic. And it's appropriate to be aware that there are reasons to at least look at whether some additional regulations around the clinic might be good."

By siding with what they see as principle and not assigning blame or railing against the decision, these elites present state law as something pure but also as something somewhat academic. On the one hand, their stories validate state law's essential legitimacy, authority, and power. On the other, because their distance from the politics of the conflicts enables their pure construction of law, it raises a question about whether or not legal principle is only allowed to exist in conditions where the issues at stake are hypothetical for those considering them.

The abortion-rights activists, for example, attest to holding the same First Amendment views as these elites. The effect of the activists' permissive and principled understanding of the First Amendment, however, appears to be limited at best during the conflict. Activists' fidelity to their espoused legal principles surfaced only as a constraint in their later narratives. The stories therefore imply that the heat of conflict gave the activists the ability to mobilize law in spite of their various misgivings. The clarity provided by the immediacy of the fight, however, seems to fade over time. That is, the more distance the activists got from the conflict, and the more academic the issues became, the more their beliefs in liberal legal principle surfaced.[82]

Conclusion

By examining legal elites, this chapter has clearly strayed from the original forms of legal consciousness research. It has, however, established that elites have a more complicated relationship with law than the typical view of their positions would suggest. While they play formal roles in creating and sustaining state law, the above analysis has shown that they can adopt movement frames and rhetoric, and thus become incorporated into movements and look like activists in many ways. Elites can also come not only to challenge state law but to do so more dramatically than the activists that recruit them. Given this, while the chapter is initially at odds with legal consciousness norms, it ultimately contributes to the "critical sociological project of explaining the durability and ideological power of law."[83] It has exposed the ways in which the legal elite narratives from both sides of these movement-countermovement conflicts have simultaneously helped sustain and hinder state law's legitimacy and power.

These elites have helped to sustain and reproduce state law by showing it to be effective and powerful. Their stories note that when state law was brought to bear, conditions significantly changed in front of the clinics. As expected, this quality appeared in a far more positive light on the abortion-rights side of the conflict than on the anti-abortion side. In spite of this, the latter's stories still strongly affirm the effectiveness of state law's coercive power.

The amici and the majority of legislators on the anti-abortion-activist side of the conflicts also affirmed state law by drawing attention to what they saw as the power of its principled core. The value of this elite construction, however, is questionable for at least three reasons. First, it comes from the actors that are most removed from the conflicts themselves. This means that they are forwarded by the elites least likely to ever directly interact with movement actors. These elites are thus unlikely to popularly spread their principled views of law. Second, the fact that law is most principled in these conflicts when the issues involved are most academic also suggests that law fails to maintain power in the times when it is seemingly most needed. Finally, these actors and their principled constructions were greatly outnumbered by the other elites involved in these disputes. They are, in effect, outliers.

The balance of the elites on both sides of these conflicts painted a portrait of state law that showed it to be powerful, but largely unprincipled and politically saturated. Instead of behaving like the street-level activists who leveled narrowly tailored criticism that limited the harm to state law's overall legitimacy, or who saw law redeem itself for perceived past failures, the majority of elites present an anemic version of law that raises significant doubts about the system's legitimacy. As a result, their stories potentially hinder state law's durability and power.

The stories' content is not the only threat to the state's legal authority, either. The storytellers themselves pose an equal or greater problem. First, the attacks come from elites who are charged with ensuring the state's legal dominance. Second, their positions within the state's legal apparatus give them accumulated experiential knowledge that provides their accounts with a high degree of authority. Compounding this, these elites are positioned to impart their beliefs to activists who can use them to justify defying the state.[84] Finally, the legal system is ill-equipped to immediately address such internal threats to its legitimacy, allowing them to live on and spread. In spite of the preponderance of problems that elites' stories pose for state law's legitimacy, the complete collection of narratives examined here suggests how the state is still able to maintain its authority. Why this is so is the subject of the following, and final, chapter.

7

Lessons from the Street Politics of Abortion

Anti-abortion activists may have been part of the socially conservative coalition that helped elect Ronald Reagan president, but they failed to see their policy goals realized through his administration. Instead of creating a Supreme Court that would see to overturning *Roe v. Wade*, Reagan appointed Sandra Day O'Connor to the bench. This proved instrumental in keeping abortion legal. Showing early signs of adaptability, the movement remained active in the formal halls of government, but it also shifted its attention to the streets. The new front that anti-abortion activists opened would not only assist their more traditional political efforts by featuring a mobilized constituency and publicizing the movement, but it would also apply direct pressure to abortion providers and seekers.

As the stories in this book have shown, clinics and abortion-rights activists responded to the burgeoning street-level activism by developing their own direct-action strategies. They found, however, that they could be more effective when they relocated the conflicts from the street to the courtroom. Grassroots anti-abortion activists were initially knocked off-balance by the change in forum, its accompanying requirements, and the penalties they suffered. They kept their movement alive, however, by finding lawyers of their own.

Raised in the Streets: The Political Legacies of the Street Politics of Abortion

Even with the coordinated help of local and national lawyers, anti-abortion forces endured substantial losses in court. These were felt at the local level with individual activists having to pay heavy fines, and at the movement-wide level with various forms of regulation being allowed to stand and spread. This correspondingly led to grassroots activists being discouraged, demobilized, or otherwise redirected to less confrontational activities (e.g., staffing anti-abortion crisis pregnancy centers), effectively ending the anti-abortion movement's widespread direct-action strategies.

In spite of the demise of the street politics of abortion, the conflicts in court appear to have brought net political and organizational gains for the anti-abortion movement. Their legal responses helped professionalize not only their movement but also the larger New Christian Right of which they are a major part. Following the cliché, that which did not kill them made them stronger. During the course of these protest-regulation conflicts, disparate socially conservative cause lawyers and activist groups were being brought together and restructured by both the demands of these cases and the greater political plans of New Christian Right leaders.[1] The resulting organizations—the ACLJ chief among them—have not only helped mold the contemporary abortion conflict, but they have become significant players in a wide range of conservative causes.

The movement's organizational transition is captured in the personal and professional histories of many of those involved on the anti-abortion sides of *Williams*, *Schenck*, and *Hill*. James Henderson, a conservative Christian lawyer involved in *Schenck* and *Hill*, is a fitting example. Henderson attended the Jesuit St. Louis University School of Law with the help of a fellowship from the Thomas White Education Foundation—a group interested in conservative educational causes such as defending school vouchers. While in law school, Henderson made contact with Thomas "Pat" Monaghan who was associated with the Catholic League and who helped to start a conservative litigation group, Free Speech Associates. Through working with Monaghan, Henderson made contact with Jay Sekulow who headed his own conservative litigation group, the Christian Advocates Serving Evangelism (CASE). Henderson joined CASE in 1989 and soon opened the organization's Washington, D.C., office where he worked with Sekulow on cases such as *Bray v. Alexandria Women's Health Clinic*—an early anti-abortion protest regulation case.[2]

While Henderson's developing career shows the existence of a loose network of Christian cause lawyers, there was ample room for institutional improvement. As many scholars have noted, the Christian Right had repeatedly tried to create lasting political institutions during the 20th century. The resulting organizations, however, were marked by limited life spans and an overwhelming emphasis on electoral politics.[3] Furthermore, the investment—or lack thereof—in the Christian Right's legal institutions was not helped by the suspicion toward lawyers that many conservative Christians have historically harbored.[4] Given this, it is not a surprise that until the 1990s there were few conservative Christian public-interest law practices, and those that existed were neither particularly well funded nor well known.[5]

This changed dramatically when a collection of wealthy, well-known Christian conservative leaders—most prominently Pat Robertson and Jerry Falwell—decided that there was a need to make a concerted effort to develop the New Christian Right's legal resources. Their massive investment in building a Christian legal movement specifically, and improving Christian Right political institutions more generally, is clearly seen through Pat Robertson's American Center for Law and Justice.

As the organization's website states, Robertson created the ACLJ in the early 1990s because he "saw the need for a legal organization to counter the growing impact of the American Civil Liberties Union."[6] Robertson started the ACLJ largely with proven talent, hiring the CASE attorneys and other known conservative lawyers like Pat Monaghan and his colleague Walter Weber. Instead of laboring at disparate organizations that potentially competed with one another for cases, talent, and funding, these lawyers were now concentrated in one place and working together. As an additional benefit, the ACLJ was able to take over CASE's litigation of *Bray* and thus announce its arrival with an immediate trip to the U.S. Supreme Court. The ACLJ has built on this solid foundation and raised its profile by continuing to select cases that make it to the Supreme Court and by maintaining a constant media presence.[7] It has also been successful in preserving its legal talent—Sekulow, Monaghan, Weber, and Henderson are all senior attorneys at the ACLJ—which contributes to ensuring its survival and growth.

Returning to James Henderson as an example of the New Christian Right's successful legal institutional development, his involvement in the *Hill* case illustrates a way that the ACLJ and similar conservative public-interest firms multiply their legal resources. While working on *Hill*, Henderson collaborated with Roger Westlund, a regional lawyer with no direct ACLJ affiliation. Lawyers like Westlund are not ACLJ staff attorneys, but they are identified by the ACLJ through their histories defending local anti-abortion protesters or being involved in other conservative causes, cases, or organizations. When they work with the ACLJ on cases like *Hill*, these local attorneys are more formally brought into the organized conservative Christian legal movement. While they often do not end up subsequently working directly for the ACLJ as staff attorneys, their involvement in ACLJ cases allows the organization—and, by extension, the larger conservative Christian legal movement—to expand its reach and cultivate a network of conservative cause lawyers and activists across the country. The resulting relationship can then work in two directions. The ACLJ can call on these lawyers and activists when it identifies issues in their region or specialty, and these lawyers and activists can call upon the ACLJ when they find a need for the organization's superior resources.[8] It is through this network that Jeannie Hill knew to contact the ACLJ in order to challenge the Colorado Bubble Bill.

Since its creation the ACLJ has not only extended its domestic network, it has also expanded its purview, geographic reach, and substantive interests. Within two years of its creation, the ACLJ started reflecting Pat Robertson's roots and launched its first foray into producing popular media. The ACLJ now has regular satellite radio and cable television shows and an active website. Jay Sekulow regularly features in these shows, on the organization's website, and in other media forums.[9] This promotes the ACLJ and increases its political importance. In the interests of continuing to highlight the links between the organization and anti-abortion protest regulation cases, it is worth noting that Paul Schenck left his position organizing direct-action demonstrations in Western New York in order to become a director at the ACLJ and edit one of its early publications.[10]

Other major changes at the ACLJ are seen in the contrast between the group's 1999 and 2012 mission statements. In 1999 the organization described itself as the "nation's pre-eminent public interest law firm and educational organization dedicated to defending and advancing religious liberty, the sanctity of human life, and the two-parent, marriage-bound family."[11] Just over a decade later, the group has repositioned itself.

The American Center for Law and Justice (ACLJ) and its globally affiliated organizations are committed to ensuring the ongoing viability of freedom and liberty in the United States and around the world. . . . [These organizations] are dedicated to the concept that freedom and liberty are universal, God-given and inalienable rights that must be protected [and they] engage in litigation, provide legal services, render advice to individuals and governmental agencies, as well as counsel clients on global freedom and liberty issues. They also support training law students from around the world in order to protect religious liberty and safeguard human rights and dignity.[12]

The narrow concern with domestic social conservative issues has been replaced by a global view and a general interest in "freedom and liberty." The ACLJ's affiliated offices in Israel, Russia, Kenya, France, Pakistan, and Zimbabwe enable the former. The latter allows the organization to move beyond abortion, gay marriage, and other Christian conservative issues so that it can spend significant time on secular domestic conservative hot-button issues as diverse as fighting the Affordable Care Act ("ObamaCare") and defending the New York City Police Department's surveillance of Muslim groups in New Jersey.[13] This broadening of substantive political interests reflects one of the important ways that the New Christian Right is different from, and more politically potent than, earlier Christian conservative political iterations.[14]

Similarly, it should be noted that organizations like the ACLJ seem to reflect the New Christian Right's abilities to successfully bridge religious doctrinal divisions. Looking at the ACLJ's leadership history, for example, the organization's first head was Keith Fournier—a conservative Catholic—and his successor, Jay Sekulow, considers himself to be a "Messianic Jew." Both men were hired by Pat Robertson, a charismatic evangelical Protestant and ordained Baptist minister. This relative ecumenicalism at the ACLJ's head also extends to its legal staff.[15] This is important because religious differences helped to undermine the Christian Right's previous political efforts.[16]

A final change noted in the contrast between the 1999 and 2012 self-descriptions is telling in terms of the ACLJ's, and the general New Christian Right's, long-term investment in legal and political resources. Like the aforementioned Roger Westlund, James Duane—an attorney from *Schenck*—was a local lawyer representing anti-abortion activists in regional courts. He, however, left the *Schenck* case before it reached the U.S. Supreme Court in order to take a teaching position at Pat Robertson's Regent University Law School where, as of 2012, he is still a professor.

Regent University Law School, as well as Jerry Falwell's Liberty University School of Law and the Ave Maria School of Law founded by Thomas Monaghan (not the ACLJ lawyer, but rather the former head of Domino's Pizza who is known for his conservative activism), show the long-term view taken in restructuring Christian Right activism. As discussed above, the ACLJ metaphorically hit the ground running because it collected leading socially conservative lawyers, and some of their ongoing cases, in one well-funded organization. To fully realize the movement's institutional goals, however, there is a need to continue growing their professional ranks. This is one way that newly created Christian law schools benefit the New Christian Right generally, and the conservative Christian legal movement specifically.

Using Falwell's description of Liberty Law School, these Christian law schools were founded with the "belief that we needed to produce a generation of Christian attorneys who could, in fact, infiltrate the legal profession with a strong commitment to the Judeo-Christian ethic."[17] These schools in part serve to continually create such lawyers for all levels of the movement. This is further made evident by how intimately entwined the schools are with leading socially conservative law and policy organizations. Regent University Law School, for example, prominently advertises its connections to Jay Sekulow and the ACLJ on its web page. Regent's students can take classes from Sekulow and other ACLJ attorneys. They can also work directly with the organization as staff members at the ACLJ's Regent office, or as summer interns at the Washington, D.C., office.[18]

Liberty University Law School is similarly connected to Liberty Counsel—an organization that describes itself as "an international nonprofit litigation, education, and policy organization dedicated to advancing religious freedom, the sanctity of life, and the family . . . by providing pro bono assistance and representation on these and related topics."[19] Like the ACLJ, Liberty Counsel was born of the same conditions and its activities now extend across and beyond the United States through its "offices in Florida, Virginia, Texas, Washington, D.C., and Jerusalem, Israel."[20] Mathew Staver, who is both the dean of Liberty Law School and the founder of the Liberty Foundation, is evidence of the tight relationship between the two institutions. The bond is more formally institutionalized through the Liberty Center for Law and Policy (LCLP). As the subtitle on the LCLP's webpage announces, it is "a partnership of Liberty University School of Law & Liberty Counsel." The webpage goes on to state that the organization "conducts legal research and writing on current legislation and policies related to religious liberties, the sanctity of life, the family, nominations and appointments, constitutional issues, and governmental oversight in order to educate members of Congress and the public about current issues *and trains a new generation of constitutional lawyers and world leaders through internship opportunities, training seminars, and conferences.*[21] These law school partnerships allow Christian Right legal and policy organizations to mentor future movement professionals. They also enable the organizations to directly recruit the best graduates, and to know that those who have worked with them while in law school, but who do not join their staffs after graduation, will still grow the decentralized social conservative professional and legal network.

Considered as a whole, these comprehensive networks stand as testament to the New Christian Right's investment in institution building and professionalization. With roots in the street politics of abortion, these organizations have matured into "advocacy conglomerates" where "the constituent parts . . . cover various portions of the public square and benefit from each other's unique resources."[22] The Christian Right is thus well situated to undertake various types of efforts in multiple political forums. They can address constituents directly through their own media outlets, educating and mobilizing voters and grassroots activists. They can also use their legal and political expertise to lobby legislatures and influence policy, nominations, and appointments. Finally, they can use their lawyers to both defend their legislative gains and pursue minority political strategies in court when they cannot directly influence electoral politics.

While some scholars may question the Christian Right's abilities to have significant effects on policy, it should be noted that the New Christian Right is at least well positioned to remain on the political scene and to continue to push for its ends.[23] This stability should not be underappreciated. Evangelicals have a history of being disorganized and withdrawing from the public political sphere. These New Christian Right political organizations provide a means to keep conservative Christians unified and their political issues alive. As a result, they can and do affect politics and policy in tangible ways.[24]

While these institutional developments were prompted by multiple factors and unfolded over many decades, abortion politics generally, and anti-abortion protest regulation cases specifically, played a significant part in the process. The institution-building activity spurred during this period, however, appears to be one-sided. A commensurate flourishing is not seen on the abortion-rights side of the conflict for multiple reasons. First, this deficit is in part due to the existence and institutional maturity of organizations—such as NARAL Pro-Choice America, the

National Organization for Women, and the ACLU—that have worked to defend reproductive rights in various governmental forums. Furthermore, while abortion rights are a notable part of the general liberal platform, the issue does not garner the same sustained, high-level attention that banning abortion does within the socially conservative coalition. Finally, these cases did not spur institutional growth because the existing strategy of using courts and legislatures was overwhelmingly successful in these conflicts. Abortion and related reproductive-rights groups had no obvious reasons to restructure or expand their efforts whereas anti-abortion activists, and social conservatives more generally, did.

While the abortion-rights movement may have had an institutional advantage and is still well served by its more mature organizations, questions arise around issues of momentum, potential for innovation, and the long-term prospects for abortion-rights advocates. Anti-abortion campaigners have been very active in developing and implementing novel strategies—from incremental strategies like instating mandatory waiting periods, ultrasounds, and Targeted Regulation of Abortion Providers (TRAP) laws, to more sweeping ones like attempting to redefine the legal definition of personhood to include fetuses. These steps can increase the costs of abortion for seekers and providers alike, and some come close to effectively reversing *Roe v. Wade*.

Beyond these more immediate strategies, the New Christian Right institution-building efforts reveal that, like a good chess player, they are thinking multiple moves ahead. The Christian conservative law schools and political/legal organizations not only provide new strategies and the lawyers to defend them, but they strive to produce the future politicians and judges that will control state policies. It remains to be seen how these new institutions will affect the form of the ongoing movement-countermovement politics of abortion. It is also an open question as to how abortion-rights organizations will respond to these changes in order to stay relevant, and if they can somehow mount an offensive of their own. Abortion-rights advocates have thus far been restricted to rebuffing their opponents' innovations, and their prospects of taking the offensive seem limited. Given all of this, the ultimate overarching question is whether or not either side will be able to do more than just prolong the existing conflict. If history is any predictor, the odds lean against such a thing happening.

Learning from Secondary Movement Litigation

Another highlight from the cases studied here is that they reveal a little-studied type of litigation.[25] Social or political movement court cases are typically conceived of as attempts to use courts to directly achieve primary policy goals. The cases seen here, however, address more immediate concerns that grow out of a movement-countermovement dynamic. As a result, they hinge on substantively unrelated or "secondary" legal matters that raise new risks and benefits for movements.

The relocation of activism, or even more common disputes, into court requires a process of translation. These conflicts must become legal disputes that meet the standards of justiciability. This requires the parties to demonstrate that they have been harmed in ways that the law recognizes and can address. Would-be litigants must translate their claims into ones that can be attached to a specific bad actor, show how they are directly harmed by that bad actor, and also show that this harm can be classified under a specific law or set of laws.

The nature of the claims made and goals sought by social movements can make this conversion process difficult. The reductionism required by courts can also hide the passion behind a given conflict and render the legal disputes unrecognizable to activists. Finally, the professional knowledge that is required to complete the translation and follow it through demands hiring lawyers who are often movement outsiders. The cumulative effect of these changes is that activists can feel alienated by the process and that movements risk losing control of their causes.[26]

The cases seen here provide an extreme version of this translation process. When the clinics decided to try to regulate anti-abortion direct-action strategies, and these activists decided to resist, actors on both sides of these conflicts were suddenly transformed into First Amendment disputants. The wholly foreign nature of the primary legal subject in *Williams*, *Schenck*, and *Hill*—that is, the vast gap between abortion and free speech—would seem to significantly increase the associated risks of entering court for both movements.

First, because these cases dealt with a sacred cow in the First Amendment, as well as the perennially controversial abortion conflict, there was no way that the cases could escape notice and scrutiny. Groups like the ACLU and labor unions that are invested in free speech issues were sure to take note, and there was a possibility that the confluence of issues would also attract the press's attention. As a result, the original disputants had to tread carefully and place significant amounts of faith in their lawyers. This made the respective movements all the more vulnerable to losing control over their cases.

Second, the newly introduced First Amendment issue invited not only the scrutiny but also the direct involvement of groups that are invested in speech rights but that may *not* be interested in abortion politics. What's more, because liberal abortion-rights advocates were championing restrictive-speech rights, and conservative anti-abortion activists were advocating broad-speech protections, the possibilities for both internal tension and uncomfortable political partnerships would seem to elevate the risk of activist alienation.

Alternatively, one can also argue that the distance between the movements and the law at issue actually insulates the movements from traditional problems associated with litigation. For example, since these groups are not seeking to obtain their major policy goals through secondary movement cases, the activists cannot be seduced by the "myth of rights."[27] Victories won in court cannot be taken for meaningful change if the cases have no direct relationship to the policy changes sought. The distance inherent in secondary movement litigation situations may also allow grassroots activists to better see the distinction between what the lawyers are striving to achieve and what their own roles are in the movement. As a result, they can avoid the problems of alienation and movement takeover related to litigation. Similarly, because these cases are secondary, one would expect the movements to not be fully invested in them. As a result, the movements may be better able to end these cases if they seem to be too great of a drain on financial or emotional resources.

The interviews show few signs of participants on either side equating these legal victories with major substantive policy advances. Rep. DeGette did conceive of the Bubble Bill as "pro-choice legislation," and the cases clearly had a recognized effect on the course of abortion politics, but no one confused the suits with a profound shift in the core conflict over abortion's legality.

In terms of the general concern with activist alienation, a first sign of the problem is seen in the interviews when activists on both sides of these conflicts flatly stated that they were disengaged from the litigation process. The cases were legal affairs handled by distant lawyers in distant courts. What's more, the interviews show that the courts frustrated some anti-abortion activists by declaring their arguments for activism legally irrelevant. This was most directly stated by one of the rescuers:

[W]e wanted to use as our defense that we were trying to save a life. And with the legal system being what it is, the Judge would not allow that defense. Now I understand that he had the power to stop it, but I thought it was wrong. In my own heart I thought it was wrong. It's like, because, essentially, I felt the jury was getting an unclear, they were not getting a clear view of everything that was going on there. They only saw us as a bunch of crazy activists that were trespassing on private property. They didn't understand our passion. They didn't understand our conviction. And I actually chose at one point to defend myself . . . and every time I would say something the Judge would have it stricken from the record . . . I think this goes beyond free speech, what we were doing, I think it went beyond free speech. . . . The courts that we were in would not allow us to use as our defense that we were intervening to save a life. That's what we wanted . . . that goes beyond free speech. That goes to practical, behavior that is justified under American law. I mean it's totally justified. . . . It was common sense. I am trying to save a life. I am intervening. . . . Wasn't that sad? We had to fall back on something [the First Amendment] that does not adequately cover our behavior.[28]

As the quote shows, the rescuer struggled to resolve how his activism fit within the First Amendment constraints that the legal case and system required, and he was ultimately deeply disappointed by the process: "Wasn't that sad? We had to fall back on something [the First Amendment] that does not adequately cover our behavior." This is a clear example of how the litigation process not only can render a dispute unrecognizable but also can be taken as a personal affront.

While aspects of alienation like this are found in the interviews, their presence did not produce the pernicious effects that are oft warned of. In fact, the distance between the anti-abortion activists and the case helped to stave off any discomfort associated with the odd political alliances created by the introduction of the free speech issue. For example, many of the anti-abortion activists interviewed were unaware that ACLU affiliates filed briefs that effectively supported the protesters' legal arguments. This is potentially a good thing for the anti-abortion movement since the Christian Right regularly demonizes the ACLU. As others have noted, the Christian Right has been hampered in the past when the realities of politics (e.g., the need to compromise, to make expedient alliances, etc.) have conflicted with the desire to maintain ideological or religious purity.[29] In this case, what was not known obviously could not cause problems for these activists.[30]

In spite of these factors helping to ward off some of the problems of activist alienation, one can point to the noticeable demobilization of street-level actors on both sides as an argument that the foreign nature of the legal battles undermined the respective grassroots movements. This, however, is out of place. Anti-abortion activists were demobilized not because they felt that the cases and the inclusion of lawyers displaced them. Rather, former anti-abortion activists made reference to being pushed away from direct action because of the increased personal financial and legal risks associated with it; because they had been worn out by the adversarial nature or other aspects of street-level activism; and because of the assassination of abortion providers like Dr. David Gunn and Dr. Barnett Slepian. For example, even the above-quoted rescuer who was so disappointed by the constraints of the legal process cited the increasing fines and penalties levied against activists as the reason that he left the movement. These issues would have been problems for the movement even if they chose not to bring in lawyers to fight the regulations in court.

Furthermore, as the close readings of street-level anti-abortion activists' stories revealed, they were *not* put off by being thrust into the role of defending expansive readings of speech rights. They may have been conservative, and they may not have necessarily seen themselves as First Amendment activists, but they were able to use the injected speech elements to their advantage. It became another means by which to attack their adversaries rather than an internal conflict that alienated them from their cause.

On the other side of the conflict, many of the activists interviewed were either still employed at or running clinics, or were still active in reproductive rights groups. One cannot say, though, that those who were no longer involved in activism were forced out by litigation's negative repercussions. If the cases pushed them out of activism it was only because litigation eliminated the problems that spurred their activism in the first place. Their reasons to be active diminished in unison with the decreased rate and intensity of sidewalk counseling and rescues. This, again, has nothing to do with the litigation process itself. As for being alienated by the introduction of speech rights into the abortion conflict, or being required to defend speech-restrictive arguments, the close readings of their stories reveals problems that these activists had using the law. These issues, however, had to do with limiting the group's use of law's cultural or symbolic aspects, rather than undermining their grassroots participation. Given this, it is hard to say that either set of activists fell victim to the traditional problems that scholars ascribe to movement litigation.

These interviews offer a less clear answer to the question of a movement's ability to relatively easily end secondary movement cases if they become too costly. It is obvious that *Williams*, *Schenck*, and *Hill*—as well as many other secondary movement cases from the abortion conflict— were *not* cut off early. Instead, these cases persisted through the appeals process even when they were quite costly for both sides. This shows that the movements were deeply invested in these cases. The comments of participants on both sides suggest that while the cases are secondary in terms of the movements' ultimate policy goals, they were personally important for many of the disputants and highly significant within the context of the ongoing movement-countermovement conflict.

Clinic members and their supporters repeatedly stated that they saw these cases as a means to stopping the violence that they, and those seeking to access the clinics, regularly experienced. Such concerns are much closer to the daily lives of these people than the more abstract and likely unobtainable notion of having confident control of abortion policy. Furthermore, the nonclinic staff members of the PCN were mobilized by the desire to combat anti-abortion direct activism. While they may have been pro-choice before, many members, like Addie Levine and Lucinda Finley, only became truly active when anti-abortion activists began appearing in front of clinics. Considering this, the cases were extensions of the work that they had begun, were correspondingly meaningful, and were therefore unlikely to be easily surrendered.

Similarly, anti-abortion activists recognized that their continued direct-action involvement in abortion politics rode on these cases. Yes, other ways to be involved in the movement could and would arise. And yes, the efforts to reverse *Roe* could and would carry on through other means. However, clinic-front activism was the known way to do both and, more importantly, it was presented to these activists as their religious and moral duty. As a result, they had good reasons to be invested in and to continue appealing these cases.

Finally, the separation between what is a secondary and a primary movement interest blurs when one is embroiled in a heated struggle. Fighting over clinic-front activism was the form that the abortion conflict took at the time, and thus was the fight that each side had to be invested in no matter how imperfect its specifics were. As a prominent anti-abortion leader from Western New York stated:

If they [the PCN] were going to push the pendulum all the way over in one direction, we were going to have to push with equal force and magnitude in the opposite direction. . . . And so, in kind, we tended to respond by, by saying, "OK, if that's the way you want it, we'll battle for, for the whole enchilada which you are battling to take away."

In such an environment that breeds extremism—where "the pendulum" has to be pushed all the way—backing out of the cases would be tantamount to showing weakness and handing one's opponents a victory. Even though it might make strategic sense to cut one's losses and move on, recognizing this would require a degree of distance that is hard to muster in a passionate and prolonged political fight.

Considering this, the risk of a movement harming itself through overinvesting in secondary movement litigation should be recognized, even when the conflict involves two national movements. It is easy to think of the anti-abortion and abortion-rights movements as being well-funded, national organizations. This, however, overlooks the fact that the movements are largely collections of multiple local and regional organizations. While these smaller entities may have access to national organizations and resources, they and their local networks are not immune to financial limitations.

Individual street-level anti-abortion activists have to violate these injunctions and laws in order to both challenge them and fully realize their conception of the law. This means that they and/or their supporters have to pay the resulting court-levied fines—a cost that can become quite substantial.[31] Furthermore, while local lawyers may volunteer services to activists, their services are not "free." Rather, the cost of litigation is borne by the volunteering lawyers. These attorneys still need to attend to their "day jobs." If the costs of volunteering become too great the lawyers have to choose between continuing with the movement and enduring the ensuing financial, personal, and/or professional harm; finding a means for handing the case off; or, failing that, disappointing the other movement actors by calling an end to litigation. Finally, for-profit clinics that don't qualify for pro bono legal work have to hire attorneys, potentially stretching or breaking their limited budgets. All of these scenarios were actual concerns faced by individuals and organizations in these three cases, and all of them threatened the movements in their own ways. Considering these concerns, the risks of overinvesting in secondary movement litigation are quite real for both individuals and movements.

This discussion of secondary movement litigation springing from the movement-countermovement context is, obviously, just a beginning. It remains to be seen how often such secondary movement litigation occurs in movement-countermovement conflicts and other contexts.[32] With more cases we will also be better able to tell how this type of legal action compares with more typical movement litigation and whether it is on balance a fruitful or detrimental strategy for movements to pursue. On their own, though, these three examples raise the above questions and illustrate how movement-countermovement conflicts foster tactical innovation; how secondary movement litigation can create new problems and benefits within a movement; and how both helped to direct the course of not just this specific conflict, but the institutional development of the larger New Christian Right.

Law in and from Street-Level Narratives

While the above succinctly states the findings derived from using stories as a scholarly means and product, the focus now shifts to examining what these narratives reveal when they become the subjects of inquiry.[33] In her critical review of legal consciousness research, Susan Silbey notes that the area "developed . . . to address issues of legal hegemony, particularly how the law sustains its institutional power despite a persistent gap between the law on the books and the law in action."[34] Silbey goes on to argue that this area of research has generally strayed from its purpose, and she therefore urges scholars to "recapture the critical sociological project of explaining the durability and ideological power of law."[35] This book has attempted to contribute to this sociological project by offering a detailed analysis of "meaning work" and the construction of legality in abortion-conflict participant stories.[36] In doing so, the book has exposed the ways in which the narratives from both sides of these disputes have ultimately sustained and reproduced state law's legitimacy and power in spite of criticism from street-level activists and elites alike.

When the state spoke in *Williams*, *Schenck*, and *Hill*, it told the parties and the general public that the clinics understood and used the law correctly, and that the anti-abortion activists had fatally flawed conceptions of speech rights. If the anti-abortion activists continued to live by the understandings of law that they used in court to justify and defend their actions, they would become subject to the state's coercive force. Given this, one would expect the clinics and their supporting abortion-rights activists to have unencumbered access to the law in their narratives, and that they would correspondingly wholly affirm state law in their stories. The anti-abortion activists, on the other hand, could be expected to have limited, if any, affirmative use of state law in their stories. Considering both their losses in court and their dependence on God's law, one could also reasonably expect these activists' stories to be outright defiant toward state law. A close reading of the respective sides' accounts, however, has shown that the use of law was more complicated than this.

Starting with the clinics and their supporters' stories, state law was at its strongest when they described how their expectations rose regarding the possibilities of using state power as a coercive force, and how they were pleased with the ultimate effects of their legal strategy. Like Nielsen's interviewees who encountered street harassment, the clinics' past negative experiences with the "law shape[d] what remedies respondents believe are possible and plausible."[37] In the *Schenck* case, for example, it took a relative outsider to move the clinics to seek legal help. Before Lucinda Finley told the PCN about the possibilities for a federal injunction, the organization had written off the judicial system as being beholden to the "Right to Life [electoral] ticket."[38] Once these groups experienced some success in federal court, however, the law transformed from something inaccessible and useless—even negative—into an effective tool. It is this latter image of the law that dominates the abortion-rights activists' stories. This turn shows that state law sustained or, more appropriately, regained its institutional power in these stories because the state delivered on the promise of being effective. In Silbey's words, it bridged the "persistent gap between the law on the books and the law in action."[39] Recognizing that the state can potentially be of assistance and then mobilizing to seek its help are two steps in affirmatively constructing and feeding state law and power. Praising the state's effectiveness in a victorious postlitigation narrative is the next move in this progression.

These activist narratives also reaffirm Nielsen's point that "past experiences with law and legal actors affect a person's legal consciousness."[40] In fact, they go further than this by suggesting that because legal consciousness is experientially rooted, new experiences can change one's consciousness. This idea is implied by Nielsen's statement, but the turn in views in these stories makes it explicit. The degree to which legal consciousness can change, the permanence of such changes, and the specific conditions related to both, however, remain to be seen. These stories have begun to contribute to answering these questions, particularly in terms of how the dimensions of time and proximity to conflict pertain to shifts in legal consciousness, but these questions are still ripe topics for future research.[41]

The question of how much one's legal consciousness can change, and how permanent these changes are, is also raised by the abortion-rights activists' difficulties in using law to succinctly convey the harms endured at clinics. The First Amendment rights that constitute the cases' core clearly interfered with their abilities to effectively employ law's normative force in their stories. Their speech-restrictive position in these cases simply denied them access to familiar and uncomplicated First Amendment–related rights claims. As a result, the storytellers' legal language was unfocused, diluting its power.[42] These problems reveal the simultaneous pliability and stickiness of conceptions of law, which in turn informs both our understanding of state law's enduring strength and the limits of movements to fully use law as an instrument.

Starting with the latter, Nielsen's interviews show that one's legal consciousness can block mobilization. She specifically finds that fidelity to a certain conception of the freedom of speech—the kind that these liberal activists attest to hold—is one of four paradigms that impeded mobilization in her group of actors.[43] This demonstrates how conceptions of law can be significant and sticky for some groups of actors or under certain conditions. In spite of the abortion-rights activists' attesting to hold a similar liberal conception of speech rights, and the activists' initial misgivings about law's effectiveness (another of Nielsen's four paradigms), the clinics *were* able to act.[44] They did effectively mobilize state law. This, however, does not mean that these actors have completely abandoned their liberal conception of speech rights.

It is true that the abortion-rights activists' typical understanding of the First Amendment appears to have had limited behavioral effects during the conflict. Fidelity to the liberal conception of the First Amendment, however, resurfaced as a constraint in the abortion-rights activists' subsequent narratives. The expected conflict between a permissive reading of speech rights and the speech-restrictive actions taken in these cases manifested both in the activists' difficulties in finding suitably expressive legal language and in their creating nuanced stories about the compromises they made between competing rights claims. Both issues work against the activists' ability to invoke rights talk in order to crystallize the conflict and convey its importance in a simple, resonant way. As a result, both show the limits of being able to fully control and use law to one's advantage. The paradox of winning in court but failing to gain lasting access to law's normative power is not an issue that is broadly discussed in sociolegal literature.[45] It is also unclear as to whether it is unique to this situation, or if it is a more pervasive issue with social movements and the law. As a result, this opens up another interesting avenue for further research into the costs and benefits of social movement litigation.

The ebb and flow of the liberal conception of speech rights also speaks to the legal consciousness discussion about state law's durability. The heat of conflict explains these activists' abilities to mobilize law in spite of their various misgivings. As one PCN member stated, "We were being activists. . . . You tend to think that all right is on your side when you are being an activist." The clarity provided by the immediacy of the fight, however, appears to fade for some over time. To use Ewick and Silbey's language, when embroiled in the fight with anti-abortion activists, the clinics and their supporters adopted a "with the law" conception that allowed them to use law as a tool. When the conflict was settled and time passed, the reverence of the "before the law" conception returned and complicated matters.[46]

New experiences, contexts, and needs can lead to different conceptions of law, but these understandings can also be temporary and expedient. This adds depth to legal consciousness. It implies that some aspects might be malleable, while other parts appear to be resilient. As Ewick and Silbey argue, this multidimensionality provides a way for law to be durable.[47] Law can be flexible and allow for action in the immediate term, but it can also resist change in the long term, providing a sense of coherence and consistency over time. The narratives examined here show that temporal and experiential proximity to conflicts matter in these shifts, but other factors are sure to be of importance. Given this, more research needs to be done to better understand when conceptions shift, when they do not, when the shifts last, when they fade, and why.

Switching to the other side of the conflicts and the reverse of the above-mentioned paradox, sociolegal scholarship has shown that people do not necessarily lose the ability to use law in various beneficial ways when they lose in the courtroom.[48] It was therefore not wholly surprising that the anti-abortion protesters retained the ability to effectively use law in their narratives even after the state ruled against them. What is surprising is that these activists did so much to positively construct and affirm state law in their narratives given their losses and the availability of a developed alternative conception of law.

All of the anti-abortion activists simultaneously held two interrelated conceptions of law. Specifically, their stories present both state law and extrastate law in the form of God's law. In this two-part construction of law, the two forms were intimately entwined but hierarchically arranged. God's law legitimated, and thus trumped, state law. The activists, and indeed many in the public, may see this two-part conception of law as one wholly integrated system. The secular nature of the U.S. government, however, reveals that they are actually two separate systems of law. To quote *A Man for All Seasons*, "This country is planted thick with laws, from coast to coast, *Man's laws, not God's*."[49] Countries such as the United States do not base their law on one conception of a divine power, and therefore these activists are rightly seen as engaging in a form of jurisgenesis.[50] That is, they are creating a conception of law that competes with state law.

The two generally discrete groups within the collection of anti-abortion activists—picketers and rescuers—emphasized one or the other conception of law. Rescuers more commonly invoked the religious, extrastate version of law in their stories, while the picketers concentrated on the state-law conception. In both groups' accounts, law functioned as a normative resource that illustrated why they were in the right, and the clinics and the courts were in the wrong. Neither group, however, condemned or even significantly challenged state law. Individuals within the state legal system were attacked, but the anti-abortion activists' stories ultimately reinforced the state's conception of law and the legitimacy of its authority.

The rescuers' stories are examples of how extrastate law can be constructed and acted upon but still allow for actors to sustain the state's institutional power and legitimacy. The rescuers do this by cordoning off the core free-speech regulation issue involved in these disputes and dealing with it independently from the larger question of abortion's legality—something that they see as clearly governed by God's law and in conflict with state law. They recognize and respect the speech issue's foreign nature in relation to their activism and can thus keep it separate from the domain of God's law. Safe from tension, the two systems of law can coexist, allowing these conservatives who value regulating aggressive demonstration to affirm the state's legitimate legal authority to do so even while they are subject to it.

Alternately, anti-abortion picketers who shared the religious conception of extrastate law, but who did not follow it to the point of intentionally breaking state law, actually amend, and therefore resist, state law in their stories. Their resistance, however, is carefully limited. Picketers present the adverse judicial rulings as aberrations—the products of ethically dubious abortion-rights advocates and a few rogue judges. This framing delegitimizes the rulings in the specific cases, but reaffirms that the state is still a legitimate source of legal authority. In short, the system is still good, but it was illegitimately manipulated by a few bad actors in these cases.

The efforts to amend but preserve state law illustrate its personal and political importance to these activists, and thus reveal an aspect of state law's durability. By emphasizing how they strove to keep—and in their view, succeeded in keeping—their activism within the First Amendment's specified boundaries, the picketers are able to maintain the personal belief that they were both "good Christians" and "good law-abiding citizens." They are also able to vilify the clinics, abortion rights activists, and judges who found against them. In doing both, the anti-abortion activists appeal to the general perception of state law's legitimacy and thus reproduce it. The work done in these narratives is an example of a circular, self-reinforcing way that law maintains its power. People assume that law is powerful and legitimate, and so they act accordingly, which in turn contributes to creating the reality of state law's legitimacy and power. These stories are also examples of how law is simultaneously flexible and fixed. The diversity of people that make up the state-law system allow for its failures to be attached to individual deviant actors and not the system itself. In doing so, the failures become unfortunate isolated peculiarities and the system as a whole is kept pure.

Finally, the supportive construction of state power seen here assists the movement's transition to its current elite-institution-based form. In preserving the legitimacy of state law, these activists allow themselves and their representatives to continue to work with the state. By contrast, it would seem far more difficult for the movement to adopt its current form if its grassroots members wholly condemned the state as corrupt.[51] Such a view would call instead for collective defiance, dropping out, or possibly revolution.

Law in and from Elite Narratives

While street-level activists' on both sides of these conflicts ultimately affirmed state law's authority in their stories, it is harder to say the same for all of the elites that sided with them. At first glance, the stories told by the elites most closely associated with the respective activists appear to mirror those of the activists. For example, cause lawyers on each side situate these cases within a larger movement context and demonize the rival camp in language similar to that used by the activists they represent. Looking more closely, elites that sided with the clinics discussed law's value as a coercive force and as binding principle, just as the street-level activists did. To this end, they affirmed state law's legitimacy. The lawyers representing the anti-abortion activists similarly recognized the place of God's law in relation to state law, treated the rescuers' and the picketers' behavior differently, and attributed the case outcomes to "activist judges" and deceitful clinics. While substantial, the connections between the elites' and street-level activists' stories largely end here.

A minority of elites that maintained more distance from the two movements exchanged the passionate language of the activists for staid professional wording to describe events and opponents. These actors were not deeply invested advocates on either side of the abortion conflict, and some clearly saw themselves as defenders of the First Amendment.[52] While these amici authors and legislators were largely sympathetic to the clinics—acknowledging that harm either was occurring or that it could occur—they thought that the regulations sought were excessive. These elites see the law and their actions in these cases as being guided by principles, not politics. As one amicus author stated, "These are neutral principles that should apply no matter what the political climate, or the issues, or the people who are advocating issues." State law's power is thus directly bolstered in these few stories by an absolute principle-over-politics, "before the law" construction.[53] The direct clarity of this endorsement, however, was an aberration.

The overwhelming majority of elites constructed images of law that were unprincipled and infused with politics and showmanship. The elites' stories illustrated how they moved freely within this system and how their professional roles and responsibilities deflected the complications that the street-level actors faced. In the telling, their stories worked to endorse and perpetuate a political and unprincipled version of law that on its own erodes state law's legitimating promise of neutrality.[54]

The construction of law as an unmoored political tool poses a particular problem for the state when one considers who is forwarding this image. First, the elites' professional experiences within the state legal system and, in the case of the lawyers, their specialized education provide their accounts with a high degree of presumptive authority. Outsiders may have ideas about the law, but these elites have insider knowledge of the *real* law.

Adding to this, the elites' roles in these conflicts—especially the lawyers—position them to impart their beliefs to activists. Thinking about a lawyer's role in comparison to a teacher's helps to clarify their ability to spread their beliefs. Lawyers are authorities that are expected not only to advise but also to instruct their clients on legal realities. The fact that they are hired to do so only strengthens the incentive for clients to listen to and internalize what their lawyers say. Returning to the threat that these elites' legal-realist views pose to state law, their activist clients can adopt these views and use them to justify overtly defying the state. Other than the threat of coercive force, why should spurned activists obey judicial rulings that come from such an unprincipled, game-like system? While scholars typically discuss how lawyers are positioned to pacify their activist clients, it should also be noted that they can also provide fuel to radicalize them.[55]

The state's potential problems with these elite stories are further complicated by the fact that lawyers are not only expected to advise and instruct their clients, but, along with legislative members, they are charged with ensuring the state's legal dominance. This does not mean that there cannot be differences in opinion, that legal realism must be ignored, or that such elites must show and instill slavish obedience to the state. Instead, the point is noted in order to acknowledge that these elites play a formal role in the state legal system, and that this system is ill-equipped to immediately address such internal threats to its legitimacy.

When lawyers, amici, and legislators abdicate responsibility by citing their institutional roles, or when they present law as a game-like system, they are portraying an anemic parallel version of state law. The legal rules are the same, and it is presented as the actual state-law system, but its justifications are thin (if at all existent) and overtly political. This version of law corrodes state law's legitimacy by denying that state law has a principled core. Typically when state law faces an externally threatening alternate construction it uses judicial decisions backed by coercive force to announce the official version of the law and either incorporate or eliminate the competition.[56] The threatening construction of law presented by the majority of elites here, however, occupies a middle space that allows it to escape or delay facing the state's jurispathic force. It is a lived version of the law—not just one that Cover would dismiss as mere "literature"—and it is thus significant.[57] However, this construction of law is not a directly competing version of law that can be immediately addressed by the state. Rather, the state must wait until someone has used this conception of the law in an act of direct defiance. This distance and delay allows the parallel threatening construction of law to live on, spread, and corrode the principled justification for state law's authority.

Interestingly, the comparisons between participant narratives suggest that this anemic understanding of law has not significantly passed from elites to the street-level activists on either side of the conflict. The activists may use the law as an instrument, and they may identify with some of the political and game-like aspects of law, but their accounts show signs of internal struggle. They have trouble accessing legal language. They work to convince themselves and others that they have not violated their personal, principled understanding of law. They attack those who are seen as letting politics enter into the legal realm.[58] These are all examples of containing the elites' realist cynicism and the continued existence of a principled understanding of law.

The street-level activists' stories suggest a combination of factors to explain these differences. First, the street-level activists have personal and political reasons to foster a purer version of state law. On the abortion-rights side of the conflict, the activists gain validation and normative justification from fostering the image of a neutral and principled legal system. If the system functions as it should, the clinics' legal actions are affirmed as being more than just politically motivated. The story becomes one where neutral courts agreed with how abortion-rights activists viewed the world (i.e., how they defined violence, harassment, permissible speech), and not one where political allies in the judiciary threw the state's coercive weight behind a cause that they were sympathetic to. More broadly, when state law remains principled the clinics are seen as rightfully asserting and defending the belief that we all deserve to be treated with respect and to be free from harassment in our daily lives. This elevates their cause, transforming it from being about their specific needs to being about our common needs as a people.

The anti-abortion protesters are likewise invested in presenting a pure version of state law. If the legal system were accepted as just another political institution, their loss would not be particularly remarkable. It would be like any loss in the legislature or electoral politics—upsetting to them and their supporters, but not a failing that should necessarily be of concern to the wider public. However, if the legal system is a principled system, one that is politically neutral and charged with defending our fundamental rights, their loss can be cast as a problem for us all. The presence of a principled legal system elevates the anti-abortion activists' First Amendment claims above simple self-interested political maneuvers. They are seen as defending a right that we all benefit from. Wholly adopting this view, the fact that the courts disagreed with them was not a sign that the activists were wrong in their assessment of the world and the application of law. Rather, it is a sign that the courts were hijacked by politics, and that this is a failing that should alarm us all.

Beyond this, the anti-abortion activists were also personally invested in sustaining a principled conception of state law. Their stories show that their Christian identities are intertwined with state law. Anti abortion activists regularly conflated the legality of their actions with their Christian identities. As one New York activist stated, "How far I went with how I expressed my freedom of speech, you know, what I believe biblically really determined a lot of that." Using the same reasoning, picketers also often argued that they could not have broken the law and harassed or otherwise harmed people at clinics because as Christians they were not able to act in that manner.

These statements begin to show a connection between state law and Christian values that is both explicit, in terms of law, and generalized in terms of the legitimating core for the entire state:

Judges should use the word of God, first and foremost, as their standard. We're a long way from that and therefore have a problem. Based on our Constitution, and the Framers of our Constitution, these men were not only excellent statesmen, but they were godly men. They didn't have trouble defining what was decent and indecent. It was right and wrong. They wrote the laws that way, and they wrote them based on the Ten Commandments. They would have no problem defining it. We have a problem today because we've thrown out the standard. But yes, you can define decency, you can define truth, you can define absolute truth absolutely.[59]

Well, for me [the line separating acceptable and unacceptable speech,] that's pretty simple. I would base it on Biblical principles and what the Bible talks about as far as what is right and what is wrong. I think that's what it boils down to because you have to have a base that laws and principles are structured to because otherwise anyone can define what is right and what is wrong according to what they consider personally. But if you don't have a bottom line that everyone agrees to, then basically you have what you have today where judges are making laws.[60]

Good Christians follow the law because the law is just, and the law is just because it is rooted in God's teachings—or at least the belief is that law was and should and can still be. These anti-abortion protesters, like the broader New Christian Right, are invested in constructing a principled conception of law because the purity of law and the state essentially motivate their activism. The New Christian Right can be understood in the unifying terms of defending or restoring their conception of God's central place in the public sphere and the political realm. For example, according to Stein, Christian Conservatives "wish to restore rules, order, and authority. . . . They wish to construct a conception of the world that is secure, unambiguous, where there are good people and bad people, and where they themselves are clearly on the side of the good and true."[61]

We may "have a problem today because we've thrown out the standard" that legitimates law and the state, but it is seen by Christian Conservatives as just that—a problem. It is the New Christian Right's mission to correct the problem and restore the system to its proper place. The anemic view of law and politics is thus firmly rejected, and the principled view is held up as a cause of its own. Given this conviction, it is not surprising that these activists do not embrace or strongly echo the elite's more political view of law. To do so would be to contradict what they see as law's very nature.

While it could not be tested in a more concrete way, street-level activists' statements also suggest that they did not wholly adopt the elites' views because there was limited interaction between the majority of activists and the various elites. Activist leaders in all of these conflicts did meet with their respective lawyers, but with a few exceptions, it did not appear that the bulk of the activists spent much time with any of the elites.[62] In fact, even the movement leaders seemed to have limited interactions with the lawyers and essentially no interaction with supportive legislators and amici. For example, when asked how involved she felt in the *Hill* case, one Colorado anti-abortion activist responded by saying, "Pretty uninvolved. I had to go down to the Attorney General's office and give a deposition. It took about three or four hours. . . . We got questioned and whatever— why we were doing it and that sort of thing. Other than that, I really was not that involved at all." A New York anti-abortion activist echoed this sentiment, saying, "I never got involved in the *Schenck* case that went forward. I mean, my name was on it for a long time, but I really got kind of bored with it." The lack of interest and involvement was not limited to the anti-abortion activists either. As one New York abortion provider flatly stated,

I will be very honest with you, there are things, I consider myself a pretty bright person, and there are things that piqued my interest and I will really need to understand the facts, I'll probably delve into them. Then there is a whole category of things that I just sort of put on the shelf and go, "I really don't need to know that much about it. I am going to let someone else take care of it." . . . A lot of legal matters that I haven't needed to be intimately involved with have also just kind of been in the category of things that don't really interest me. As long as we can just function day-to-day . . . then I am OK. And that is sort of how I felt about the issue.

Instead of being their fight in their world, the various disputes had become legal fights in a foreign world being waged by distant surrogates. While many studies of social movements and the law warn that this sort of separation between elites and the rank-and-file in a movement can cause problems, limiting the transfer of the anemic view of state law is one possible benefit of this separation for state law.[63]

This returns us to "the critical sociological project of explaining the durability and ideological power of law."[64] While the state-law system cannot directly combat the anemic version of law that its elites present, the activists' stories show that state law is still able to maintain its power by other, nonstate means. Some powerful actors may construct weakened or problematic versions of state law, but many other actors are invested in preserving state law's purer image. The latter, as represented by the street-level activists, are aware of law's failings, and even at times express severe disenchantment with the law. One Colorado anti-abortion activist went so far as to say that the case "decreased my faith, my faith in the system. That's kind of general. But if they can make a law like this then I can see how China came to be what it was. You just lose your rights a little bit at a time." In spite of this disillusionment, the unsullied conception of law maintained its value, even for her. Consciously or not, she, like the rest of the street-level activists, primarily constructed principled images of law. In doing so, the activists collectively worked to sustain such a conception of law.

Furthermore, the earlier discussions of the inverse relationship between the strength of legal principle's presence in these narratives, and the storyteller's proximity to actual conflict, reaffirm what was found in the clinics' and abortion-rights activists' narratives. While principle may be sacrificed or ignored in the heat of conflict, it tends to return when some distance is gained. The same is true for those who are only marginally involved in the disputes. If one maintains a degree of distance from the heat of the conflict, law is more easily seen as principled. This point can be generalized and thus inform our understanding of state law's stability. Given that most people are not constantly embroiled in conflicts like those seen in these cases, the purer conception of state law is largely left undisturbed. This provides a sense of coherence and consistency over time that contributes to state law retaining its power.

In Ewick and Silbey's excellent book, *The Common Place of Law*, the authors identify and label three legal typologies and argue that while these different forms of legal consciousness first appear to be in conflict with one another, they actually work together to "sustain legality as hegemonic. The multiple images of legality . . . mediate the mundane, incomplete world of concrete particularities . . . with the demands for legitimacy and consent required of all social institutions, including the law."[65] While the collective participant narratives from the *Williams*, *Schenck*, and *Hill* cases lead to similar conclusions, they add new details in terms of how, when, and why the different dimensions of law surface in particular political conflicts. What's more, the inclusion of elites' stories in the analysis—something that Ewick and Silbey consciously avoid doing—raises new questions about how the differing conceptions of law work together to sustain hegemony.

Ewick and Silbey's typologies of being "before the law" and "with the law" are of particular interest in terms of these conflict participants' stories. The "before the law" typology "envisions legality animated by an aspiration for disinterested decision making and impersonal treatment. This normative dimension justifies legality."[66] Being "with the law" offers, "by contrast . . . a view of law as a ground for strategic engagements orchestrated to win in competitive struggles . . . a pragmatic, perhaps vulgar, account of the routine practices of biased, differentially endowed, and fallible actors."[67] Ewick and Silbey go on to note how these typologies are linked in that each requires the other in order for law's power to endure. The everyday failings and injustices of law would soon overwhelm and break the idealist purity of the "before the law" conception if it were our only understanding of law. Left on its own, the unprincipled and self-interested bent of being "with the law" fails to provide a compelling reason to be obedient to law. Together, though, the two conceptions of law balance one another. We may be temporarily angered or discouraged when we are on the losing end of what we see as someone else manipulating the legal system, but we are able to put it aside as an aberration when we also believe that the system as a whole is fair.

At first look, it appears clear how the different understandings of law within the activist groups work together to maintain legality's hegemonic status. The picketers encountered adversity, exhibited negative aspects of the "with the law" conception, but contained them and returned to a state more closely aligned with the "before the law" view. The abortion-rights activists' stories of law's redemption are another example of the moves made between the differing legal typologies. The actors have access to an understanding of the legal world that accounts for difficulty, unfairness, and failure, but the actors eventually return to a more reverent and stable stance "before the law." When one moves away from the street-level actors, however, the pattern in the distribution of these two typologies across the stories raises some questions and new possibilities about how they work together to preserve law's power.

While the street-level actors' stories display both conceptions of law, but ultimately land on the side of being "before the law," the elites' stories are concentrated distillations of one typology or the other. The more removed elites (i.e., the amici authors and the pro-choice, no-vote legislative members) present a highly principled "before the law" conception of legality. Conversely, the elites that are much closer to the actual disputes present a highly political "with the law" conception. The pattern here suggests that the competing versions of law that are usually held within one person are, in these disputes, separated out and distributed according to one's place in the conflict. This one-sidedness seems to work against the typologies' abilities to combine in order to sustain law's power, exposing it to the risk of breaking under the weight of idealism or cynicism.

The apparent imbalance in the distribution of the typologies is, how-ever, addressed in various ways. First, the purity of the "before the law" view held by the minority of elites is, as mentioned above, attributable to their distance from these conflicts. Their positions as detached amicus authors and legislators specifically asked to defend legal principles gives them little reason to rely on or to discuss the more imperfect and profane aspects of their roles within the legal system or of the law in general as it pertains to these cases. In spite of this, one can assume that their practi-cal legal and political experiences have given them a healthy accompany-ing "with the law" view. In fact, it is hard to imagine them being able to continue as lawyers and legislators without some realist understandings of their professions and the law. The presence of the "with the law" typology is in fact suggested by some of these elites recognizing that these cases caused tensions and political infighting within the ACLU and the wider progressive legal community.[68]

The more compelling and supported means to balance are found within the stories themselves and their immediate and extended audi-ences. With a closer reading one can see that the "with the law" views taken in the majority of elite stories are not without their own claims to principle. The lawyers appeal to their duty to serve their clients, and the legislators say the same in terms of their legislative responsibilities. Where there is duty, there is principle and therefore a means to restore needed balance.

The gritty political details of law in action, combined with the call of professional duty and, more importantly, one's own beliefs with respect to the causes that the elites fought on behalf of, allow audiences to divide the majority of the elites into saints and sinners. To the unsympathetic audi-ence, the elites on one side of the conflict are the bad actors who corrupt the legal and political systems. They simultaneously personify, externalize, and contain law's problems. They therefore become the "whipping boys" that allow the greater system to continue to be pure.

The remaining elites, those with whom the audience politically aligns, are seen as telling stories that demonstrate how they rightfully fol-lowed their hearts and convictions as they "fought the good fight." They may have to play the game of law and politics, but they are playing for the "right" reasons. They are thus seen as principled actors both in terms of fulfilling their professional duties and, more importantly, in serving worthy political ends. When pressed, the sympathetic audience can also borrow from the "before the law" view and grant their subset of elites the benefit of the doubt that, as good servants of the law, they will take care to not abuse it.

The elites therefore collectively embody legality's virtues as well as its vices. While they appear to be nearly pure distillations of each typology, law's multidimensionality is still evident through them when they are taken as a collective whole. As a result, they, like the street-level activists, present us with the means to continue to believe in law and for the state's legal power to endure.

Methodological Appendix

Of the 50 interviews involved in this project, 22 were conducted with street-level activists and 28 were conducted with elites (i.e., lawyers, legislators, and amicus brief authors). Of the street-level activists, 14 are from the anti-abortion side, and eight are from the abortion-rights side. Looking more closely at the 14 anti-abortion activists, seven are from *Planned Parenthood v. Williams,* five are from *Schenck v. Pro-Choice Network*, and two are from *Hill v. Colorado.* The eight abortion-rights activists and clinic managers include two from *Planned Parenthood v. Williams* and six from *Schenck v. Pro-Choice Network*. Since *Hill v. Colorado* was a facial challenge to a state law, there are no ground-level activists involved in the case on the abortion-rights side.

Of the 28 elites interviewed, 13 sided with the anti-abortion activists and 15 sided with the clinics. Looking more closely at those who aligned with the anti-abortion activists, they include one lawyer from *Planned Parenthood v. Williams,* six lawyers (including three amici authors) from *Schenck v. Pro-Choice Network*, and four legislators and two lawyers from *Hill v. Colorado.* The 15 elites who sided with the abortion-rights activists and clinics include three lawyers from *Planned Parenthood v. Williams,* four lawyers (including two amici authors) from *Schenck v. Pro-Choice Network*, and six legislators and two state lawyers from *Hill v. Colorado.*

The street-level and lawyer interviewees were selected from the lists of named plaintiffs, defendants, attorneys, and amici authors in each court case. The legislators were selected using the Bubble Bill's voting records. All of the "yes" vote interviewees were either sponsors or cosponsors of the bill. The "no" vote interviewees were selected from the 15 total legislators who opposed the bill. The interviewees were initially contacted by mail or email, and then by phone. Some snowball sampling was also used in order to gain access to those whose contact information was unavailable, who initially failed to respond, or who were named in the cases via organizational affiliation (e.g., Pro-Choice Network of Western New York) rather than by a personal name.

The interviews took place between January and November 2004. The author conducted all interviews. The interviews with Paul Schenck and those related to *Hill v. Colorado* were the only interviews not conducted in person. Of the eight clinic members and supporters, all were highly educated, six were women, two were men, five worked in some official capacity for the clinic (e.g., as a doctor and/or manager), and three were volunteers. Of the 14 anti-abortion activists, education levels varied significantly (e.g., ranging from some college education to holding graduate degrees), eight were women, six were men, and all strongly identified as being "Christian."

Of the elites who supported the clinics and abortion-rights activists, four of the legislators and four of the lawyers were women, and two of the legislators and five of the lawyers were men. On the other side of these conflicts, all nine of the lawyers and three of the four legislators were men. Although the interviewee sample size limits the ability to make conclusive or causal claims, the interviews are compelling and allow for the in-depth examination required by the interpretive approach. Furthermore, it is unlikely that a wider sample of people involved in these cases would be significantly demographically different.[1]

The recruitment letter or email told the participants that the interviews would be used to write a narrative history of the events surrounding the court cases they were involved in, as well as to address how they thought about the limits of free speech. The interviews began with general questions about the person's background and how they became involved in activism, lawyering, and/or politics. Questions then moved to such topics as: the protest or countermovement activities they were involved in; how the activist groups they were associated with were organized; how they understood the purpose of protest or countermovement activities; how they understood their opponents' actions; whether they ever felt conflicted about their, or their associates', actions; their involvement in the court cases; whether they felt that they were affected by the cases; and, finally, how they understood the limits of the First Amendment—both in general and in relation to their specific case.

Since these were open-ended interviews, questions were largely used to initiate conversations, giving the interviewee a significant amount of control over the direction of the interview. Interviews ranged in length between 35 and 127 minutes, with the average interview lasting just over an hour. All but one of the interviews were recorded, transcribed, and analyzed using a grounded theory approach.[7]

After numerous readings, interview responses were initially put into spreadsheets according to question/response type and movement alignment (anti-abortion or abortion-rights). Examples of question/response type categories include explaining why the case was brought and what it was about; responding to or expressing the notion that protesters were causing harm; explaining what motivated one's activism; reactions to the injunctions or state statutes; expressing comfort or discomfort with positions taken in legal arguments; and portrayal of the court system.

Further review of the interviews led to organizing interviewee responses according to emerging themes regarding how law mattered in respondents' narratives. Examples of such themes for the clinics and their supporters include law being portrayed as a coercive resource, law limiting desired action, and the nature of the violations committed by anti-abortion protesters. Legal themes that emerged from the anti-abortion activist interviews include the relationship between law and morality/religion, the clarity of law, and types of responses to the claim that they were causing harm through their activism. Related themes that surfaced across both sets of interviews include the understanding of the First Amendment, separating or distancing oneself from the law and the state, and negative experiences with the law. These emergent themes were used to identify and critique how interviewees use, resist, are constrained by, and construct law.

Finally, in addition to the interview data, court decisions and filings; clinic and protest materials; organization newsletters; audio recordings of the Colorado legislative hearings and debates; the Pro-Choice Network of Western New York archives at SUNY Buffalo; and local newspaper accounts of the protests, cases, and legislative action were used in order to understand the context of each case.

Notes

Chapter 1

1. See Williams 2011 for a thorough explanation of how abortion migrated from being a fringe "Catholic issue" to being a significant plank in the Republican Party platform.

2. As Ginsburg 1998, Luker 1985, and Zald and Useem 1987 argue, both abortion as a political issue and anti-abortion activism subsume many concerns beyond the status of the fetus. For example, anti-abortion activism and the political issue of abortion also include concerns over traditional gender roles, secular humanism, and, as I am focusing on here, the growth of federal government power and the general liberalizing of domestic policy.

3. For example, see *Brown v. Board of Education* 347 U.S. 483 (1954) and *Brown v. Board of Education* 349 U.S. 294 (1955) in terms of racial integration; *Engel v. Vitale* 370 U.S. 421 (1962) and *Abington School District v. Schempp* 374 U.S. 203 (1963) for school prayer; *Gideon v. Wainwright* 372 U.S. 335 (1963) and *Miranda v. Arizona* 384 U.S. 436 (1966) for criminal justice; and *Griswold v. Connecticut* 381 U.S. 479 (1965) in relation to sexual taboos.

4. I have chosen to refer to the opposing sides of this conflict as "anti-abortion" and "abortion-rights" as opposed to using the terms "pro-life movement" and "pro-choice movement." While these labels are less common and not the chosen titles of the respective groups, they are more directly related to the subject of contention—the legality of abortion.

5. As Meyer and Staggenborg 1996; 2008 note, an increase in the perception of an organized and successful threat to established interests is a condition that helps to both spawn and sustain movement-countermovement (or, as they refer to them, "opposing movement") conflicts. While the abortion conflict had already produced competing movements, the direct-action tactics of the anti-abortion movement helped to reignite concerns about the security of reproductive rights and thus to remobilize abortion-rights activists. For more on this dynamic within the abortion conflict, see Blanchard 1995; Risen and Thomas 1999; and Staggenborg 1991.

6. As will be shown in the following chapters, examples of direct-action strategies include organizing volunteers to escort women into clinics or to create human corridors that provided access to clinic entrances.

7. This maneuver failed in a series of U.S. Supreme Court cases that matched NOW against Joseph Scheidler and a collection of other anti-abortion activists. See *National*

Organization for Women, Inc. v. Scheidler (1994), *Scheidler v. National Organization for Women* (2003), and *National Organization for Women v. Scheidler* (2006).

8. The eight cases heard by the Court are *Frisby v. Schultz* (1988), *Bray v. Alexandria Women's Health Clinic* (1993), *National Organization for Women, Inc. v. Scheidler* (1994), *Madsen v. Women's Health Center, Inc.* (1994), *Schenck v. Pro-Choice Network of Western New York* (1997), *Hill v. Colorado* (2000), *Scheidler v. National Organization for Women* (2003), and *National Organization for Women v. Scheidler* (2006).

9. The latest abortion protest RICO case is *National Organization for Women v. Scheidler*, 547 U.S. (2006).

10. The three dissents are *Winfield v. Kaplan* (1994), *Williams v. Planned Parenthood Shasta-Diablo, Inc.* (1997), and *Cloer v. Gynecology Clinic, Inc.* (2000). Justice Scalia authored, and was joined by Justice Thomas, in all three of these dissents. Justice Kennedy joined Scalia and Thomas in *Winfield* and *Williams*. The two concurrences, both authored by Justice Scalia, are *Lawson v. Murray* (1995) and *Lawson v. Murray* (1998).

11. According to the U.S. Supreme Court's website, "The Court receives approximately 10,000 petitions for a writ of certiorari each year. The Court grants and hears oral argument in about 75–80 cases" ("Frequently Asked Questions").

12. The term "New Christian Right" refers to the collective political mobilization and institutionalization of previously divided Christian sects (e.g., Evangelical, Fundamentalist, Pentecostal, and Charismatic Christians) within the Republican Party in the late 20th century. For more on the formation of, and the underlying tensions within, the New Christian Right, see Wilcox 1992; D. Williams 2010.

13. Rescues existed both before and beyond Operation Rescue. Diamond, for example, notes that Operation Rescue's founder, Randall Terry, was inspired by Joseph Scheidler's clinic blockades in the mid-1980s (1998, 136).

14. Colo. Rev. Stat., 18-9-122(3).

15. DeGette 2004.

16. 18 U.S.C. § 248.

17. Anti-abortion activists' involvement in both federal and state legislative politics predates, runs concurrently with, and follows the period dominated by the street politics of abortion. For example, early anti-abortion activists sought a federal constitutional amendment to overturn *Roe v. Wade*. Furthermore, at the state level, both *Webster* (1989) and *Casey* (1992) are examples of anti-abortion activists working and succeeding in state legislatures in the mid- to late 1980s. I refer, however, to the movement's more recent efforts in the state legislative arena as a distinct phase that follows the demise of the street politics of abortion. This is because the movement has concentrated resources, developed expertise, and devised a coordinated state-level strategy that outshines earlier efforts. Again, this does not deny that such strategies existed earlier, or that direct street-level activism does not still occur. Rather, the distinctions between periods are drawn in terms of the concentration of resources, effort, and publicity.

18. Meyer and Staggenborg 1996; Meyer and Staggenborg 2008.

19. See *Hague v. Congress of Industrial Organizations*, 307 U.S. 496 (1939); and *Schneider v. State*, 308 U.S. 147 (1939).

20. However, as the *Williams* case illustrates, the ownership of certain spaces is not always clear.

21. *Police Department of the City of Chicago v. Mosley*, 408 U.S. 92 (1972), 95–96.

22. *Cox v. New Hampshire*, 312 U.S. 569 (1941), 576.

23. *Ward v. Rock Against Racism*, 491 U.S. 781 (1989).

24. Ibid., 791.

25. Ibid.,798.

26. Ibid., 802.

27. For an argument that the content-neutrality requirement and the time, place, and manner test can be used to subordinate speech, see Post 1995.

28. *Cohen v. California*, 403 U.S. 15 (1971).

29. *Frisby v. Schultz* 487 U.S. 474 (1988), 487.

30. Scheingold 2004.

31. For example, see Rosenberg 2008.

32. For example, see Galanter 1974.

33. For a critical review of this literature, see McCann 1998, 83–89.

34. For examples, see Albiston 1999; Bumiller 1992; Kennedy 2002; Glendon 1993.

35. For examples, see Feeley and Rubin 2000; Keck 2009.

36. For example, see Ashar 2007.

37. For examples, see McCann 1994; NeJaime 2011; Polletta 2000. For a thorough review of the risks and benefits of movement litigation, see Albiston 2011.

38. For examples, see Coglianese 2001; Frymer 2003; Keck 2009; McCann 1994; Polletta 2000; Rosenberg 2008; Scheingold 2004; G. Williams and Williams 1995.

39. There is admittedly variation within the law and social movement scholarship in terms of how researchers define law and connect it to the goals that a group is seeking to obtain. For example, Gerald Rosenberg (2008) considers the link between positive judicial rulings and realizing actual policy change, rates of giving to a movement, and other quantifiable and tangible effects. In contrast, Michael McCann (1994) looks at litigation, even when unsuccessful, and its ability to mobilize activists and provide a language for their activism. Both, however, are still considering how the use of law directly connects to the realization of the movement's ultimate ends.

40. For examples of movement-countermovement research, see Meyer and Staggenborg 1996; Meyer and Staggenborg 2008; Oliver and Myers 2002; Peckham 1998; Rohlinger 2002; Zald and Useem 1987.

41. For example, see Meyer and Staggenborg 1996.

42. Kagan 2003.

43. McCann 1994; Frymer 2003.

44. Epp 1998; Teles 2010.

45. Both law and litigation are seen in discussions of opposing movement framing and shifts in tactics and venues, but they do not draw specific attention in the law and social movements literature. In terms of the law and social movements literature, Thomas Keck (2009), for example, examines litigation in a movement-countermovement context, but he does not directly engage with the movement-countermovement literature.

46. Meyer and Staggenborg 1996, 1655–56.

47. I refer to these cases as micro-studies of movement-countermovement conflicts because Meyer and Staggenborg (1996; 2008) use a macro-longitudinal view of the ongoing abortion conflict to develop and illustrate their theories on movement-countermovement conflicts. That is, they look at the large policy and strategy shifts from the conflict over time. This book, in contrast, takes one era within the ongoing history, and specific battles within the larger conflict, to both illustrate and further develop movement-countermovement theories.

48. In her book *Unleashing Rights* (1996a), Helena Silverstein discusses "human law" cases brought by animal rights activists that create "secondary battles" (133, 147–52). These secondary battles that employ human law are related to what I am terming "secondary movement litigation" in that they both involve an indirect relationship between the legal issue being litigated and the movements' ultimate goals. The two types of cases are, however, differentiated from one another in at least two important ways.

First, the origins for the two types of cases are different. Silverstein's human law cases "are used by activists as a legal alternative in light of the lack of animal laws and the limitations of environmental laws" (ibid., 133). That is, animal rights activists employ human law in creative ways in order to circumvent problems of legal standing and to generally compensate for the lack of law that directly relates to their goal of recognizing animal rights. As will be discussed in the remainder of this chapter, the secondary movement cases examined here spring from the movement-countermovement context.

Second, as Silverstein notes, the animal rights activists were able to use these unrelated legal issues in order to "raise issues of animal rights and protection" (ibid., 147). While they may have been raising First Amendment and other issues, they were sometimes able to bring it back to their movement goal of creating animal-rights-related policy. For example, activists were able to get universities to offer "alternative classes for students who take a moral stand against dissection" and animal rights lawyers "are increasingly trying to distinguish pets from property and have had some success getting judges to recognize the 'sentimental value' of animals" (ibid., 148, 152). The secondary movement litigation seen in the anti-abortion protest regulation cases does not return to abortion policy in such a direct way.

49. Meyer and Staggenborg 1996, 1632–33. In opposing movement conflicts, there is an initial action or event that creates a movement, and another that creates the corresponding countermovement. Up to this point, the progression appears linear. Once the two sides are established, though, they can become locked together in a continuing cycle of tactical innovation and response. With strong competition between opposing movements, conflicts appear to spiral. Researchers can therefore find themselves in the position of Laurence Sterne's satiric title character in *Tristram Shandy* (1980), who, when faced with deciding where to begin telling his autobiography, continually moves to more distant points that predate his birth.

50. Furthermore, the regulations aim to control protest activities so that there is not a need for enforcement cases. These subsequent cases only happen because the protesters violate, or are thought to have violated, the regulations. It is worth noting, though, that

clinics and their supporters stand to benefit from bringing enforcement cases that bleed the anti-abortion activists' resources and discourage future activism. Still, the bringing of civil enforcement suits takes time and resources that the movement could otherwise use for different ends.

51. Meyer and Staggenborg 1996, 1649–51.

52. As others have noted, the translation process that is required for a dispute to become a *legal dispute* is often both unsettling and disorienting for the original disputants. See n. 39.

53. See Guth and Green 1991; McClosky and Brill 1983.

54. Cook, Jelen, and Wilcox 1992; Fiorina, Abrams, and Pope 2010.

55. Clyde Wilcox (1992), for example, argues that many social conservatives have more varied beliefs about what abortion policy should be than the general public assumes, or than these same conservatives may admit to one another.

56. Meyer and Staggenborg 1996, 1655–56.

57. Scheingold 2004.

58. Silverstein's work (1996) is one related example of secondary movement litigation but, as discussed in note 48, there are important differences between the cases examined.

59. For examples of law and society scholarship that illustrates the cultural dimensions of law and legal power, see Ewick and Silbey 1998; Greenhouse 1994; Marshall 2003; Merry 1990.

60. For the law governing both situations, see N.Y. Vehicular and Traffic Law §1112, and Lincoln Municipal Code §10.48.170.

61. Ewick and Silbey describe at least three ways in which narrative enters scholarly work. It can be present as either "the object of inquiry, the method of inquiry . . . [and/ or] the product of inquiry" (1995, 201). This book employs narrative in all three of these forms. In this final section the role of narrative shifts from being the *product* and *means* of inquiry, to being the *object* of inquiry. For more on narrative as the means, product, and subject of inquiry, see Berger and Quinney 2004; Ewick and Silbey 1995; Orbuch 1997; Polletta 2006; Polletta et al. 2011.

62. The term "state law" is in reference to the law that is formally controlled, defined, and executed by state authorities like the police and court officials. It stands in contrast to "extrastate law," which refers to law as it is constructed, and possibly lived, outside of the official state.

63. This is a process that Robert Cover referred to as the court's "jurispathic" function. He noted it in part to highlight the inherently violent nature of courts. "Judges are people of violence. Because of the violence they command, judges characteristically do not create law, but kill it. Theirs is the jurispathic office. Confronting the luxuriant growth of a hundred legal traditions, they assert that this one is law and destroy or try to destroy the rest" (1983, 53). While not citing Cover or litigation directly, Alan Hunt makes a very similar argument about legal pluralism and conflicts with the state one decade later. "My project is to articulate a conception of law that starts out from an interrogation of the law as a mode of regulation. / At the heart of this endeavor is a concern to give full recognition to the lessons of legal pluralism . . . while at the same time to give due recognition to the

importance of both the state as a political agency and to state-law. . . . [The] important recognition of the diversification and pluralization of law and regulation should not lead us to forget about the role that law plays as the medium of an ever-expanding state. These spheres of diversification and of centralization exist in complex tension. *Provisionally we can express the role of the central state apparatus as being continuously engaged in the 'project of regulatory unification'*; this project is pursued with varying vigor and commitment; it is never more than partially successful [in controlling legal meaning] . . . the unificatory project is always present and must inform our theorization of law just as must our recognition of the reality of legal pluralism" (Hunt 1993, 307–8, emphasis added). Roughly speaking, the means that are employed in the court's jurispathic or regulatory unification function fall along a continuum of possibilities—with persuasion in the shadow of violence at one end of the spectrum, and outright state oppression at the other. Noting the inherent violence of law is important here because it reveals the high stakes that accompany the choices that social movements and other litigants make.

64. See, for example, Cover 1983; Cover 1986; Hunt 1993; Minow 1987; McCann 1994.

65. Judicial violence, however severe, does not guarantee that the state will succeed in eliminating competing forms of law. Rather, the very real possibility of violence forces those who create divergent versions of law to consider why, if, and how they may resist law as articulated by the judge. "For a group to live its law in the face of the predictable employment of violence against it requires a new elaboration of 'law'—the development of an understanding of what is right and just in the violent contexts that the group will encounter. The group must understand the normative implications of struggle and the meaning of suffering and must accept responsibility for the results of the confrontations that will ensue" Cover 1983, 49).

66. Cover refers to the creation of extrastate legal meaning as "jurisgenesis" (1983, 46).

67. Silbey 2005, 334.

68. Researchers interested in the constitutive uses of law by social movements often study the ways that organizations make meaning and compete to utilize law via framing and mobilizing.

69. While clearly related, this path to understanding the place of law in movements does not pay particular attention to individuals or how the movements' use of law affects law's hegemonic power. For examples of framing and mobilizing literature, see Snow et al. 1986; Snow and Benford 1992; McCann 1994; Benford and Snow 2000.

70. MCann1997, 466.

71. McCann 1996, 480.

72. McCann 1994; McCann 1996; McCann 2006; NeJaime 2011.

73. McCann 1994, 65.

74. Some work is beginning to appear on the legal consciousness of elites. See, for example, Dudas 2009; Sarat and Scheingold 2008.

75. See, for example, Barclay and Marshall 2005; McCann and Silverstein 1998; Levitsky 2006.

76. For a critical review of this literature, see McCann 1998, 83–89; Polletta 2000, 367–83.

Chapter 2

Portions of Chapter 2 were previously published in "Anti-Abortion Protests and the Ideological Dilemma in Planned Parenthood Shasta Diablo, Inc. v. Williams," in *Studies in Law, Politics, and Society*, ed. Austin Sarat, vol. 35 (London: Elsevier, 2005).

1. Luker 1985; Risen and Thomas 1999.
2. Hammer 2004.
3. Williams 1990b.
4. DeMers 2004.
5. Williams 2004.
6. Williams 1990a, 3, 4.
7. Sallade 1990.
8. Estes 2004.
9. Ibid.
10. Rouche 2004.
11. Estes 2004.
12. Planned Parenthood 1990.
13. Williams 2004.
14. Ibid.
15. Street 2004.
16. Bunting 1990.
17. Williams 1990c.
18. Ibid.
19. Hammer 2004.
20. Palmer 2004.
21. DeMers 2004.
22. Street 2004.
23. Ryer 2004.
24. Rouche 2004.
25. Williams 1991.
26. Bunting 1991.
27. California Supreme Court 1993.
28. California Supreme Court 1994.
29. Ibid.
30. USSC 1994, 512:2527.
31. California Supreme Court 1995, 43:1026.
32. USSC 1997a.
33. USSC 1997b, 1135.
34. USSC 1997b, 1136.
35. Williams 1991.
36. Williams 2004.
37. Ibid.
38. Bartels 2004.
39. Street 2004.

40. Palmer 2004.
41. Williams 2004.

Chapter 3

1. Levine 2004.
2. Ibid.
3. Luker 1985; Risen and Thomas 1999.
4. Others involved with the Pro-Choice Network of Western New York who have or had connections to the local academic community are Lucinda Finley and Isabelle Marcus of the SUNY Buffalo Law School, Murray Levine of the Dept. of Psychology at SUNY Buffalo, and Elizabeth "Babs" Conant of Canisius College.
5. Conant 1989, 1.
6. Levine 2004.
7. Ibid.
8. Ibid.
9. Ibid.
10. Levine 1990, 1.
11. Ibid., 2.
12. Schenck 2004.
13. Ibid.
14. Ibid.
15. Ibid.
16. Ibid.
17. Ibid..
18. Certo 2004.
19. Mueller 2004.
20. Ibid.
21. Project Rescue Western New York 1990.
22. G. Warner 1989, A9.
23. Escort Committee 1990; Finley 2004.
24. Finley 2004.
25. Operation Rescue 1988, emphasis in original.
26. M. Green 1988.
27. Finley 2004.
28. Wortman 2004.
29. Levine 2004.
30. Buckham 2004.
31. Baran 2004.
32. Mueller 2004.
33. Cadwallader 2004.
34. Baran 2004.
35. Levine 1990, 2.
36. Escort Committee 1990.

37. Dalley 2004.

38. Steering Committee 1990, 3.

39. Conant 1989, 3.

40. Conant 1989, 1.

41. Buckham 2004.

42. Conant 1989, 1.

43. Mueller 2004.

44. Steering Committee 1989, 2.

45. Finley 2004.

46. Ibid.

47. Board of Directors 1990a, 1.

48. Finley 2004.

49. Board of Directors 1990a, 2.

50. Ibid.

51. Ibid.

52. Ibid.

53. Ibid.

54. Ibid., 3.

55. Ibid., 2.

56. Ibid., 3.

57. Ibid., 2.

58. Ibid.

59. Board of Directors 1990a, 3.

60. Ibid., 2. Emphasis in original.

61. Ibid.

62. Ibid.

63. Ibid. Board of Directors 1990a, 2.

64. Ibid., 2, 3.

65. Ibid., 3.

66. Ibid., 3.

67. Finley 2004.

68. Ibid.

69. Arcara 1990.

70. Board of Directors 1990c, 1.

71. Board of Directors 1990b, 1. Emphasis in original.

72. Pro-Choice Network 1992, 1.

73. Ibid., 4.

74. Finley 2004.

75. Finley 2004.

76. Ibid.

77. Board of Directors 1991, 1.

78. Ibid., 2.

79. The complete February 14, 1992 Preliminary Injunction reads:

Upon consideration of the evidence introduced at a hearing held on plaintiffs' motion for a preliminary injunction, and at hearings on plaintiffs' motions to find defendants Nancy Walker, Bonnie Behn, Carla Rainero, Rev. Paul Schenck, Rev. Robert Schenck and Project Rescue in civil contempt for violations of this Court's Temporary Restraining Order, and upon consideration of the complaint and supporting documents, and upon consideration of defendants' stipulations pertaining to the entry of a preliminary injunction against certain conduct and to the binding nature of any preliminary injunction on all named individual and organizational defendants, it is hereby

ORDERED that defendants, the officers, directors, agents, and representatives of defendants, and all other persons whomsoever, known or unknown, acting in their behalf or in concert with them, and receiving actual or constructive notice of this Order, are:

1. Enjoined and restrained in any manner or by any means from:

(a) trespassing on, sitting in, blocking, impeding, or obstructing access to, ingress into or egress from any facility, including, but not limited to, the parking lots, parking lot entrances, driveways, and driveway entrances, at which abortions are performed in the Western District of New York;

(b) demonstrating within fifteen feet from either side or edge of, or in front of, doorways or doorway entrances, parking lot entrances, driveways and driveway entrances of such facilities, or within fifteen feet of any person or vehicle seeking access to or leaving such facilities, except that the form of demonstrating known as sidewalk counseling by no more than two persons as specified in paragraph (c) shall be allowed;

(c) physically abusing, grabbing, touching, pushing, shoving, or crowding persons entering or leaving, working at or using any services at any facility at which abortions are performed; provided, however, that sidewalk counseling consisting of a conversation of a non-threatening nature by not more than two people with each person or group of persons they are seeking to counsel shall not be prohibited. Also provided that no one is required to accept or listen to sidewalk counseling, and that if anyone or any group of persons who is sought to be counseled wants to not have counseling, wants to leave, or walk away, they shall have the absolute right to do that, and in such event all persons seeking to counsel that person or group of persons shall cease and desist from such counseling, and shall thereafter be governed by the provisions of paragraph (b) pertaining to not demonstrating within fifteen feet of persons seeking access to or leaving a facility. In addition, it is further provided that this right to sidewalk counseling as defined herein shall not limit the right of the Police

Department to maintain public order or such reasonably necessary rules and regulations as they decide are necessary at each particular demonstration site;

(d) using any mechanical loudspeaker or sound amplification device or making any excessively loud sound which injures, disturbs, or endangers the health or safety of any patient or employee of a health care facility at which abortions are performed, nor shall any person make such sounds which interfere with the rights of anyone not in violation of this Order;

(e) attempting, or inducing, directing, aiding, or abetting in any manner, others to take any of the actions described in paragraphs (a) through (d) above; and it is further

ORDERED that nothing in this Order shall be construed to limit defendants and those acting in concert with them from exercising their legitimate First Amendment rights; and it is further

ORDERED that the defendant organizations and their officers and agents, and all individual defendants and those acting in concert with them, shall make a good faith effort to instruct all organizations and individuals they believe to be planning to participate in any of the activities enumerated above not to engage or participate in the activities enjoined in paragraphs (a) through (e) above;

2. IT IS FURTHER ORDERED that the failure to comply with this Order by any defendant or anyone acting in their behalf or in concert with them shall be subject to civil damages of $10,000 per day for the first violation of this Order and/or may subject them to criminal contempt proceedings; and it is further

ORDERED that each successive violation of this Order shall subject the contemnor to a civil contempt fine double that of the previous fine and/or criminal contempt proceedings; and it is further

ORDERED that any amounts collected thereunder shall be paid to the Plaintiff health care facility at which the violation occurred, or to the Registry of the Court if the targeted health care facility is not a Plaintiff; and it is further

ORDERED that each contemnor shall be jointly and severally liable for all attorney's fees and related costs incurred by plaintiffs in relation to the enforcement of this Order.

3. Violations of this Order shall be enforced by appropriate motion.

4. IT IS FURTHER ORDERED that the United States Marshal for the Western District of New York shall read this Order as set forth above in Paragraphs 1 and 2 in their entirety at the site of a demonstration or protest at a facility at which abortions are performed in the Western District of New York. Plaintiffs'

counsel shall be responsible for notifying the Marshal in a timely manner of the location of such demonstration or protest activity.

5. It is the Court's intention that nothing contained in this Order shall supersede or diminish the obligation of local and state law enforcement authorities to fulfill their duties and responsibilities in enforcing state laws and local ordinances.

6. This Order shall remain in full force and effect until modified by further Order, or until final resolution by this Court of the claims for permanent injunctive relief in the above captioned matter.

It is so ordered.

80. Arcara 1992.
81. Conant 1992, 1.
82. Ibid., 1.
83. G. Warner 1992, 6.
84. Ibid.
85. Edmonds 1992.
86. G. Warner 1991.
87. USSC 1993.
88. Dist. Court, WD NY 1993, 828, 1020.
89. Ibid., 1032.
90. U.S. Court of Appeals, Second Circuit 1994, 67, 369.
91. Ibid., 371.
92. Ibid., 372.
93. U.S. Court of Appeals, Second Circuit 1995, 67, 394.
94. Ibid., 398.
95. Gene Warner 1994, 1.
96. Ibid., 6.
97. Board of Directors 1991, 2.
98. Waples 2004.
99. As compared to internal controversies in the past, such as over who to support in *National Socialist Party v. Skokie*, 432 U.S. 43 (1977), also know as the "Nazis in Skokie" case.
100. Heins 2004.
101. Waples 2004.
102. J. Green 2004.
103. Waples 2004.
104. Buckham 2004.
105. Levine 2004.
106. Finley 2004.
107. Murray 2004.
108. Anon. 1996.

109. USSC 1997, 519:377.

110. USSC 1997, 519:378.

111. USSC 1997, 519:381; emphasis in original.

112. USSC 1997, 519:383, 384; emphasis added.

113. USSC 1997, 519:384, 385; emphasis added.

114. USSC 1997, 519:386; emphasis in original.

115. USSC 1997, 519:388. Justice Scalia leveled a similar criticism at the California Supreme Court in his dissent from the court's rejection of cert in *Williams v. Planned Parenthood Shasta-Diablo, Inc.*, 1997.

116. USSC 1997, 519:390, 391; emphasis in original.

117. Conant 1997, 3.

118. Finley 2004.

119. Conant 1997, 3; emphasis in original.

120. Mueller 2004.

121. Schenck 2004.

Chapter 4

1. Sanko 1992, 7.

2. Ibid.

3. Ibid.

4. DeGette 2004.

5. Ibid.

6. Ibid.

7. Feeley 2004.

8. Ibid.

9. Ibid.

10. Ibid.

11. DeGette 2004.

12. Feeley 2004.

13. DeGette 2004.

14. Ibid.

15. Colo. Rev. Stat. 1999, § 18-9-122(3).

16. Ibid.:

(1) The general assembly recognizes that access to health care facilities for the purpose of obtaining medical counseling and treatment is imperative for the citizens of this state; that the exercise of a person's right to protest or counsel against certain medical procedures must be balanced against another person's right to obtain medical counseling and treatment in an unobstructed manner; and that preventing the willful obstruction of a person's access to medical counseling and treatment at a health care facility is a matter of statewide concern. The general assembly therefore declares that it is appropriate to enact legislation that prohibits a person from knowingly obstructing another person's entry to or exit from a health care facility.

(2) A person commits a class 3 misdemeanor if such person knowingly obstructs, detains, hinders, impedes, or blocks another person's entry to or exit from a health care facility.

(3) No person shall knowingly approach another person within eight feet of such person, unless such other person consents, for the purpose of passing a leaflet or handbill to, displaying a sign to, or engaging in oral protest, education, or counseling with such other person in the public way or sidewalk area within a radius of one hundred feet from any entrance door to a health care facility. Any person who violates this subsection (3) commits a class 3 misdemeanor.

(4) For the purposes of this section, 'health care facility' means any entity that is licensed, certified, or otherwise authorized or permitted by law to administer medical treatment in this state.

(5) Nothing in this section shall be construed to prohibit a statutory or home rule city or county or city and county from adopting a law for the control of access to health care facilities that is no less restrictive than the provisions of this section.

(6) In addition to, and not in lieu of, the penalties set forth in this section, a person who violates the provisions of this section shall be subject to civil liability, as provided in section 13-21-106.7, C.R.S.

17. DeGette 2004.
18. Feeley 2004.
19. Ibid.
20. Sanko 1993a, 18.
21. Colorado House Judiciary Committee 1993a.
22. Ibid.
23. Ibid.
24. Ibid.
25. Hill 2004.
26. Ibid.
27. Ibid.
28. Ibid.
29. Hill 1989, 5.
30. Ibid., 7.
31. Ibid., 4.
32. Ibid., 25; emphasis in original.
33. Hill 2004.
34. U.S. Court of Appeals, Tenth Circuit 1993.
35. Ibid., 869.
36. Ibid., 878.
37. California Supreme Court 1995; USSC 1997a.
38. Hill 2004.
39. Colorado House Judiciary Committee 1993b.
40. Ibid. 1993c.
41. Ibid.

42. Ibid.

43. Ibid.

44. Ibid.

45. Colorado House 1993.

46. Ibid.

47. Ibid.

48. Ibid.

49. Colorado Senate Judiciary Committee 1993a.

50. Colorado Senate 1993.

51. Colorado Senate Judiciary Committee 1993b.

52. Sanko 1993b, 19.

53. Colorado Senate Judiciary Committee 1993b.

54. Ibid.

55. Colorado Senate 1993.

56. Ibid.

57. Sanko 1993d, 6A.

58. Sanko 1993c, 12. Such "personhood" bills and amendments have since enjoyed a resurgence in popularity in state legislatures (Lohr 2011).

59. Sanko 1993c, 12.

60. Sanko 1993d, 6A.

61. Henderson 2004.

62. Ibid.

63. Himmelmann 2004.

64. Westlund 2004.

65. Henderson 2004.

66. Angel 2004.

67. Ibid.

68. Ibid.

69. Col. Ct. of Ap. 1995.

70. USSC 1997b.

71. Col. Ct. of Ap. 1997, 949:109.

72. Col. Ct. of Ap. 1997, 949:110.

73. Col. Ct. of Ap. 1997, 949:110.

74. Col. S.Ct. 1999, 973:1252–3.

75. Col. S.Ct. 1999, 973:1255.

76. Col. S.Ct. 1999, 973:1257.

77. Col. S.Ct. 1999, 973:1258.

78. Col. S.Ct. 1999, 973:1258.

79. USSC 2000b.

80. Ibid.

81. USSC 2000a, 530:707–8.

82. USSC 2000a, 530:714.

83. USSC 2000a, 530:719–20.

84. USSC 2000a, 530:723.

85. USSC 2000a, 530:737.

86. USSC 2000a, 530:738.

87. USSC 2000a, 530:741, 742.

88. USSC 2000a, 530:743, 744.

89. USSC 2000a, 530:749.

90. USSC 2000a, 530:765.

91. USSC 2000a, 530:765, 766.

92. USSC 2000a, 530:791, 792.

93. Hill 2004.

94. Himmelmann 2004.

95. Ibid.

96. See National Abortion Federation, NAF Violence and Disruption Statistics, http://www.prochoice.org/pubs_research/publications/downloads/about_abortion/stats_table2010.pdf.

97. The Guttmacher Institute is a good source for a detailed cataloguing of the anti-abortion movement's state regulatory successes.

98. USSC 1989.

99. Medoff 2002, 482.

100. USSC 1992.

101. USSC 1992, 505:846.

102. USSC 1992, 505:846. Emphasis added.

103. Frontline; State Regulation of Abortion, http://www.pbs.org/wgbh/pages/frontline/clinic/etc/map.html.

104. Davey 2006.

105. Lohr 2011.

106. Pickert 2013.

107. Pickert, for example, notes that 4 states possess only one surgical abortion clinic, 13 states have less than one abortion provider per 100,000 women ages 15–44, and only 7 states have more than 5 abortion providers per 100,000 women ages 15–44 (2013, 42–3).

108. See http://www.guttmacher.org/media/inthenews/2013/04/11/. For more on the regulatory battle over abortion policy, see Rose 2007.

109. For more on the creation of New Christian Right legal infrastructure, see Den Dulk 2006; Wilson 2011; Wilson and Hollis-Brusky 2012.

110. For more on the general conservative legal movement and its development, see Hollis-Brusky 2011; Southworth 2008; Teles 2010.

111. Center for Reproductive Rights 2009. Emphasis in original.

Chapter 5

Portions of Chapter 5 were previously published in "Sustaining the State: Legal Consciousness and the Construction of Legality in Competing Abortion Activists' Narratives," *Law & Social Inquiry* 21, no. 2: 455–83. ©2011 American Bar Foundation.

1. Foucault 1995; Puzo 1983.

2. The point of citing *The Godfather*'s Book III, and of the repeated contrasts between the Don and the more overtly violent characters, is arguably to illustrate this point.

3. Edelman 1985, 114.

4. Puzo 1969, 10.

5. The one narrow exception to this stems from the limited anti-abortion judicial victory in *Schenck* regarding the unconstitutionality of floating buffer zones.

6. Cover 1983, 53.

7. Cover, for example, would argue that even though such speakers assert legal authority in one sense, the fact that they are living the state's version of the law negates any claims that they are *creating* law and wielding it in a strong sense. "The creation of legal meaning cannot take place . . . without the committed action that distinguishes law from literature. . . . Those who would offer a law different from that of the state will not be satisfied with a rule that permits them to speak without living their law" (Cover 1983, 49).

8. Ibid.

9. In this and the following chapters, interviewees' names have been replaced with general category titles in order to protect their privacy.

10. McCann 1994, 63–68.

11. Clinic Manager, Schenck 2004.

12. PCN Activist, Schenck 2004.

13. PCN Activist, Schenck 2004.

14. Clinic Manager, Williams 2004.

15. Clinic Manager, Schenck 2004.

16. Clinic Manager, Williams 2004.

17. Manager/Doctor, Schenck 2004.

18. Clinic Manager, Schenck 2004.

19. Planned Parenthood Shasta-Diablo 1993; Board of Directors 1990a; Board of Directors 1990b; Board of Directors 1990c; Board of Directors 1991; Pro-Choice Network 1992; Conant 1992; Conant 1997; G. Warner 1992; Gene Warner 1994.

20. McCann 1994, 65.

21. PCN Activist, Schenck 2004.

22. Clinic Manager, Williams 2004.

23. Clinic Manager, Williams 2004.

24. PCN Activist, Schenck 2004.

25. PCN Activist, Schenck 2004.

26. Clinic Manager, Williams 2004.

27. Clinic Manager, Williams 2004.

28. Clinic Manager, Schenck 2004.

29. PCN Activist, Schenck 2004.

30. Clinic Manager, Williams 2004.

31. Manager/Doctor, Schenck 2004.

32. McCann 1994, 65.

33. Clinic Manager, Williams 2004. Emphasis added.

34. Interestingly, one of the PCN members cited a study that quantified the medical harm in terms of increased blood pressure and stress levels that can lead to medical complications.

35. The actual legal standing of the property in the *Williams* case was in question since it was not clear who owned the parking lot. Regardless, the injunction applied to the public sidewalk and not just the parking lot.

36. For a more complete discussion of master frames, see Snow, David, and Benford 1992; Benford and Snow 2000.

37. Cover 1983.

38. Rescuer, Schenck 2004.

39. Four interviewees (all of whom were involved in the *Schenck* case) self-identified as "rescuers." Nine participants from all three cases self-identified as "sidewalk counselors" or "picketers." One final activist from the *Schenck* case straddled the line between the two categories.

40. McCann 1994; McCann 1996; McCann 2006. Also see NeJaime 2011.

41. McCann 1994, 65.

42. Cover 1983, 49.

43. Rescuer, Schenck 2004.

44. Rescuer, Schenck 2004.

45. Rescuer, Schenck 2004.

46. Rescuer, Schenck 2004.

47. Picketer, Williams 2004.

48. Picketer, Hill 2004.

49. Picketer, Schenck 2004.

50. Picketer, Williams 2004.

51. Picketer, Williams 2004.

52. Picketer, Williams 2004.

53. Picketer, Schenck 2004.

54. Picketer, Williams 2004.

55. Picketer, Hill 2004.

56. Picketer, Hill 2004.

57. Picketer, Williams 2004.

58. Picketer, Williams 2004.

59. Picketer, Hill 2004.

60. Picketer, Schenck 2004.

61. Picketer, Williams 2004.

62. Picketer, Williams 2004.

63. Many picketers and rescuers even left the movement shortly after or during these court cases. The reasons given for compliance and leaving street-level activism range from age and the passing of the protest season, to the fear of state violence and being dispirited by the legal process.

64. Cover 1983, 51.

65. For example, the perceived mistreatment of anti-abortion activists in these cases can be used as evidence of systemic, nationwide ills that mobilize the Religious Right

more generally. Some of these activists freely make such connections to wider conservative themes such as mobilizing against judicial activism and the secular "crusade against the Bible and Christianity" (Picketer, Williams 2004).

66. Ewick and Silbey 1995, 211.

67. McCann 1994; McCann 1996; McCann 2006; NeJaime 2011.

68. McCann 1994, 65.

Chapter 6

1. As noted in the introductory chapter, work is beginning to appear elsewhere on the legal consciousness of elites. See, for example, Dudas 2009; Sarat and Scheingold 2008.

2. Silbey 2005, 334.

3. See, e.g., Jones 2005.

4. Scheingold 2004.

5. For a critical review of this literature, see McCann 1998, 83–89.

6. See McCann 1994; Marshall 2003; Jones 2006. For more on framing generally, see Snow et al. 1986; Snow, David, and Benford 1992; Benford and Snow 2000.

7. As other chapters note, a diversity of factors (e.g., the murdering of abortion providers, activist age, etc.) contributed to the decline of more aggressive and participatory movement strategies. Securing protest regulations, however, also clearly played a major role.

8. See Hilbink (2006) as a rare example of examining the effects of movements on elites.

9. Stein 2001, 115.

10. Anti-Abortion Lawyer, Schenck 2004.

11. Anti-Abortion Lawyer, Hill 2004.

12. PCN Lawyer, Schenck 2004.

13. Clinic Lawyer, Williams 2004.

14. For comprehensive discussions of "cause lawyers" and cause lawyering, see Sarat and Scheingold 1998; Sarat and Scheingold 2001; Scheingold and Sarat 2004; Sarat and Scheingold 2005; Sarat and Scheingold 2006; Sarat and Scheingold 2008.

15. State Lawyer, Hill 2004.

16. State Lawyer, Hill 2004.

17. State Lawyer, Hill 2004. This quote directly reflects the frustration expressed by a ground-level activist involved in the *Schenck* case concerning what she saw as the unwillingness of the protesters to challenge the moral authority of the injunction by accepting the penalty for breaching it. "I think making your stand and taking it on the chin is the way to do it . . . I didn't have much respect for them. . . . And that in a way made it all the more aggravating that they were getting away with stuff" (PCN Activist, Schenck 2004).

18. Admittedly, movements will face the anxiety of wondering how aligned their and the state's interests are every time that there is a change in administration and thus a reordering of enforcement priorities, or whenever a new case brings a new set of lawyers. There are also no convenient ways for movements to check or affirm the lawyers' political sympathies.

19. State Lawyer, Hill 2004.

20. Silverstein 1998, 280.

21. Appellate Lawyer, Williams 2004.

22. Appellate Lawyer, Williams 2004.

23. Appellate Lawyer, Williams 2004.

24. Pro-Bill Legislator, Hill 2004.

25. Anti-Bill Legislator, Hill 2004.

26. In fact, one state legislator said that the media formed his view of the events. This anecdotally shows the extent of the abortion-rights activists' control of the narrative.

27. It is true that something can be appropriate but ineffective, just as the opposite is also true. However, the most appropriate solution to a problem should also be the most effective, and so appropriateness typically assumes effectiveness. Furthermore, if a response seems appropriate, but proves to be ineffective, it is likely that one would note this as being incongruous.

28. PCN Lawyer, Schenck 2004.

29. Clinic Lawyer, Williams 2004.

30. PCN Lawyer, Schenck 2004.

31. State Lawyer, Hill 2004.

32. Clinic Amici, Schenck 2004.

33. PCN Lawyer, Schenck 2004.

34. Clinic Lawyer, Williams 2004.

35. PCN Lawyer, Schenck 2004.

36. Appellate Lawyer, Williams 2004.

37. State Lawyer, Hill 2004.

38. Pro-Bill Legislator, Hill 2004.

39. Pro-Bill Legislator, Hill 2004.

40. Appellate Lawyer, Williams 2004.

41. PCN Lawyer, Schenck 2004.

42. Emphasis added.

43. Emphasis added.

44. PCN Lawyer, Schenck 2004.

45. Clinic Lawyer, Williams 2004.

46. Clinic Lawyer, Williams 2004.

47. Appellate Lawyer, Williams 2004.

48. PCN Lawyer, Schenck 2004.

49. State Lawyer, Hill 2004.

50. Clinic Amici, Schenck 2004.

51. Pro-Bill Legislator, Hill 2004.

52. Pro-Bill Legislator, Hill 2004.

53. Pro-Bill Legislator, Hill 2004.

54. Pro-Bill Legislator, Hill 2004.

55. Pro-Bill Legislator, Hill 2004.

56. Pro-Bill Legislator, Hill 2004.

57. Colorado House 1993.

58. Anti-Abortion Lawyer, Hill 2004.

59. *Anti-Abortion Lawyer, Schenck 2004.*

60. Anti-Abortion Lawyer, Schenck 2004.

61. Anti-Abortion Lawyer, Hill 2004.

62. Anti-Abortion Lawyer, Schenck 2004.

63. Anti-Abortion Lawyer, Schenck 2004.

64. Anti-Abortion Lawyer, Williams 2004.

65. Anti-Abortion Lawyer, Williams 2004.

66. Anti-Abortion Lawyer, Hill 2004.

67. Anti-Abortion Lawyer, Schenck 2004.

68. Anti-Abortion Lawyer, Schenck 2004.

69. Anti-Abortion Lawyer, Williams 2004.

70. This issue will be developed in the following chapter.

71. Anti-Bill Legislator, Hill 2004.

72. Anti-Bill Legislator, Hill 2004.

73. Anti-Bill Legislator, Hill 2004.

74. Overrule Amici, Schenck 2004.

75. Overrule Amici, Schenck 2004.

76. It should be noted, though, that the amici authors who herald law's principle also nod toward its political aspects by referencing the tensions that these cases created within the liberal legal community.

77. Overrule Amici, Schenck 2004.

78. Overrule Amici, Schenck 2004.

79. Overrule Amici, Schenck 2004.

80. Anti-Bill Legislator, Hill 2004.

81. Anti-Bill Legislator, Hill 2004.

82. Factors beyond the proximity to the instigating conflict must also be at work here. In spite of their professed liberal reading of the First Amendment, the abortion-rights lawyers' conception of law does not seem to shift in the same way with increased distance from the conflicts. Rather, their realist view of law appears to be more fixed.

83. Silbey 2005, 358.

84. Hilbink (2006), for example, finds that lawyers can sometimes encourage or facilitate radicalism in activists.

Chapter 7

Portions of Chapter 7 were previously published in "Sustaining the State: Legal Consciousness and the Construction of Legality in Competing Abortion Activists' Narratives," *Law & Social Inquiry* 21, no. 2: 455–83. ©2011 American Bar Foundation.

1. While this book has focused on three specific conflicts, it is important to recall the Supreme Court has written opinions for thirteen cases related to the regulation of anti-abortion activism in less than 20 years (see chapter 1, nn. 8, 9, and 10), and this is to say nothing of the numerous cases that never reached the USSC.

2. *Bray v. Alexandria Women's Health Clinic* (1993).

3. For more on earlier attempts to create Christian Right and evangelical political institutions, see Den Dulk 2008; W. C. Wilcox 1992; Williams 2010.

4. For example, see Den Dulk 2006; 2008; Southworth 2008; Wilson and Hollis-Brusky 2012.

5. See, Diamond 1998, 84–88; Brown 2002, 24–31.

6. "About the ACLJ" 2012.

7. Jay Sekulow's online ACLJ bio touts that he has appeared in the USSC 12 times ("Jay Sekulow" 2013).

8. In this way, lawyers like Westlund begin to comprise the conservative Christian legal movement's "B Team" that Teles argues is missing from the general conservative legal movement (2010, 254).

9. Jay Sekulow's ACLJ bio notes that he "brings insight and education to listeners daily with his national call-in radio program, Jay Sekulow Live!, which is broadcast on more than 850 radio stations . . . [He] hosts a weekly television program, ACLJ This Week, which is broadcast on a number of networks nationwide . . . [that] He is a popular guest on nationally televised news programs on FOX News, ABC, CBS, NBC, CNN, MSNBC, CNBC, and PBS . . . and is often quoted in the nation's leading newspapers including USA Today, New York Times, Los Angeles Times, Washington Post, and Washington Times" ("Jay Sekulow" 2013).

10. Warner 1994b; Zremski 1996.

11. "ACLJ—About the ACLJ" 2012. This sentiment concerning the organizations stature is also echoed by Sara Diamond (1998, 85–88).

12. "Our Mission | American Center for Law and Justice ACLJ" 2012.

13. "ObamaCare" 2012; "ACLJ & 20,000 Americans Defend NYPD Surveillance—Telling DOJ It's 'Legitimate' Response to Terrorism" 2012.

14. For more on issue diversification and its effect on the Christian Right as an organized political entity, see Boyer 2008; W. C. Wilcox 1992; Williams 2010.

15. See Mauro 2005; Gross 1995; "Pat Robertson, Part 1," 2012; Harell 2010. Fournier quote in Harrell (2010, 263). This same section of Harrell's book, however, reveals that the organization's ecumenicalism is not as harmonious as New Christian Right leaders might want.

16. For works discussing the religious tensions between Christian sects and how it undermined political effectiveness, see W. C. Wilcox 1992; Williams 2010; Woodberry and Smith 1998.

17. Quoted in Anderson 2007.

18. "Regent Law—Center for Advocacy Skills" 2012.

19. "Liberty Counsel—About" 2012.

20. "Liberty Counsel—About" 2012.

21. "About Liberty Center for Law and Policy | Liberty Center for Law and Policy" 2012. Emphasis added.

22. Den Dulk 2008, 71.

23. Williams quips, for example, "At the end of Bush's presidency, abortion was still legal, and school prayer was not" (2010, 8). Smith also adds, "In sum, whatever their

deepest aspirations, nothing in recent litigation, legislation, or social experience suggests that Religious Right groups are likely to succeed in displacing secular social service providers, community groups, or broadcasters in law, public policies, or in social practices, only that they exist alongside them within a highly pluralistic society."

Smith does, however, temper this assessment by conceding, "It is true, nonetheless, that Religious Right litigants have altered major constitutional doctrines over the last three decades, and that they have done so in ways that have directly assisted their institutions and programs. Religious Right activists and their political allies have also influenced numerous public policies to bring them in accordance with their religious convictions, particularly on topics seen as matters of sexual morality, including abortion and contraception. *In the early 1970s few would have predicted such success*" (2009, 350–51). Emphasis added.

24. For more on the ebb and flow of Christian conservatives in politics, see Conger 2009; Hall 2009; C. Wilcox and Robinson 2010.

25. As noted in chapter 1, nn. 48 and 58, Helena Silverstein also discusses a related, but different, form of secondary movement litigation that she refers to as starting "secondary battles" in the animal rights movement (1996, 133).

26. For a thorough catalogue of the possible risks and benefits of traditional movement litigation, see Albiston 2011.

27. Scheingold 2004.

28. Rescuer, Schenck 2004.

29. See, for example, Brown 2002; Southworth 2008; W. C. Wilcox 1992; Woodberry and Smith 1998.

30. As for the ACLU affiliates whose national organization defends abortion rights, they tried to mitigate the awkwardness of the situation by formally filing the briefs in support of neither party. This allowed them to make their legal arguments in defense of free speech, but to do so in a way that maintained a degree of separation from the anti-abortion activists.

31. For example, multiple anti-abortion activists in Western New York were individually fined $10,000, payable to specific abortion providers, and were required to pay a total of $110,976 in legal fees. Paul Schenck was also fined $20,000 payable to the federal government. The PCN even sought to fine one activist $40,000. See Warner 1992; Warner 1994a; Herbeck 1991.

32. As mentioned earlier, Silverstein 1996. See chapter 1, nn. 48 and 58.

33. Ewick and Silbey 1995, 201. See chapter 1, n. 61.

34. Silbey 2005, 323.

35. Ibid, 358.

36. For more on meaning work, see Benford and Snow 2000, 613.

37. Nielsen 2000, 1087.

38. Clinic Manager, Schenck 2004.

39. Silbey 2005, 323.

40. Nielsen 2000, 1087.

41. One is left to wonder, for example, if changes from viewing the state as ineffective to effective are also possible when people lose in court. Tom Tyler's (2006) research on the

creation of legitimacy through process, as opposed to outcome, suggests that it is possible. Further work would need to be done in the attempt to separate process and outcome, but initial review here suggests that process *may* influence these actors' legal consciousness. The clinic and PCN members do at times refer to how they were particularly impressed by the behavior of court officials and their treatment in these cases. Picketer narratives that attack individual judges also suggest, albeit negatively, that process is important. Fully separating outcome and process here, however, is not possible.

42. As stated earlier, the difficulty in employing law in this way is not to be confused with the law alienating the activists. Their stories show that their ultimate experience with the law was positive.

43. Nielsen 2000, 1072.

44. The clinics' abilities to mobilize law in the courtroom, versus Nelsen's interviewees' lack thereof, can be linked to a number of things including certain individual catalysts discussed above, the existence of structured organizations, and possibly the more visible and political nature of the clinics' problem versus the everyday street harassment experienced by Nielsen's interviewees.

45. Catherine Albiston discusses winning initial litigation fights but losing the larger reform effort in her article (1999). The losses that she discusses, however, are in reference to failing to produce published judicial opinions that will assist in setting the rules for future cases and disputes.

46. Ewick and Silbey 1998, 227–30.

47. Ibid.

48. For examples see Albiston 2011; McCann 1994; McCann 1996; McCann 2006; NeJaime 2011.

49. Zinnemann 1966. Emphasis added.

50. For more on jurisgenesis, see Cover 1983.

51. While Christian conservatives may be mobilized by the belief that the state has been infected by Secular Humanists, they still create room to save the state. Like the anti-abortion activists seen here, den Dulk notes, "The typical story plays on some kind of mass-based alienation from a small yet influential group of cultural elites whose machinations have resulted in moral decay, poverty, or some other social ill." In other words, "the 'ungodly' had not yet won the hearts and minds of the American majority," and so the American majority, and by extension, the democratically elected state, is still inherently good (2008, 64).

52. This is most clearly seen in the amici who filed in favor of neither party in order to "remind the court that we have a position . . . that is driven more by the First Amendment than by . . . the plaintiff's support for abortion, or the protesters, defendant's opposition to abortion" (Overrule Amici, Schenck 2004).

53. Ewick and Silbey 1998, 227–30.

54. For more on the legitimating promise of judicial neutrality, see Shapiro 1986; Tyler 2006.

55. The literature on the problems caused by entering the legal system is nicely summarized and critically engaged in Albiston 2011, 61–77; Lobel 2006; Olson 1984.

56. The latter being Cover's "jurispathic" regulation (1983).

57. Cover 1983, 51.

58. While this last point has primarily been discussed in terms of the anti-abortion activists criticizing specific judges, it is worth remembering that the PCN similarly dismissed the state court judges that they first encountered.

59. Picketer, *Williams* 2004.

60. Picketer, *Hill* 2004.

61. Stein 2001, 115.

62. It is not uncommon for there to be distance between lawyers and other movement actors. For example, see Levitsky 2006.

63. Lobel (2006, 952–54) highlights divisions between legal professionals and more traditional movement actors.

64. Silbey 2005, 358.

65. 1998, 230.

66. Ewick and Silbey 1998, 227.

67. Ibid.

68. That is, recognizing the crosscutting political interests—the right to access abortion, or the right to unencumbered political speech—that these cases presented, and that these organizations had to make political decisions regarding how to frame these cases and who to support in them.

Appendix

1. For comparison, see Luker 1985; Munson 2009.

2. Unfortunately, a technical failure resulted in the inability to record an interview with one legislator who voted in favor of the Bubble Bill. Detailed notes were taken in place of the interview transcription.

Bibliography

Cases, Orders, and Statutes

Arcara, Richard. 1990. "Temporary Restraining Order."

———. 1992. "Preliminary Injunction."

Bunting, Dennis. 1990. "Planned Parenthood Shasta-Diablo Inc. v. Williams—Temporary Restraining Order."

———. 1991. "Planned Parenthood Shasta-Diablo Inc. v. Williams—Permanent Restraining Order."

California Supreme Court. 1993. *Planned Parenthood Shasta-Diablo Inc. v. Williams*, 16 California Reporter 540. California Court of Appeals.

———. 1994. *Planned Parenthood Shasta-Diablo Inc. v. Williams*, 30 California Reporter 629. California Supreme Court.

———. 1995. *Planned Parenthood Shasta-Diablo Inc. v. Williams*, 43 California Reporter 88. California Supreme Court.

Col. Ct. of Ap. 1995. *Hill v. City of Lakewood*, 911 P. 2d 670. Court of Appeals, 5th Div.

———. 1997. *Hill v. City of Lakewood*, 949 P.2d 107. Colorado Court of Appeals.

Col. S.Ct. 1999. *Hill v. Thomas*, 973 P. 2d 1246. Colorado Supreme Court.

Colo. Rev. Stat. 1999. *Bubble Bill. Colo. Rev. Stat.*

Dist. Court, WD NY. 1993. *Pro-Choice Network v. Project Rescue*, 828 F. Supp. 1018. Dist. Court, WD New York.

U.S. Court of Appeals, Second Circuit. 1994. *Pro-Choice Network v. Schenck*, 67 F.3d 359. U.S. Court of Appeals, Second Circuit.

———. 1995. *Pro-Choice Network v. Schenck*, 67 F.3d 377. U.S. Court of Appeals, Second Circuit.

U.S. Court of Appeals, Tenth Circuit. 1993. *Cannon v. City and County of Denver*, 998 F. 2d 867. Court of Appeals, 10th Circuit.

U.S. Supreme Court. 1989. *Webster v. Reproductive Health Services*, 492 U.S. 490. Supreme Court.

———. 1992. *Planned Parenthood of Southeastern Pa. v. Casey*, 505 US 833. Supreme Court.

———. 1993. *Bray v. Alexandria Women's Health Clinic*, 506 U.S. 263. Supreme Court.

———. 1994. *Madsen v. Women's Health Center, Inc.*, 512 U.S. 753. Supreme Court.

———. 1997a. *Schenck v. Pro-Choice Network of Western NY*, 519 U.S. 357. Supreme Court.

———. 1997b. *Hill v. Colorado*, 117 U.S. 1077. Supreme Court.

————. 1997c. *Christine Williams and Solano Citizens for Life v. Planned Parenthood Shasta-Diablo, Inc.* U.S. U.S. Supreme Court.

————. 2000a. *Hill v. Colorado*, 530 U.S. 703. Supreme Court.

Interviews

Angel, Carol. 2004.

Anti-Abortion Lawyer, *Hill*. 2004.

Anti-Abortion Lawyer, *Schenck*. 2004.

Anti-Abortion Lawyer, *Williams*. 2004.

Anti-Bill Legislator, *Hill*. 2004.

Appellate Lawyer, *Williams*. 2004.

Baran, Jeffrey. 2004.

Bartels, David. 2004.

Buckham, Marilyn. 2004.

Cadwallader, Ted. 2004.

Certo, Gilbert. 2004.

Clinic Amici, *Schenck*. 2004.

Clinic Lawyer, *Williams*. 2004.

Clinic Manager, *Schenck*. 2004.

Clinic Manager, *Williams*. 2004.

Dalley, Helen. 2004.

DeGette, Diana. 2004.

DeMers, Bridget. 2004.

Estes, Heather. 2004.

Feeley, Michael. 2004.

Finley, Lucinda. 2004.

Green, James. 2004.

Hammer, Jeannette. 2004.

Heins, Marjorie. 2004.

Henderson, James. 2004.

Hill, Jeannie. 2004.

Himmelmann, Audrey. 2004.

Levine, Adeline. 2004.

Manager/Doctor, *Schenck*. 2004.

Mueller, Doug. 2004.

Murray, Glenn. 2004.

Overrule Amici, *Schenck*. 2004.

Palmer, Romona. 2004.

PCN Activist, *Schenck*. 2004.

PCN Lawyer, *Schenck*. 2004.

Picketer, *Hill*. 2004.

Picketer, *Schenck*. 2004.

Picketer, *Williams*. 2004.

Pro-Bill Legislator, *Hill*. 2004.

Rescuer, *Schenck*. 2004.

Rouche, Lynde. 2004.

Ryer, Karen Anderson. 2004.

Schenck, Paul. 2004.

State Lawyer, *Hill*. 2004.

Street, John. 2004.

Waples, Richard. 2004.

Williams, Christine. 2004.

Wortman, Morris. 2004.

Online Resources

"About the ACLJ." 2012. *American Center for Law and Justice*. Accessed August 1. http://aclj.org/our-mission/about-aclj. Accessed November 20, 2012.

"About Liberty Center for Law and Policy | Liberty Center for Law and Policy." 2012. http://www.libertyclp.org/index.cfm?PID=23472. Accessed November 20, 2012.

"ACLJ & 20,000 Americans Defend NYPD Surveillance—Telling DOJ It's 'Legitimate' Response to Terrorism." 2012. *American Center for Law and Justice*. http://aclj.org/war-on-terror/aclj-20-000-americans-defend-nypd-surveillance---telling-doj-legitimate-response-to-terrorism. Accessed July 3, 2012.

"ACLJ—About the ACLJ." 2012. http://web.archive.org/web/19990427234259/http://www.aclj.org/AboutA.html. Accessed November 20, 2012.

Center for Reproductive Rights. 2009. *Targeted Regulation of Abortion Providers (TRAP)*. Center for Reproductive Rights. http://reproductiverights.org/en/project/targeted-regulation-of-abortion-providers-trap. Accessed June 27, 2012.

"Frequently Asked Questions." http://www.supremecourt.gov/faq.aspx#faqgi9.

Frontline. "State Regulation of Abortion." Accessed June 27, 2012. http://www.pbs.org/wgbh/pages/frontline/clinic/etc/map.html.

Gross, Terry. 1995. "Keith Fournier, Head of the American Center for Law and Justice." *NPR.org*. http://www.npr.org/templates/story/story.php?storyId=1108449. Accessed August 2, 2012.

Hill v. Colorado, Oral Argument. http://www.oyez.org/cases/1990-1999/1999/1999_98_1856. Accessed January 8, 2013.

"Jay Sekulow." 2013. *American Center for Law and Justice*. http://aclj.org/jay-sekulow. Accessed January 11, 2013.

"Liberty Counsel—About." 2012. http://www.lc.org/index.cfm?pid=14096. Accessed November 20, 2012.

Lohr, Kathy. 2011. "Miss. Set to Vote on Measure Defining a Person: NPR." *Morning Edition*. NPR. http://www.npr.org/2011/11/02/141900772/miss-set-to-vote-on-measure-making-fetus-a-person. Accessed June 27, 2012.

National Abortion Federation. 2013. "NAF Violence and Disruption Statistics." http://www.prochoice.org/pubs_research/publications/downloads/about_abortion/stats_table2010.pdf. Accessed January 8, 2013.

"ObamaCare." 2012. *American Center for Law and Justice.* http://aclj.org/obamacare. Accessed July 3, 2012.

"Our Mission | American Center for Law and Justice ACLJ." 2012. http://aclj.org/our-mission. Accessed November 20, 2012.

"Regent Law—Center for Advocacy Skills." 2012. http://www.regent.edu/acad/schlaw/academics/centerforadvocacy.cfm. Accessed November 20, 2012.

Schenck v. Pro-Choice Network of Western New York, Oral Argument. 1996. http://www.oyez.org/oyez/resource/case/838/resources. Accessed June 26, 2012.

Works

Albiston, Catherine. 1999. "The Rule of Law and the Litigation Process: The Paradox of Losing by Winning." *Law & Society Review* 33, no. 4: 869–910.

———. 2011. "The Dark Side of Litigation as a Movement Strategy." *Iowa Law Review* 96: 61–77.

Anderson, Lisa. 2007. "Falwell Saw Law School as Tool to Alter Society." *Chicago Tribune*, May 21. E1.

Ashar, Sameer. 2007. "Public Interest Lawyers and Resistance Movements." *California Law Review* 95: 1879–1926.

Barclay, Scott, and Anna-Maria Marshall. 2005. "Supporting a Cause, Developing a Movement, and Consolidating a Practice: Cause Lawyers and Sexual Orientation Litigation in Vermont." In *The Worlds Cause Lawyers Make*, ed. Austin Sarat and Stuart Scheingold, 171–202. Stanford, CA: Stanford University Press.

Benford, Robert, and David A. Snow. 2000. "Framing Processes and Social Movements: An Overview and Assessment." *Annual Review of Sociology* 26: 611–39.

Berger, Ronald J., and Richard Quinney, eds. 2004. *Storytelling Sociology: Narrative as Social Inquiry.* Illustrated ed. Boulder, CO: Lynne Rienner.

Blanchard, Dallas A. 1995. *The Anti-Abortion Movement and the Rise of the Religious Right: From Polite to Fiery Protest.* New York: Twayne.

Board of Directors. 1990a. "Pro-Choice Network of Western New York Board of Directors Meeting Minutes, September 10, 1990." Box 2, Folder 11. SUNY Buffalo Archives.

———. 1990b. "Pro-Choice Network of Western New York Board of Directors Meeting Minutes, October 15, 1990." Box 2, Folder 11. SUNY Buffalo Archives.

———. 1990c. "Pro-Choice Network of Western New York Board of Directors Meeting Minutes, November 19, 1990." Box 2, Folder 11. SUNY Buffalo Archives.

———. 1991. "Pro-Choice Network of Western New York Board of Directors Meeting Minutes, February 11, 1991." Box 3, Folder 1. SUNY Buffalo Archives.

Boyer, Paul S. 2008. "The Evangelical Resurgence in 1970s American Protestantism." In *Rightward Bound: Making America Conservative in The 1970s*, ed. Bruce J. Schulman and Julian E. Zelizer. Cambridge, MA: Harvard University Press.

Brown, Steven P. 2002. *Trumping Religion: The New Christian Right, the Free Speech Clause, and the Courts.* 1st ed. Tuscaloosa: University of Alabama Press.

Bumiller, Kristin. 1992. *The Civil Rights Society: The Social Construction of Victims.* Baltimore: Johns Hopkins University Press.

Coglianese, Cary. 2001. "Social Movements, Law, and Society: The Institutionalization of the Environmental Movement." *University of Pennsylvania Law Review* 150: 85.

Colorado House. 1993. *House Chambers Reading Tape 3*. Tape. Vol. 3.

Colorado House Judiciary Committee. 1993a. *House Judiciary Committee Meeting*. Tape. Vol. 1.

———. 1993b. *House Judiciary Committee Meeting*. Tape. Vol. 2.

———. 1993c. *House Judiciary Committee Meeting*. Tape. Vol. 3.

Colorado Senate. 1993. *Senate Chamber Second Reading*. Tape. Vol. 6.

Colorado Senate Judiciary Committee. 1993a. *Senate Judiciary Committee Meeting*. Tape. Vol. 4.

———. 1993b. *Senate Judiciary Committee Meeting, Tape 5, March 3, 1993*. Tape. Vol. 5.

Conant, Elizabeth. 1992. "Pro-Choice Victory in Federal Court: Arcara Grants Preliminary Injunction." *SPEAK OUT!* (March). Box 6, Folder 7. SUNY Buffalo Archives.

———. 1997. "U.S. Supreme Court Upholds PCN's Preliminary Injunction." *SPEAK OUT!* (February/March). Box 6, Folder 4. SUNY Buffalo Archives.

Conant, Elizabeth, ed. 1989. "SPEAK OUT!" *SPEAK OUT!* (May). Box 6, Folder 4. SUNY Buffalo Archives.

Conger, Kimberly H. 2009. "Moral Values and Political Parties: Cycles of Conflict and Accommodation." In *Evangelicals and Democracy in America*. Vol. 2, *Religion and Politics*, ed. Steven Brint and Jean Reith Schroedel, 280–304. New York: Russell Sage.

Cook, Elizabeth Adell, Ted Jelen, and Clyde Wilcox. 1992. *Between Two Absolutes: Public Opinion and the Politics of Abortion*. Boulder, CO: Westview Press.

Cover, Robert M. 1983. "Foreword: Nomos and Narrative." *Harvard Law Review* 97: 4.

———. 1986. "Violence and the Word." *Yale Law Journal* 95: 1601–29.

Crean. 2009. "Pat Robertson, Part 1." *CBS News*. http://www.cbsnews.com/8301-3445_162-1481775.html. Accessed August 2, 2012.

Davey, Monica. 2006. "South Dakota Bans Abortion, Setting Up a Battle." *New York Times*, March 7, A1.

Diamond, Sara. 1998. *Not by Politics Alone: The Enduring Influence of the Christian Right*. New York: Guilford Press.

Dudas, Jeffrey R. 2009. "Little Monsters, Wild Animals, and Welfare Queens: Ronald Reagan and the Legal Constitution of American Politics." *Studies in Law, Politics, and Society* 49: 157–210.

Den Dulk, Kevin R. 2006. "In Legal Culture, But Not of It: The Role of Cause Lawyers in Evangelical Legal Mobilization." In *Cause Lawyers and Social Movements*, ed. Austin Sarat and Stuart Scheingold. Stanford, CA: Stanford University Press.

———. 2008. "Purpose-Driven Lawyers: Evangelical Cause Lawyering and the Culture War." In *The Cultural Lives of Cause Lawyers*, ed. Austin Sarat and Stuart Scheingold, 56–78. New York: Cambridge University Press.

Edelman, Murray Jacob. 1985. *The Symbolic Uses of Politics: With a New Afterword*. Champaign: University of Illinois Press.

Edmonds, P. 1992. "Abortion Fight: Twins Lead Charge." *USA Today*, April 24, 3A.

Epp, Charles R. 1998. *The Rights Revolution: Lawyers, Activists, and Supreme Courts in Comparative Perspective.* 1st ed. Chicago: University of Chicago Press.

Escort Committee. 1990. "Pro-Choice Network of Western New York Escort Committee Meeting Minutes, April 20, 1990." Box 2, Folder 11. SUNY Buffalo Archives.

Ewick, Patricia, and Susan S. Silbey. 1995. "Subversive Stories and Hegemonic Tales: Toward a Sociology of Narrative." *Law & Society Review* 29: 197.

——. 1998. *The Common Place of Law: Stories from Everyday Life.* 1st ed. Chicago: University of Chicago Press.

Feeley, Malcolm M., and Edward L. Rubin. 2000. *Judicial Policy Making and the Modern State: How the Courts Reformed America's Prisons.* New York: Cambridge University Press.

Fiorina, Morris P., Samuel J. Abrams, and Jeremy C. Pope. 2010. *Culture War? The Myth of a Polarized America.* 3rd ed. New York: Pearson.

Foucault, Michel. 1995. *Discipline and Punish: The Birth of the Prison.* New York: Random House.

Frymer, Paul. 2003. "Acting When Elected Officials Won't: Federal Courts and Civil Rights Enforcement in U.S. Labor Unions, 1935–85." *American Political Science Review* 97, no. 3: 483–99.

Galanter, Marc. 1974. "Why the Haves Come Out Ahead: Speculations on the Limits of Legal Change." *Law & Society Review* 9: 95.

Ginsburg, Faye D. *Contested Lives: The Abortion Debate in an American Community.* Berkeley: University of California Press, 1998.

Glendon, Mary Ann. 1993. *Rights Talk: The Impoverishment of Political Discourse.* New York: Free Press.

Green, Melody. 1988. "Pamphlet: Why I Got Arrested in Atlanta." Binghamton, NY: Operation Rescue.

Greenhouse, Carol J. 1994. *Law and Community in Three American Towns.* Ithaca, NY: Cornell University Press.

Guth, James L., and John C. Green. 1991. "An Ideology of Rights: Support for Civil Liberties among Political Activists." *Political Behavior* 13, no. 4: 321–44.

Hall, Peter Dobkin. 2009. "The Decline, Transformation, and Revival of the Christian Right in the United States." In *Evangelicals and Democracy in America.* Vol. 2, *Religion and Politics*, ed. Steven Brint and Jean Reith Schroedel, 249–79. New York: Russell Sage.

Harrell, David Edwin. 2010. *Pat Robertson: A Life and Legacy.* 1st ed. Grand Rapids, MI: Wm. B. Eerdmans.

Herbeck, Dan. 1991. "Fine of $40,000 Sought against Pro-life Protester." *Buffalo News,* February 6, B1, B4.

Hilbink, Thomas. 2006. "The Profession, the Grassroots, and the Elite: Cause Lawyering for Civil Rights and Freedom in the Direct Action Era." In *Cause Lawyers and Social Movements,* ed. Austin Sarat and Stuart A Scheingold, 60. Stanford, CA: Stanford University Press.

Hill, Jeannie. 1989. *Sidewalk Counseling Workbook.* Wheat Ridge, CO: Sidewalk Counselors for Life, Inc.

Hollis-Brusky, Amanda. 2011. "Support Structures and Constitutional Change: Teles, Southworth, and the Conservative Legal Movement." *Law & Social Inquiry* 36, no. 2: 516–36.

Hunt, Alan. 1993. *Explorations in Law and Society: Toward a Constitutive Theory of Law.* New York: Routledge.

Jones, Lynn. 2005. "Exploring the Sources of Cause and Career Correspondence among Cause Lawyers." In *The World's Cause Lawyers Make: Structure and Agency in Legal Practice*, ed. Austin Sarat and Stuart Scheingold. Stanford, CA: Stanford University Press.

———. 2006. "The Haves Come Out Ahead: How Cause Lawyers Frame the Legal System for Movements." In *Cause Lawyers and Social Movements*, ed. Austin Sarat and Stuart Scheingold. Stanford, CA: Stanford University Press.

Kagan, Robert A. 2003. *Adversarial Legalism: The American Way of Law.* Cambridge, MA: Harvard University Press.

Keck, Thomas. 2009. "Beyond Backlash: Assessing the Impact of Judicial Decisions on LGBT Rights." *Law & Society Review* 43, no. 1 (March): 151–86.

Kennedy, Duncan. 2002. "The Critique of Rights in Critical Legal Studies." In *Left Liberalism/Left Critique*, ed. Wendy Brown and Janet Halley, 178. Durham, NC: Duke University Press Books.

Levine, Adeline. 1990. *First Annual Report for the Pro-Choice Network of Western New York, Inc.* Box 1, Folder 6. SUNY Buffalo Archives.

Levitsky, Sandra R. 2006. "To Lead with Law: Reassessing the Influence of Legal Advocacy Organizations in Social Movements." In *Cause Lawyers and Social Movements*, ed. Austin Sarat and Stuart Scheingold, 145. Stanford, CA: Stanford University Press.

Lobel, Orly. 2006. "The Paradox of Extralegal Activism: Critical Legal Consciousness and Transformative Politics." *Harvard Law Review* 120: 937.

Luker, Kristin. 1985. *Abortion and the Politics of Motherhood.* Berkeley: University of California Press.

Marshall, Anna-Maria. 2003. "Injustice Frames, Legality, and the Everyday Construction of Sexual Harassment." *Law & Social Inquiry* 28, no. 3: 659–89.

Mauro, Tony. 2005. "LegalTimes.com—Jay Sekulow's Golden Ticket." http://www.law.com/jsp/nlj/PubArticleNLJ.jsp?id=900005439857 . Accessed October 31, 2005.

McCann, Michael. 1994. *Rights at Work: Pay Equity Reform and the Politics of Legal Mobilization.* 1st ed. Chicago: University of Chicago Press.

———. 1996. "Causal versus Constitutive Explanations (or, On the Difficulty of Being So Positive . . .)." *Law & Social Inquiry* 21, no. 2: 457–82.

———. 1998. "How Does Law Matter for Social Movements." In *How Does Law Matter?: Fundamental Issues in Law And Society*, ed. Bryant Garth and Austin Sarat, 76–108. 1st ed. Chicago: Northwestern University Press.

———. 2006. "Law and Social Movements: Contemporary Perspectives." *Annual Review of Law and Social Science* 2, no. 1: 17–38.

McCann, Michael, and Helena Silverstein. 1998. "Rethinking Law's 'Allurements': A Relational Analysis of Social Movement Lawyers in the United States." In *Cause*

Lawyering: Political Commitments and Professional Responsibilities, ed. Austin Sarat and Stuart Scheingold, 261–92. New York: Oxford University Press.

McClosky, Herbert, and Alida Brill. 1983. *Dimensions of Tolerance: What Americans Believe about Civil Liberties*. New York: Russell Sage.

Medoff, Marshall H. 2002. "The Determinants and Impact of State Abortion Restrictions." *American Journal of Economics and Sociology* 61, no. 2: 481–93.

Merry, Sally Engle. 1990. *Getting Justice and Getting Even: Legal Consciousness among Working-Class Americans*. Language and Legal Discourse Series. 1st ed. Chicago: University of Chicago Press.

Meyer, David S., and Suzanne Staggenborg. 1996. "Movements, Countermovements, and the Structure of Political Opportunity." *American Journal of Sociology* 101, no. 6: 1628–60.

———. 2008. "Opposing Movement Strategies in U.S. Abortion Politics." *Research in Social Movements, Conflicts and Change* 28 (June 16): 207–38.

Minow, Martha. "Interpreting Rights: An Essay for Robert Cover." *Yale Law Journal* 96, no. 8 (July 1987): 1860.

NeJaime, Douglas. 2011. "Winning through Losing." *Iowa Law Review* 96: 941–1012.

Nielsen, Laura Beth. 2000. "Situating Legal Consciousness: Experiences and Attitudes of Ordinary Citizens about Law and Street Harassment." *Law and Society Review* 34: 1055.

Oliver, Pamela E., and Daniel J. Myers. 2002. "The Coevolution of Social Movements." *Mobilization* 8, no. 1: 1–24.

Olson, Susan. 1984. *Clients and Lawyers: Securing the Rights of Disabled Persons*. New York: Praeger.

Operation Rescue. 1988. "Pamphlet Operation Rescue New York January 12–14, 1989." Operation Rescue. Box 31, Folder 1. SUNY Buffalo Archives.

Orbuch, Terri. 1997. "People's Accounts Count: The Sociology of Accounts." *Annual Review of Sociology* 23: 455–78.

Peckham, Michael. 1998. "New Dimensions of Social Movement/Countermovement Interaction: The Case of Scientology and Its Internet Critics." *Canadian Journal of Sociology* 23: 317–47.

Pickert, Kate. 2013. "What Choice?" *Time*, January 14, 38.

Planned Parenthood Shasta-Diablo. 1990. "Complaint for Injunctive Relief, Filed with Solano Superior Court."

———. 1993. *Planned Parenthood Newsletter*.

Polletta, Francesca. 2000. "Structural Context of Novel Rights Claims: Southern Civil Rights Organizing, 1961–1966." *Law & Society Review* 34: 367.

———. 2006. *It Was Like a Fever: Storytelling in Protest and Politics*. Chicago: University of Chicago Press.

Polletta, Francesca, Pang Ching, Bobby Chen, Beth Gharrity Gardner, and Alice Motes. 2011. "The Sociology of Storytelling." *Annual Review of Sociology* 37, no. 1: 109–30.

Post, Robert. 1995. "Recuperating First Amendment Doctrine." *Stanford Law Review* 47: 1249–81.

Pro-Choice Network. 1992. *Third Annual Report for the Pro-Choice Network of Western New York, Inc. April 1, 1991 to March 31, 1992*. Annual Report. Pro-Choice Network of Western New York. Box 31, Folder 6 9. SUNY Buffalo Archives.

Project Rescue Western New York. 1990. "Pamphlet Project Rescue Western New York, Regional Rescue Mission September 28, 1990." Project Rescue. Box 31, Folder 1. SUNY Buffalo Archives.

Puzo, Mario. 1969. *The Godfather*. New York: G. P. Putnam's Sons.

Risen, James, and Judy L. Thomas. 1999. *Wrath of Angels: The American Abortion War*. New York: Basic Books.

Rohlinger, Deana A. 2002. "Framing the Abortion Debate: Organizational Resources, Media Strategies, and Movement-Countermovement Dynamics." *Sociological Quarterly* 43, no. 4: 479–507.

Rose, Melody. 2007. *Safe, Legal, and Unavailable?: Abortion Politics in the United States*. Washington, DC: CQ Press.

Rosenberg, Gerald N. 2008. *The Hollow Hope: Can Courts Bring about Social Change?* 2nd ed. Chicago: University of Chicago Press.

Sallade, C. R. 1990. "City of Vallejo Police Department Letter to Solano Citizens for Life."

Sanko, John J. 1992. "State Legislative Races to Watch." *Rocky Mountain News*, October 26.

———. 1993a. "Bill Would Shield Women Entering Abortion Clinics." *Rocky Mountain News*, January 29.

———. 1993b. "Committee Approves Abortion Clinic Buffer." *Rocky Mountain News*, March 4.

———. 1993c. "Session Tough for Abortion Foes." *Rocky Mountain News*, March 15.

———. 1993d. "Romer Signs Abortion 'Bubble' Bill into Law." *Rocky Mountain News*, April 20.

Sarat, Austin, and Stuart Scheingold, ed. 1998. *Cause Lawyering: Political Commitments and Professional Responsibilities*. New York: Oxford University Press.

———. 2001. *Cause Lawyering and the State in a Global Era*. New York: Oxford University Press, USA.

———. 2005. *The Worlds Cause Lawyers Make: Structure and Agency in Legal Practice*. 1st ed. Stanford, CA: Stanford University Press.

———. 2006. *Cause Lawyers and Social Movements*. Stanford, CA: Stanford University Press.

———. 2008. *The Cultural Lives of Cause Lawyers*. 1st ed. New York: Cambridge University Press.

Scheingold, Stuart A. 2004. *The Politics of Rights: Lawyers, Public Policy, and Political Change*. 2nd ed. Ann Arbor: University of Michigan Press.

Scheingold, Stuart A., and Austin Sarat, ed. 2004. *Something to Believe In: Politics, Professionalism, and Cause Lawyering*. 1st ed. Stanford Law and Politics series. Stanford, CA: Stanford University Press.

Shapiro, Martin. 1986. *Courts: A Comparative and Political Analysis*. Chicago,: University of Chicago Press.

Silbey, Susan S. 2005. "After Legal Consciousness." *Annual Review of Law and Social Science* 1, no. 1: 323–68.

Silverstein, Helena. 1996. *Unleashing Rights: Law, Meaning, and the Animal Rights Movement*. Ann Arbor: University of Michigan Press.

Smith, Roger M. 2009. "An Almost-Christian Nation? Constitutional Consequences of the Rise of the Religious Right." In *Evangelicals and Democracy in America*, ed. Steven Brint and Jean Reith Schroedel. Vol. 1, *Religion and Society*, 329–55. New York: Russell Sage.

Snow, David A., E. Burke Rochford Jr., Steven K. Worden, and Robert Benford. 1986. "Frame Alignment Processes, Micromobilization, and Movement Participation." *American Sociological Review* 51 (August): 464–81.

Snow, David, and Robert Benford. 1992. "Master Frames and Cycles of Protest." In *Frontiers in Social Movement Theory*, ed. Aldon D. Morris and Carol McClurg Mueller. New Haven: Yale University Press.

Southworth, Ann. 2008. *Lawyers of the Right: Professionalizing the Conservative Coalition*. Chicago: University of Chicago Press.

Staggenborg, Suzanne. 1991. *The Pro-Choice Movement: Organization and Activism in the Abortion Conflict*. New York: Oxford University Press.

Steering Committee. 1989. *Steering Committee of the Pro-Choice Network of Western New York Meeting Minutes, November 6, 1989*. Box 2, Folder 11. SUNY Buffalo Archives.

———. 1990. *Steering Committee of the Pro-Choice Network of Western New York Meeting Minutes, March 12, 1990*. Box 2, Folder 11. SUNY Buffalo Archives.

Stein, Arlene. 2001. "Revenge of the Shamed: The Christian Right's Emotional Culture War." In *Passionate Politics: Emotions and Social Movements*, ed. Jeff Goodwin, James M. Jasper, and Francesca Polletta. Chicago: University of Chicago Press.

Sterne, Laurence. 1980. *Tristram Shandy*. Ed. Howard Anderson. 1st ed. New York: W. W. Norton.

Teles, Steven. 2010. *The Rise of the Conservative Legal Movement: The Battle for Control of the Law*. Princeton, NJ: Princeton University Press.

Tyler, Tom R. 2006. *Why People Obey the Law*. Princeton, NJ: Princeton University Press.

Warner, G. 1989. "WNY Is Seen as Key Locale for Abortions." *Buffalo News*, July 4, A1, A9.

———. 1991. "Pro-lifers Use Fetuses for 'Reality.'" *Buffalo News*, June 15, n.p.

———. 1992. "Tactics of Anti-Abortionists Add Bitter Element to Struggle." *Buffalo News*, April 29, B1, B6.

Warner, Gene. 1992. "Fines Hang over Heads of 2 Pro-life Activists." *Buffalo News*, October 23, C1, C13.

———. 1994a. "Pro-Choice Activists Boost Efforts to Collect Fines Imposed on the Opposition." *Buffalo News*, June 4, C1, C4.

———. 1994b. "Schenck Brothers Bid Farewell to Pro-Life Activism in Buffalo." *Buffalo News*, August 11, A1, A6.

Westlund, Roger. 2004. Interview with author.

Wilcox, Clyde, and Carin Robinson. 2010. *Onward Christian Soldiers?: The Religious Right in American Politics*. 4th rev. ed. Boulder, CO: Westview.

Wilcox, William Clyde. 1992. *God's Warriors: The Christian Right in Twentieth-Century America*. Baltimore: Johns Hopkins University Press.

Williams, Christine. 1990a. "Written Record Provided by Christine Williams."

———. 1990b. "Solano Lifelines." *Solano Lifelines* 3, no. 2 (April).

———. 1990c. "Solano Lifelines." *Solano Lifelines* 3, no. 3 (September).

———. 1991. "Solano Lifelines." *Solano Lifelines* 3, no. 3 (September).

Williams, Daniel. 2010. *God's Own Party: The Making of the Christian Right*. New York: Oxford University Press.

———. "The GOP's Abortion Strategy: Why Pro-Choice Republicans Became Pro-Life in the 1970s." *Journal of Policy History* 23, no. 4 (2011): 513–39.

Williams, Gwyneth, and Rhys Williams. 1995. "'All We Want Is Equality': Rhetorical Framing in the Father's Rights Movement." In *Images of Issues: Typifying Contemporary Social Problems*, ed. Joel Best. 2nd ed. New York: Aldine Transaction.

Wilson, Joshua C. 2011. "A Class of Their Own: An Initial Look at the Influence of Conservative Christian Law Schools." Unpublished paper presented at Annual Meeting of the Law and Society Association, San Francisco. http://citation.allacademic.com/meta/p_mla_apa_research_citation/4/9/3/4/7/p493478_index.html. Accessed June 27, 2012.

Wilson, Joshua C., and Amanda Hollis-Brusky. 2012. "Lawyers for God & Neighbor: The Emergence of 'Law as a Calling' as a Mobilizing Frame for Christian Lawyers." Unpublished paper.

Woodberry, Robert D., and Christian S. Smith. 1998. "Fundamentalism et al.: Conservative Protestants in America." *Annual Review of Sociology* 24, no. 1: 25–56.

Zald, Mayer N., and Bert Useem. 1987. "Movement and Countermovement Interaction: Mobilization, Tactics, and State Involvement." In *Social Movements in an Organizational Society*, ed. Mayer N. Zald and John McCarthy. New Brunswick, NJ: Transaction Publishers.

Zinnemann, Fred. 1966. *A Man for All Seasons*. Biography, Drama.

Zremski, Jerry. 1996. "Schencks Find New Ways to Goals." *Buffalo News*, February 18, final ed., 1C.

Index

"abortion distortion," 30, 35–37, 102–3, 128–29, 180, 210n65, 217n58. *See also* anti-abortion activists' narratives; judicial bias

abortion politics: contentious and visible period of, 1–4, 194n17; free speech ideological tension as affected by, 16, 186, 217n68; *Hill* and, 102; legal power and, 1, 193n2; legislation and, 106–10; liberalization of domestic policy and, 1, 193n2; litigation effects on, 14, 106–10, 208n107; methodological approach and, 189–91, 217n61; New Christian Right's relation to, 3–5, 158–65, 210n65; reproductive rights and, 40–42, 61, 80, 110, 115, 121, 164–65, 193n5; Republican Party leaders and, 5; social conservative movement's connections with, 1, 66, 106–10, 158–65, 197n55; state law and courts and, 2, 4, 106–10; street-level activists and, 1–4, 13–15, 194n17, 196n50. *See also* free speech; *Hill v. Colorado;* legacies of street-level abortion politics; *Planned Parenthood Shasta-Diablo Inc. v. Christine Williams; Schenck v. Pro-Choice Network of Western New York*

abortion-rights activists: abortion-rights as term of use, 193n4; academic community's connections with, 39, 41, 53, 64, 200n4; amici narratives and, 139–48, 145, 178, 216n51; construction of law and, 24, 141–44, 146–47, 149–50, 153; culture wars and, 13, 106–10, 158–65; defensive stance taken by, 4, 110; development of movements and, 164–65; free speech ideological tension and, 15–16, 21–22, 115, 117–22, 174–75, 186, 210nn34–35, 216n42, 216nn44–45, 217n68; ideological tension within, 15–16, 21–22, 186, 217n68; judicial bias claims made by, 55–56, 173, 217n58; law and courts and, 2, 11, 14, 20, 54, 105–6, 114, 180–81, 193n7, 196n50; legal representation for, 29, 30–33, 96, 100; litigation in context of mission of, 14–16; primary cases and, 14–15; regulations' effects on, 74, 105, 114; reproductive rights and, 40–42, 61, 80, 110, 115, 121; street-level activism and, 2, 13, 51, 158, 193nn5–6, 193n6, 196n50; *Williams* and, 25–29, 32–33, 37, 121, 137–38, 140–41, 144, 210n35, 210n35. *See also* anti-abortion activists; movement-counter-movement conflict; Pro-Choice Network of Western New York

abortion-rights activists and "Bubble Bill," 87; coercive force by the state and, 141–42; construction of law for, 115–22, 141–44, 146–47, 149–50, 153; free speech and, 142–44, 146–47; legal representation for, 96; legislators' narratives and, 76–81, 87–89, 90–94, 142–44, 146–47; Planned Parenthood and, 81; reproductive rights and, 80;

The Cultural Lives of Law
Edited by Austin Sarat

The Cultural Lives of Law series brings insights and approaches from cultural studies to law and tries to secure for law a place in cultural analysis. Books in the series focus on the production, interpretation, consumption, and circulation of legal meanings. They take up the challenges posed as boundaries collapse between as well as within cultures, and as the circulation of legal meanings becomes more fluid. They also attend to the ways law's power in cultural production is renewed and resisted.

Zooland: The Institution of Captivity
Irus Braverman
2012

After Secular Law
Edited by Winnifred Fallers Sullivan, Robert A. Yelle, and Mateo Taussig-Rubbo
2011

All Judges Are Political—Except When They Are Not: Acceptable Hypocrisies and the Rule of Law
Keith J. Bybee
2010

Riding the Black Ram: Law, Literature, and Gender
Susan Sage Heinzelman
2010

Tort, Custom, and Karma: Globalization and Legal Consciousness in Thailand
David M. Engel and Jaruwan S. Engel
2010

Law in Crisis: The Ecstatic Subject of Natural Disaster
Ruth A. Miller
2009

The Affective Life of Law: Legal Modernism and the Literary Imagination
Ravit Reichman
2009

Fault Lines: Tort Law as Cultural Practice
Edited by David M. Engel and Michael McCann
2008

Lex Populi: The Jurisprudence of Popular Culture
William P. MacNeil
2007

The Cultural Lives of Capital Punishment: Comparative Perspectives
Edited by Austin Sarat and Christian Boulanger
2005